World Religions

Biographies

World Religions

Biographies VOLUME 1

Michael J. O'Neal and J. Sydney Jones
Neil Schlager and Jayne Weisblatt, Editors

U•X•L
An imprint of Thomson Gale,
a part of The Thomson Corporation

THOMSON
GALE

Detroit • New York • San Francisco • New Haven, Conn. • Waterville, Maine • London

World Religions: Biographies

Written by Michael J. O'Neal and J. Sydney Jones
Edited by Neil Schlager and Jayne Weisblatt

Project Editor
Nancy Matuszak

Editorial
Julie L. Carnagie

Rights and Acquisitions
Edna Hedblad, Emma Hull, and Sue Rudolph

Imaging and Multimedia
Lezlie Light, Michael Logusz, Christine O'Bryan, and Robyn Young

Product Design
Jennifer Wahi

Composition
Evi Seoud

Manufacturing
Rita Wimberley

For more information, contact
Thomson Gale
27500 Drake Rd.
Farmington Hills, MI 48331-3535
Or you can visit our Internet site at http://www.gale.com

LIBRARY OF CONGRESS CATALOGING-IN-PUBLICATION DATA

Jones, J. Sydney.
World religions reference library / edited by Neil Schlager and Jayne Weisblatt; written by J. Sydney Jones and Michael O'Neal; Nancy Matuszak, content project editor.
p. cm. -- (World religions reference library)
Includes bibliographical references and index.
ISBN-13: 978-1-4144-0227-7 (Almanac : set : alk. paper) --
ISBN-10: 1-4144-0227-9 (Almanac : set : alk. paper) --
ISBN-13: 978-1-4144-0228-4 (Almanac : vol. 1 : alk. paper) --
ISBN-10: 1-4144-0228-7 (Almanac : vol. 1 : alk. paper) --
[etc.]
1. Religions.I. O'Neal, Michael, 1949-II. Schlager, Neil, 1966-III. Weisblatt, Jayne.
IV. Title.V. Series.
BL74.J66 2006
200--dc22
2006012295

ISBN-13:
978-1-4144-0229-1 (Almanac vol. 2)
978-1-4144-0230-7 (Biographies set)
978-1-4144-0231-4 (Biographies vol. 1)
978-1-4144-0232-1 (Biographies vol. 2)
978-1-4144-0232-8 (Primary Sources)
978-1-4144-0234-5 (Cumulative Index)

ISBN-10:
1-4144-0229-5 (Almanac vol. 2)
1-4144-0230-9 (Biographies set)
1-4144-0231-7 (Biographies vol. 1)
1-4144-0232-5 (Biographies vol. 2)
1-4144-0233-3 (Primary Sources)
1-4144-0234-1 (Cumulative Index)

This title is also available as an e-book.
ISBN-13: 978-1-4144-0232-1, ISBN-10: 1-4144-0612-6
Contact your Thomson Gale sales representative for ordering information.
Printed in the United States of America

10 9 8 7 6 5 4 3 2

Contents

Reader's Guide

Religion influences the views and actions of many people in the world today in both political and personal ways. In some instances religious fervor compels people to perform selfless acts of compassion, while in others it spurs them to bitter warfare. Religion opens some people to all humanity but restricts others to remain loyal to small groups.

In general, religion can be described as a unified system of thought, feeling, and action that is shared by a group and that gives its members an object of devotion—someone or something sacred to believe in, such as a god or a spiritual concept. Religion also involves a code of behavior or personal moral conduct by which individuals may judge the personal and social consequences of their actions and the actions of others. Most of the time, religion also deals with what might be called the supernatural or the spiritual, about forces and a power beyond the control of humans. In this function, religion attempts to answer questions that science does not touch, such as the meaning of life and what happens after death.

Perhaps one of the most amazing things about religion is that there is no commonly held way of looking at it. Yet most of the world's population participates in it in one way or another. Though hard to define, religion seems to be a universal experience and need. Of the nearly 6.5 billion people on Earth, only about 16 percent (about 1.1. billion) say they do not believe in a god or do not believe in a specific religion. The rest of the world's population belongs to one of more than twenty different major religions.

Features and Format

World Religions: Biographies presents the biographies of fifty men and women who have played a critical role in the world's religions throughout history. Among those profiled are Abraham, whose influence is seen in three of the modern world's most dominant religions: Judaism, Christianity, and Islam; Muhammad, considered the final and most important prophet by Muslims; and Siddhartha Gautama, who became known as the Buddha. More modern figures are also included, from the Hindu teacher Swami Vivekananda to Bahá'u'lláh, who founded the Bahá'í faith. Women who made significant impacts on religion are also featured, including Mother Teresa, the Buddhist nun Dipa Ma, and the ancient Mesopotamian priestess Enheduanna.

Nearly one hundred black-and-white photos and maps illustrate the text, while sidebars highlight interesting concepts and fascinating facts connected to the individuals being profiled. The set also includes a glossary, a timeline, sources for further reading, and a subject index.

World Religions Reference Library

World Religions: Biographies is only one component of the three-part World Religions Reference Library. The set also includes two almanac volumes and one volume of primary source documents:

- *World Religions: Almanac* (two volumes) covers the history, traditions, and worldviews of dominant and less prominent religions and their sects and offshoots. This title examines the development of religions throughout history and into modern times: their philosophies and practices, sacred texts and teachings, effects on everyday life, influences on society and culture, and more. The set features eighteen chapters on today's prominent world religions and also explores ancient beliefs, such as those of Egypt and Mesopotamia; smaller movements like that of neo-paganism and Bahá'í; and philosophies, including those of ancient Greece and Rome, agnosticism, and atheism. In addition, an introductory chapter explores the concept of religion in more depth.
- *World Religions: Primary Sources* (one volume) offers eighteen excerpted writings, speeches, and sacred texts from across the religious spectrum. These include selections from the Bible, including both the Old and New Testament (Judaism and Christianity); the Qur'an (Islam); and the Dhammapada (Buddhism). Among the other selections are the Daoist text Dao De Jing; the Avesta, the sacred scripture of Zoroastrianism; the Sikh sacred scripture, Shri Guru Granth Sahib; and Thomas Henry Huxley's essay "Agnosticism and Christianity."

Acknowledgments

U•X•L would like to thank several individuals for their assistance with the *World Religions: Biographies.* At Schlager Group, Jayne Weisblatt and Neil Schlager who oversaw the writing and editing, while Michael J. O'Neal and J. Sydney Jones wrote the text. Thanks also to Shannon Kelly, who assisted with copyediting, Nora Harris for indexing, and Gloria Lam for proofing.

Special thanks are due for the invaluable comments and suggestions provided by U•X•L's World Religions Reference Library advisors and consultants:

- George Alscer, Associate Professor and Chair of Religious Studies, Philosophy and Pastoral Ministry, Marygrove College, Detroit, Michigan.
- Janet Callahan, Ford Interfaith Network, Dearborn, Michigan.
- Mary Ann Christopher, Librarian, Yellow Springs High School, Yellow Springs, Ohio.
- Margaret Hallisey, Retired library media specialist and former board member of the American Association of School Librarians; the Massachusetts School Library Media Association; and the New England Educational Media Association.
- Fatima al-Hayani, Professor of Religious Studies, University of Toledo, Toledo, Ohio.

- Madan Kaura, Bharatyia Temple, Ford Interfaith Network, Dearborn, Michigan.
- Ann Marie LaPrise, Huron School District, Monroe, Michigan.
- Ann W. Moore, Librarian, Schenectady County Public Library, Schenectady, New York.
- Chuen Pangcham, Midwest Buddhist Meditation Center (Buddha Vihara Temple), Warren, Michigan.
- Gene Schramm, Retired professor of Semitic Languages and Near Eastern Studies, University of Michigan, Ann Arbor, Michigan.
- Cheryl Youse, Media specialist, Hatherly Elementary School, Plymouth, Michigan.

Comments and Suggestions

We welcome your comments on *World Religions: Biographies* and suggestions for other topics in history to consider. Please write to Editors, *World Religions: Biographies,* U•X•L, 27500 Drake Road, Farmington Hills, Michigan 48331-3535; call toll-free 800-877-4253; send faxes to 248-699-8097; or send e-mail via http://www.gale.com.

Timeline of Events

c. 2300–c. 2260 BCE Life span of **Enheduanna.** The daughter of the Sumerian ruler Sargon of Akkad, Enheduanna is made High Priestess to the Sumerian Moon God, Nanna, beginning a tradition that will last for the next five hundred years among the princesses of the kings of the Middle Eastern region of Mesopotamia. Enheduanna also establishes the religious cult of Inanna, the daughter of the Moon God.

c. 2050–c. 1950 BCE Life span of **Abraham,** a central figure in three major religions: Judaism, Christianity, and Islam.

1353 BCE **Akhenaten,** also known as Amenhotep IV, becomes pharaoh of Egypt.

c. thirteenth century BCE According to Judeo-Christian belief, **Moses** leads the Israelites, the Jewish people, out of slavery from Egypt.

c. 1200 BCE Date perhaps marking the life of **Zarathushtra,** the founder of Zoroastrianism.

c. 604 BCE **Laozi,** considered the founder of Daoism, is born in China.

c. 569 BCE Vardhamana, who later takes the name **Mahavira** and is considered the founder of Jainism, gives up all of his worldly possessions to live a life of piety.

c. 551–479 BCE Life span of the scholar Kong zi, who is known in the West by his Latinized name, **Confucius.**

528 According to Buddhist belief, Siddhartha Gautama achieves enlightenment after a night of meditation, thus becoming **the Buddha.**

c. 483 BCE Death of the Buddha.

c. 476 BCE Greek philosopher **Anaxagoras** produces his major work *On Nature.*

c. 390 BCE The Greek philosopher **Plato** writes his most influential work, *The Republic.*

384–322 BCE Life span of the Greek philosopher **Aristotle.** Believing that achieving happiness is humanity's chief goal, he organizes all human behavior into a pyramid of actions that all lead to one supreme activity or goal for the individual.

c. 6 BCE **Jesus Christ,** also known as Jesus of Nazareth, is born.

c. 30 CE Jesus Christ is put to death by crucifixion by Roman authorities in Jerusalem.

c. 35 Saul of Tarsus, later known as **Saint Paul,** converts to Christianity.

610 According to Islamic belief, **Muhammad** begins receiving revelations and prophecies from the archangel Jabraʾil (Gabriel).

661 **ʿAlī ibn Abī Tālib,** the fourth caliph, or leader, of Islam, is murdered. His followers, part of the Shiʾa sect, believe that ʿAli is the first imam, or leader with divinely inspired powers.

c. 717–c. 801 Life span of **Rābiʾah al-Adawiyah,** a poet and a founding member of the mystical branch of Islam called Sufism. Her verses and prayers will become part of the literature and oral tradition of Islam.

1017–1137 Life span of **Ramanuja,** one of the great Hindu teachers of medieval India.

c. 1105 The Islamic philosopher **Abu Hāmid Muhammad al-Ghazālī** publishes his greatest work, *The Revival of the Religious Sciences.* The book explains the doctrines or rules and practices of Islam, especially Sufi Islam.

1177 **Moses Maimonides,** a Jewish scholar best known for his "thirteen principles of faith," is officially appointed head of Cairo's Jewish community.

c. 1199–c. 1287 Life span of **Madhva,** the founder of a sect of Hinduism called Madhvism.

1253 Japanese Buddhist monk **Nichiren** claims that the only true Buddhist religion is Nichiren Buddhism.

c. 1270 The Sufi Muslim poet **Jalāl ad-Dīn ar-Rūmī** finishes his most important work, the *Masnavi.* After his death in 1273, his name becomes associated with the Muslim sect known as the Whirling Dervishes, who are noted for their ecstatic body movements or dances as they chant the many names of Allah.

1377 The Muslim historian **Ibn Khaldūn** publishes his *Muqaddima,* in which he presents his theory for the rise and fall of civilizations.

1517 The German Augustinian monk **Martin Luther** launches the Protestant Reformation, which divides Christianity into two denominations, or branches: Catholicism and Protestantism.

1534 The Spanish nobleman **Ignatius of Loyola** establishes the Society of Jesus, or the Jesuit order, in 1534.

1536 **John Calvin** publishes the first edition of *Institutes of the Christian Religion.* In it, he argues that the authority of the pope should be rejected, that all humans are sinful and without any free will, and that eternal life is predetermined by God.

1698–1760 Life span of **Israel ben Eliezer,** the founder of Hasidism, a Jewish mystical movement that emphasizes a direct connection to God through prayer and through joyous experiences such as music and dance.

1699 The Sikh leader **Gobind Singh** founds the Khalsa, a militant brotherhood that gives identity to Sikhism and empowers Sikhs to resist persecution.

1783 Publication of *Jerusalem; or, On Religious Power and Judaism,* by the German Jewish scholar **Moses Mendelssohn.** In the book, Mendelssohn calls for freedom of conscience and argues that the state should play no role in determining the religious beliefs of its citizens.

1804 The Islamic leader **Usuman dan Fodio** leads a successful *jihad* (holy war) to become the ruler of the Fulani Empire in West Africa.

1844 The Communist philosopher **Karl Marx** publishes *Critique of the Hegelian Philosophy of Public Law.* In it, he explains his atheist views, writing that "Man makes religion, religion does not make man."

1866 **Bahá'u'lláh,** founder of the Bahá'í faith, publicly declares himself the Messenger of God.

1873 Jewish rabbi **Isaac Mayer Wise** forms the Union of American Hebrew Congregations; two years later he forms Hebrew Union College. In so doing, Wise becomes a key figure in the development of Reform Judaism in the United States.

1875 **Dayananda Sarasvati** founds the Arya Samaj, a Hindu reform movement. This organization will play a major part in the growth of Indian nationalism.

1893 The paper "What Is Hinduism?" by **Swami Vivekananda,** presented at the World Parliament of Religions in Chicago, exposes many Westerners to Hinduism for the first time. Also in Chicago at this conference, **Anagarika Dharmapala** speaks movingly of his religion, Theravada Buddhism. He gains converts in the United States and opens a U.S. chapter of the Maha Bodhi Society.

1911–1989 Life span of **Dipa Ma,** who becomes a beloved Buddhist teacher.

1932 **Black Elk** works with poet John G. Neihardt to write the work *Black Elk Speaks.* This book brought the traditional religious practices of the Lakota Sioux tribe to a wider audience.

1942 Israeli scholar **Nechama Leibowitz** begins providing weekly lessons about the Torah to students via the mail. She will continue the lessons for fifty years.

1945 **Mother Maria Skobtsova,** a nun in the Eastern Orthodox Church, dies in the concentration camp at Ravensbrück in Germany.

1947 India gains its independence from Britain, due in large part to the nonviolent protest movement led by **Mahatma Gandhi,** a devout Hindu.

1950 In Calcutta, India, **Mother Teresa** founds a new order of Catholic nuns, eventually called the Missionaries of Charity. Mother

Teresa and the order establish hospices, orphanages, and schools throughout India and eventually throughout the world.

1954 **Gerald Brousseau Gardner** publishes *Witchcraft Today,* which places witchcraft as the surviving piece of pagan or pre-Christian religion in the modern world. With the book's popularity, Gardner is dubbed by the English media as "Britain's Chief Witch."

1966 The Buddhist teacher **Thich Nhat Hanh** is exiled from Vietnam.

1986 The Anglican priest **Desmond Mpilo Tutu** becomes the Archbishop of Cape Town, South Africa. He continues his efforts to gain civil rights for South Africa's black population.

1989 The **Dalai Lama** wins the Nobel Peace Prize for his work on behalf of his homeland, Tibet, which has been under Chinese control since 1950.

1994 **Malidoma Patrice Somé** publishes his autobiography, *Of Water and the Spirit.* In it, he describes his youth as a member of the Dagara tribe in West Africa.

Words To Know

A

acupuncture: Traditional Chinese medical treatment that uses needles inserted into the body at specific locations to stimulate the body's balanced flow of energy.

adur aduran: The "fire of fires" that burns in Zoroastrian temples.

agnosticism: The view that the existence or nonexistence of God is unknown and is probably unknowable.

ahimsa: The principle of nonviolence, or not doing harm to any living creature.

Ahura Mazda: The supreme God of Zoroastrianism.

Akaranga Sutra: One of the sacred texts of Jainism, which contains the teachings of Mahavira.

Akhand Paath: Any occasion, such as a marriage or a death, when the Granth Sahib is read in its entirety.

alchemy: An ancient science that aimed to transform substances of little value into those of greater value, such as lead into gold.

Allah: The name of God in Islam, derived from the Arabic word *al-ilah,* meaning "the One True God."

Amaterasu: The Sun-goddess.

Amesha Spentas: The "Bounteous Immortals," aspects, or sides, of Ahura Mazda.

amrit: A solution of water and sugar, used in the ceremony when Sikhs are initiated into the faith.

Amrit Sanskar: The initiation ceremony for young Sikhs.

Anand Karaj: The Sikh wedding ceremony.

animism: The worship of trees, rocks, mountains, and such, which are believed to have supernatural power.

anthropomorphism: Attributing human shape or form to nonhuman things, such as the gods.

apathia: Stoic belief that happiness comes from freedom from internal turmoil.

apeiron: Anaximander's term for the first principle, an undefined and unlimited substance.

archē: The beginning or ultimate principle; the stuff of all matter, or the building block of creation.

arihant: An enlightened person.

Ark of the Covenant: A cabinet in which the Ten Commandments were kept in the First Temple of Jerusalem.

artha: Prosperity and success in material affairs.

Asatru: A neo-pagan religion based on worship of the Norse (Scandanavian) gods.

ascetic: A person who practices rigid self-denial, giving up all comforts and pleasures, as an act of religious devotion. Jain monks and nuns are ascetics.

asha: Righteousness that derives from natural law.

Ashkenazic: Term used to refer to Jews of France, Germany, and Eastern Europe.

astrology: The study of the movement of the planets and stars in relation to one another in order to predict future events.

ataraxia: Serenity, tranquility, or peace of mind.

atheism: A disbelief in the existence of God or a belief that there is no God.

atomism: The belief that matter is composed of simple, indivisible, physical particles that are too tiny to be observed by human beings.

atonement: In Christianity, the sacrifice and death of Jesus to redeem humankind from its sins.

aum: Often spelled Om, the sacred syllable and symbol of Hinduism; a symbol of the unknowable nature of Brahma.

Avesta: The chief sacred scripture of Zoroastrianism.

B

baptism: A religious ceremony in which a person is dipped in or sprinkled with water as a sign of being cleansed of sin.

bar mitzvah: The Jewish coming-of-age ceremony for boys.

bat mitzvah: The Jewish coming-of-age ceremony for girls.

belief: A conviction of the truth of a proposition either by close examination or trust.

Beltane (Beltaine): Neo-pagan holiday on April 30.

benevolence: The tendency to do good and to be kind to others.

Bhagavad Gita: A Sanskrit poem regarded as a Hindu scripture; part of the epic *Mahabharata,* which means "Great Epic of the Bharata Dynasty"; examines the nature of God and how mortals can know him.

bhakti: Devotion.

blasphemy: Disrespectful comments or actions concerning a religion or its God.

bodhisattva: A person who has attained enlightenment but, rather than entering a state of nirvana, chooses to stay behind to help others reach enlightenment.

Bon: An indigenous religion of Tibet.

Brahma: The creator-god.

The Buddha: The title of Siddhartha Gautama after he attained enlightenment.

C

caliph: One of Muhammad's successors as leader of the faith.

Candomblé: A South American religion with many similarities to Santería, often used synonymously with Santería.

canon: The official, sacred texts of a religion.

caste: Social classes in Hinduism, the dominant religion in India.

Celtic: A term referring to an ethnic group that spread throughout Europe, particularly the British Isles, and is the source of many modern neo-pagan movements.

church: From the Greek, this word refers to the community of all Christians. It is also the place where Christians go to worship.

consciousness: The condition of being aware of one's thoughts, feelings, and existence.

conservative: A movement in modern Judaism that tries to strike a balance between Orthodox and Reform Judaism.

conversion: A change in which a person adopts a new set of religious beliefs.

coven: A group of neo-pagans, such as Wiccans. Alternately referred to as circles, groves, kindreds, garths, hearths, and other terms.

covenant: In religion, a covenant refers to an agreement between God or a messenger of God and his followers.

creed: A statement of belief or basic principles.

crucifixion: The suffering and death by nailing or binding a person to a cross.

cuneiform: Sumerian writing, so-called because of its wedge-shaped marks.

D

daevas: Ancient Persian deities.

Dao: The path or way; the rhythmic balance and natural, flowing patterns of the universe.

***de*:** Political power that is the result of a ruler's virtue and honesty.

deity: A god or goddess.

dharma: Righteousness in one's religious and personal life.

Diaspora: The scattering of the Jews throughout the world.

Digambara: Literally "sky-clad"; one of the two major sects of Jainism.

disciple: A person who accepts and assists in spreading the teachings of a leader. In the Bible, a follower of Jesus.

doctrine: A set of ideas held by a religious group.

druidism: A neo-pagan religion based in the Celtic region of the British Isles.

dynasty: A sequence of rulers from the same family.

E

Eightfold Path: The path of the Buddha's teachings that can lead to the end of suffering.

Ek Onkar: The "True God" of Sikhism.

emanation: That which inevitably flows outward from the transcendental (spiritual, beyond human experience) central principle of reality, "the One," in the Neoplatonic philosophy of Plotinus.

empiricism: Belief that knowledge comes through the senses.

enlightenment: The state of realization and understanding of life, a feeling of unity with all things.

Epicureanism: The philosophy of Epicurus and others that states that the highest good is pleasure and the avoidance of pain.

equinox: Either of two points during the year when the Sun crosses the equator and the hours of day and night are equal. The spring, or vernal, equinox occurs generally on March 21 and the autumn equinox occurs on or about September 23.

Esbat: Wiccan celebration of the full Moon.

ethics: The study of moral values and rules or a guide to such values and rules.

etiquette: Proper behavior; good manners.

Evangelical: Describing a Protestant group that emphasizes the absolute authority of the Bible and forgiveness of sin through belief in Jesus.

excommunicate: To exclude or officially ban a person from a church or other religious community.

F

faith: Belief and trust in God, accompanied by a sense of loyalty to the traditional doctrines, or principles, of religion.

Faravahar: A figure of a bird with its wings spread that is a chief symbol of Zoroastrianism.

filial piety: The respect and devotion a child shows his or her parents.

***fitrah*:** An inborn tendency to seek the creator.

Five Classics: The original texts used by Confucius in his practices and teachings: *Liji, Shijing, Shujing, Chunqui,* and *Yijing.*

Five Pillars: The core of Islamic belief referring to declaring faith, daily prayer, charitable giving, fasting, and pilgrimage.

folk beliefs: The beliefs of the common people.

Folk (*Minzoku*) Shinto: Shinto that emphasizes folk beliefs, or common beliefs, of rural agricultural laborers.

Four Affirmations: A code of conduct by which Shintoists live, including emphases on tradition and family, nature, cleanliness, and worship of the kami.

Four Books: The most prominent of Confucian sacred texts, established by Zhu Xi: the Analects, the Mencius, *Da Xue* (Great Learning), and *Zhongyong* (Doctrine of the Mean).

Four Noble Truths: The foundations of the Buddhist religion: that all life is suffering, that desire causes suffering, that suffering can end, and that ending suffering happens by following the path of the Buddha's teachings.

G

Gahambars: Seasonal festivals.

Gathas: A portion of the Zend-Avesta that contains holy songs; believed to be the words of Zarathushtra himself.

God: The supreme or ultimate being or reality; creator of the universe.

Goddess worship: Term that refers generally to any neo-pagan practice that elevates the status of goddesses over that of gods.

Golden Temple: The chief Sikh temple, located in the city of Amritsar in India; more formally, the Sri Harmandir Sahib.

gurdwara: A Sikh temple or place of worship.

guru: A religious teacher.

H

Ha-ne-go-ate-geh: The "Evil-Minded," the evil spirit of the Iroquois nation.

Ha-wen-ne-yu: The Great Spirit of the Iroquois nation.

hadiths: The sayings of the prophet Muhammad recorded by his followers.

Haj: Pilgrimage to the holy city of Mecca.

halal: Permissible activities for Muslims.

Hanukkah: The Jewish Festival of Lights commemorating the rededication of the First Temple.

haram: Prohibited activities for Muslims.

heretic: A person whose beliefs oppose his or her religion's official doctrines, or defining principles.

Ho-no-che-no-keh: The Invisible Agents, or lesser spirits, of the Iroquois.

Holocaust: The systematic slaughter of Jews by the Nazi regime in Germany before and during World War II (1939–45).

householders: Laypeople; Jains who are not monks or nuns.

I

idol: A statue or other image that is worshipped as a god.

Imbolc: Neo-pagan holiday generally held on February 2 to mark the lengthening of the days and the emergence of the world from winter.

Immaculate Conception: The principle of the Roman Catholic Church that Mary, the mother of Jesus, was conceived with a soul free from original sin.

incarnation: In Christianity, the belief that God took on bodily form through Jesus, making Jesus fully human and fully divine.

indigenous: A word that describes a people, culture, or religion that is native to a particular geographical region.

indulgence: In the Roman Catholic Church, the belief that paying money to the Church would allow a person to get into heaven or be forgiven for sins that were not yet committed.

Izanagi: The male figure in the Shinto creation myth.

Izanami: The female figure in the Shinto creation myth.

J

jinja: Shrine.

jinn: Evil spirits that tempt a person away from dedication to Allah.

jinn: Literally, "conquerors"; the great teachers of Jainism who have conquered their earthly passions.

jiva: The soul.

***junzi*:** A gentleman or superior man.

K

***Ka'aba*:** The shrine built by the prophet Abraham in the holy city of Mecca and the focal point of pilgrimages to the city.

kama: Gratification of the senses.

kami: The gods or divinities of Shinto; the life force or spirit associated with places, natural objects, and ancestors.

kami-dana: A "kami shelf" or altar in a private home.

kara: A steel bracelet, worn by Sikhs as a symbol of God.

karma: The result of good or bad actions in this lifetime that can affect this or later lifetimes.

kasha: The white shorts worn by Sikhs as a symbol of purity.

kesh: Uncut hair, a symbol of Sikhism.

kevalnyan: Enlightenment.

Khalsa: The militant "brotherhood" of Sikhism, founded by Guru Gobind Singh.

Khanda: The emblem of Sikhism.

kirpan: A sword or dagger worn by Sikhs as a symbol of their willingness to fight to defend their faith.

Kojiki: The chief text of Shinto, a work that combines history, myth, and folk belief.

kosher: Dietary laws, referred to in Hebrew as *kashrut.*

kungha: The wooden comb used to groom hair, a symbol of Sikhism.

kushti: The sacred cord, or belt, that Zoroastrians wear.

kusti: The "holy path" one has to follow to be a Zoroastrian.

L

laity: Body of worshippers who are not members of the clergy.

***li*:** The rules of behavior a person must follow to reach the Confucian ideal of correct living.

Logos: Word, logic, or defining pattern of the universe, similar to the Dao in Chinese philosophy.

Lughnasadh: Neo-pagan harvest festival on August 1.

M

maat: Divine order and justice; a central concept in the religion of ancient Egypt.

Mabon: Neo-pagan celebration of the autumn equinox; the completion of the harvest season.

Magen David: The so-called Star of David, a symbol of the Jewish faith and nation.

magick: The ability to focus mental and physical energies to affect the natural world or to achieve a goal.

Mahavira: The twenty-fourth tirthankara often regarded as the founder of Jainism.

Mahavira jayanti: Mahavira's birthday, an important holy day for Jains.

mantra: A formula repeated over and over to create a trancelike state.

materialism: A belief that matter and the motion of matter constitute the universe. All phenomena, even those of mind, are the result of material interactions.

***matsuri*:** Festival.

Mecca: A city in present-day Saudi Arabia, the holiest site of Islam, where the religion was founded.

meditation: Quiet reflection on spiritual matters.

menorah: A seven-branched candelabrum; at Hanukkah, a nine-branched candelabrum is used.

Messiah: The expected deliverer and king of the Jews, foretold by the prophets of the Old Testament; used by Christians to refer to Jesus Christ.

metaphysical: Having to do with the philosophical study of the nature of reality and existence.

metaphysics: The branch of philosophy that deals with explanations for the most general questions of being, such as what brought the world into being, and the nature of space, time, God, and the afterlife.

metempsychosis: Transmigration of souls, or the migration of the soul into a different form, animal, or object after death.

mezuzah: A small case containing Torah passages that observant Jews attach to the doorposts of their houses.

midrashim: Stories that expand on incidents in the Hebrew Bible.

Mishnah: The written text of the Talmud.

mitzvoth: The laws of Judaism contained in the Torah.

moksha: Salvation; liberation from rebirth.

monastery: A place where religious people such as monks live, away from the world and following strict religious guidelines.

monotheism: Belief in one supreme being.

morality: Following the rules of right behavior and conduct.

Moshiach: The expected Messiah in Jewish belief.

***muezzin*:** The person who issues the call to prayer.

murti: Image of a god.

Muslim: A follower of Islam, from the Arabic phrase *bianna musliman,* meaning "submitted ourselves to God."

myth: A legendary story, often with no basis in historical fact, that frequently tells of the actions of deities and helps to explain some naturally occurring event or some supernatural occurrence.

mythology: The collected stories of a culture or religion, especially those dealing with the origins, heroes, gods, and beliefs of a group of people.

N

Naam Karam: The naming ceremony for children.

namaskar: The basic prayer of Jainism, recited each morning and at night before bedtime.

Neo-paganism: A term referring to modern religions based on ancient pagan religions.

nirvana: The end of suffering, beyond time and space; the goal of all Buddhists.

nivritti: People who choose to withdraw from the world to lead a life of renunciation and contemplation.

***norito*:** Prayers to the kami.

O

Offering of Eightfold Puja: An important Jain temple ritual in which the worshipper makes eight offerings to the tirthankara.

Olódùmarè: The name of the supreme god in Santería.

Om: Often spelled Aum; the sacred syllable and symbol of Jainism (and Hinduism), used for purposes of meditation.

Oral Torah: Interpretations of the Torah and ways to apply their laws.

orders: Religious communities.

Original Sin: The sin that fell upon humankind when Adam and Eve ate of the forbidden fruit in the Garden of Eden; this act, in turn, led to the separation of humans from God.

orishas: Name given to the lesser gods of Santería.

orthodox: The name of one of the sects of Judaism, generally referring to traditional Jews who are conservative in their outlook.

Oshogatsu: The Shinto new year.

Ostara: Neo-pagan holiday held at the time of the spring equinox.

P

pagan: Pre-Christian or non-Christian; also referring to those who worship many gods.

pantheon: The class or collection of all gods and goddesses in a system of belief.

Parshva: The twenty-third tirthankara, who lived about 250 years before Mahavira.

Parsis (Parsees): Zoroastrians who live in India.

Paryushana: An eight-day festival, the most important holy observance for Jains during the year.

Pesach: The feast of Passover, commemorating the flight of the Jews from Egypt.

philosophical Daoism: A form of Daoism by which followers seek knowledge and wisdom about the unity of everything in existence and how to become closer to it.

philosophy: The study of morals and reality by logical reasoning to gain a greater understanding of the world.

polytheism: A religion worshiping many gods.

pravritti: People who choose to live in the world rather than withdraw from it.

prophecy: Prediction of future events.

prophet: A person chosen to serve as God's messenger.

***pu*:** Uncarved or unformed; the state of simplicity to which Daoists try to return.

puja: Worship.

purusharthas: The four aims of Hinduism or "the doctrine of the four-fold end of life."

Purva: The original Jain sacred texts, now lost.

pyramid: A stone tomb constructed to house a deceased pharaoh of Egypt.

Q

***qi*:** The breath of life or vital energy that flows through the body and the earth.

Qur'an: The sacred scriptures of Islam; contains the revelations given to the prophet Muhammad revealed to him beginning in 610.

R

***ra'kah*:** A unit of prayer.

rationalism: Belief that knowledge can come exclusively from the mind.

reform: One of the sects of Judaism, generally used to refer to the less traditional branch of the faith.

Regla de Ocha: The formal name for the Santerían religion.

Rehit Maryada: The Sikh code of ethical conduct.

religious Daoism: A form of Daoism that recognizes gods, ancestor spirits, and life after death.

***ren*:** Empathy, the ability to feel for and sympathize with others; the highest Confucian ideal.

Resurrection: The rising of Jesus Christ from the dead three days after his Crucifixion, or death on a cross.

Rig Veda: The central scripture of Hinduism, a collection of inspired hymns and songs.

Rosh Hoshanah: The Jewish "New Year."

S

Sabbat: Holidays practiced by Wiccans throughout the year, including the summer and winter solstices, the vernal and autumnal equinoxes, and four additional holidays between these four.

sacrament: A sacred rite, or ceremony.

sadhana: Ascetic person.

saint: A deceased person who has been recognized for living a virtuous and holy life.

***salat*:** Daily prayer.

salvation: The deliverance of human beings from sin through Jesus Christ's death on the cross.

Samhain (Samhuinn): Neo-pagan holiday celebrated on October 31.

samsara: The ongoing cycle of birth, life, death, and rebirth.

Samyak charitra: Right conduct; one of the Three Jewels of Jain ethical conduct.

Samyak darshana: Right faith, or right perception; one of the Three Jewels of Jain ethical conduct.

Samyak jnana: Right knowledge; one of the Three Jewels of Jain ethical conduct.

Sanskrit: An ancient Indo-European language that is the language of Hinduism, as well as of much classical Indian literature.

Santería: The "way of the saints"; an African-based religion practiced primarily in Cuba and other Central and South American countries.

Santero: A practitioner of Santería.

***saum*:** Fasting.

sect: A small religious group that has branched off from a larger established religion.

Sect (*Kyoha*) Shinto: Shinto as it is practiced by a number of sects, or groups, formed primarily in the nineteenth century.

secular: Worldly things, of the physical world, as opposed to religious and spiritual.

Sedreh-pushi: The Zoroastrian initiation rite.

Sephardic: Term used to refer to Jews of North Africa, the Middle East, Spain, and Portugal.

***Shahadah*:** The Islamic declaration of faith. It consists of the words "*Ashahadu an la ilaha ill Allah wa ashahadu ann Muhammadar Rasulullah,*" or "I declare there is no god except God, and I declare that Muhammad is the Messenger of God."

shaman: In indigenous tribes, an intermediary between the gods and the tribal members; also one who controls various spiritual forces, can look into the future, and can cure the ill with magic.

shamanism: A term used generally to refer to indigenous religions that believe in an unseen spirit world that influences human affairs.

***shariʾah*:** Islamic law.

Shiʾite: One of the main sects of Islam; from the phrase *Shiʾat Ali,* or the party of ʿAli.

***Shinbutsu bunri*:** The separation of Shinto and Buddhism when Shinto was declared the official state religion.

***Shinbutsu shugo*:** The combination of Shinto and Buddhism.

Shinto: Literally, "the way of the gods" or "the way of the kami."

Shiva: The destroyer god, embodying the erotic and sexual.

Shivaism: A major sect of Hinduism, which sees Shiva ("the Destroyer") as the central god.

Shrine (*Jinja*) Shinto: The traditional, mainstream practice of Shinto, with emphasis on the local shrine.

skepticism: Doubt or disbelief toward a particular proposition or object.

Skepticism: A philosophical system that doubted the possibility of ever discovering real truth through the senses.

Socratic: Having to do with the philosopher Socrates and his method of asking questions of students to develop an idea.

solstice: The points in the year when the day is longest (the summer solstice, generally on June 21) and the shortest (the winter solstice, generally on December 21).

Sophists: A group of traveling teachers in ancient Greece who doubted the possibility of knowing all the truth through the physical senses.

State Shinto: Shinto as it was practiced after it was declared the official state religion in the late nineteenth century until 1945.

Stoicism: The philosophical system that holds that people should pursue the knowledge of human and divine things through the use of logical systems. It also says that humans may not be able to control natural events, but that they can control the way they react to them.

stupas: Originally a mound marking the spot where the Buddha's ashes were buried. Rock pillars carved with the words of the Buddha are also sometimes called stupas.

Sufism: A trend in or way of practicing Islam; characterized by an ecstatic, trancelike mysticism.

Sunnah: The example of the prophet Muhammad, containing the hadiths, or sayings; provides guidance to everyday questions of faith and morality.

Sunni: The main sect of Islam.

supernatural: That which is beyond the observable world, including things relating to God or spirits.

supreme being: The central God responsible for creating the cosmos.

***sura*:** Any chapter in the Qur'an.

Susano-o: The Shinto god of violence and the ruler of the oceans.

Svetambara: Literally, "white-clad"; one of the two main sects of Jainism.

swastika: A pictorial character that symbolizes the eternal nature of Brahma because it points in all directions; also used as the official emblem of the Nazi Party during World War II (1939–45).

T

takhts: Seats of spiritual authority in Sikhism. The "Five Takhts" are gurdwaras located in India.

Talmud: Traditions that explain and interpret the Torah.

Tanakh: The chief Jewish scripture; the Hebrew Bible.

***tawba*:** Repentance.

theism: Belief in the existence of gods or God.

theocracy: A form of government in which God or some supreme deity is the ruler. God's laws are then interpreted by a divine king or by a priest class.

theology: The study of God and of religions truths.

Three Jewels: The Jain code of ethical conduct, consisting of right faith, right knowledge, and right conduct.

Tian: Heaven, or the principle of ordering the universe.

Tipitaka: The Buddhist sacred texts accepted by all branches of Buddhism.

tirthankara: Literally, "makers of the ford,"; those souls who have attained enlightenment and have been freed from the cycle of death and rebirth; the twenty-four leaders of Jainism.

Torah: The first five books of the Tanakh: Genesis, Exodus, Leviticus, Numbers, and Deuteronomy.

***tori*:** The gate that marks the entrance to a shrine. Its shape is regarded as a symbol of Shinto.

totem: Some sort of object or, perhaps, animal that assumes a spiritual symbolism for a clan or tribe.

transcendent: Going beyond the ordinary, beyond the universe and time, into spiritual dimensions.

Trinity: In Christianity, the union of the Father, Son, and Holy Spirit as three divine persons in one God.

Tsukiyomi: The Shinto moon-god and the ruler of night.

U

***ujiko*:** A "named child" whose name is entered at birth at the local Shinto shrine.

Upanishads: The core of Hindu philosophy; collections of texts, originally part of the Vedas, that explain such core Hindu beliefs as karma, reincarnation, nirvana, the soul, and Brahman.

urvan: The soul.

V

Vaishnavaism: A major sect of Hinduism, which sees Vishnu ("the Preserver") as the central god.

Vedas: The chief sacred scriptures of Hinduism; knowledge, wisdom, or vision.

Virgin Birth: The Christian belief that Jesus Christ was the Son of God and born of a virgin mother.

Vishnu: Also called Krishna; the preserver-god.

Vodou: An African-based religion practiced primarily in Haiti and in other Central and South American countries.

Vodouisant: An uninitiated practitioner of Vodou.

W

Wakan: The incomprehensibility of life and death for the Sioux.

Wakan tanka: The world's motivating force for the Sioux.

***wen*:** The arts of music, poetry, and painting.

Wicca: The name of a neo-pagan religion that generally worships the God and the Goddess.

***wu wei*:** Nonaction, or deliberate and thoughtful action that follows the Dao.

Y

Yahweh: One of the names for God in the Tanakh.

yazata: Guardian angel.

Yin and yang: Literally, "shady" and "sunny"; terms referring to how the universe is composed of opposing but complementary forces.

Yom Kippur: The Day of Atonement.

Z

***zakat*:** Annual charitable giving.

ziggurat: A stepped foundation or structure that held a shrine or temple in the Mesopotamian religion.

Zionism: A movement that began in the nineteenth century to find a permanent home for Jews.

Abraham

BORN: c. 2050 BCE • Ur, Mesopotamia

DIED: c. 1950 BCE • Hebron, Canaan

religious leader

Abraham.

"I will make you into a great nation and I will bless you; . . . and all the peoples on earth will be blessed through you."

— God to Abraham, Genesis 12:2–3

Abraham is considered by many scholars to be one of the most important figures in religious history. His belief in one supreme being had a significant effect on the development of Western religion, and his life is often seen as a symbol of the power of faith and loyalty.

Abraham plays a central role in the major religions of Judaism, Christianity, and Islam. Christians believe that Abraham had much in common with **Jesus Christ** (c. 6 BCE–c. 30 CE; see entry), since both received promises from God to bless humanity. In the Islamic faith he is regarded as the first prophet, or messenger of God, as well as the ancestor (through his first son, Ishmael) of the Arab people. Both Christianity and Islam, as well as Judaism, look to Abraham as a founding father of their faith. In a 2002 *Time* magazine article, David Van Biema noted: "In fact, excluding God, Abraham is the only biblical figure who enjoys the unanimous acclaim of all three faiths, the only one . . . referred to by all three as Father."

The only records of Abraham's life come from oral tradition and passages in the Bible and the Islamic holy book, the Qur'an. This has made it difficult for historians to write a completely factual biography of him. The life of Abraham is thus a mixture of historical reconstruction, religious legend, and guesswork.

A child of Mesopotamia

Abraham was born in Ur, the major city of Mesopotamia, near modern-day Baghdad. According to the Bible, he was originally given the name of Abram or Avram, which means "exalted father" in Hebrew. It was much later in his life that God supposedly gave him the name Abraham, which means "father of many nations."

Abram's father, Terah, was well over seventy when Abram and his brothers, Haran and Nahor, were born. Abram was raised in a wealthy family. Terah owned property and livestock and also is said to have made idols (images worshipped as gods) of various gods of ancient Babylonia. Polytheism, or belief in many gods, was common among Mesopotamians and Babylonians during this period. Ur was the center of a cult, or group of religious followers, that worshipped Nanna, the moon god. Around the time of Abram's birth, the Babylonians began to recognize one god, Marduk, as having power over all the other gods. Some historians consider this an early move in the direction of monotheism, or the belief in one supreme being.

Many stories grew around the fact that Terah produced idols and his son Abram did not believe in worshipping them. People would pray to the idols, which represented various gods. One legend had young Abram breaking all the idols in a shop except for one, which was said to be an early hint that his later beliefs would turn to monotheism. Other tales have him criticizing older customers for buying idols. Several later stories relate how Abram burned his father's idols. The Qur'an recounts that because of his disapproval of idols, Abram was condemned to burn in the furnace of the king of Babylon, but God protected him. Abram's brother, Haran, also did not believe in idols, but he was not saved by God. He is said to have died in the furnace because his faith in God was not strong enough.

Promise of a new land

Terah decided to leave Ur around the time Abram married his half sister, Sarai. Terch took his family, including Abram, Sarai, and Haran's son, Lot, with him. They settled in the city of Haran (later part of Turkey). After Terah died, Abram received his first message from God, telling him to leave his homeland behind and to go to the land that God would show him.

Abram was seventy-five at the time, and, according to the account in Genesis from the Old Testament, or the Hebrew Bible, he had not demonstrated any specific religious beliefs or devotion. The tales of his destruction of the idols were a much later addition to the Abraham legend. According to the passages in Genesis numbered chapter 12, verse 2 (12:2) and 12:3, God told Abram: "I will make you into a great nation and I will bless you; will make your name great, and you will be a blessing. I will bless those who bless you, and whoever curses you I will curse; and all the peoples on earth will be blessed through you." This passage from the Old Testament became an important part of a later Christian argument from the Apostle **Paul** (c. 3 BCE–c. 67 CE; see entry). An apostle was one of a group of people in the New Testament of the Bible who were sent out to preach the words of Jesus Christ. Paul believed that these words showed that Abraham passed on God's blessing to all humankind, not just to Jews, paving the way for the rise of Christianity.

Into Canaan

Abram listened to the word of God and set out from Haran with his wife, his nephew, Lot, and the community that had gathered around them. The group traveled west to the Euphrates River, crossing it and perhaps stopping temporarily at ancient Damascus, now a part of Syria. From there they traveled south and east, crossing the Jordan River and reaching the plain of Schechem. God again appeared to Abram and promised him and his offspring the surrounding land of Canaan (modern-day Israel), even though it was already populated by Canaanites, the descendants of Noah and his son, Ham. Abram built an altar to God at Schechem and then moved on to Bethel, north of Jerusalem, where he built another altar.

According to Genesis, Abram and his followers remained in Canaan until a famine drove them farther south into Egypt. There, fearful that the sight of his beautiful wife, Sarai, might cause the Egyptians to murder

ב
עזר אלהי קדם שוכן
מעונה: אחל לפרש
תפלות כל השנה:

The first page from the Book of Abraham, written in Hebrew. Details of Abraham's life are relayed in the Old Testament, a holy text of the Jewish and Christian faiths, and in the Islamic holy book, the Qur'an. © CHRISTEL GERSTENBERG/ CORBIS.

him in order to win his bride, Abram told Sarai that they would travel as brother and sister. When the Egyptian pharaoh saw her, he took Sarai into his harem, not knowing that she was Abram's wife. Abram became wealthy as a result of this, acquiring sheep, cattle, and servants from the pharaoh. Such payments were compensation from the pharaoh for taking Sarai into the harem. When God learned of this, however, it displeased Him and He punished the pharaoh with a plague. As a result, the pharaoh became angry with Abram, returned Sarai, and ordered Abram and his people to leave Egypt with their carts of wealth.

They returned to Canaan. There, Lot and Abram decided to part company because of arguments between the men who tended their livestock. Lot and his followers set off for the lands east of the Jordan River and southwest of the Dead Sea, where the cities of Sodom and Gomorrah were located. Again God appeared to Abram and told him that the lands to the north were his, so Abram and his group traveled to Hebron, where they settled and built another altar to God. Abram then heard that Lot and his group had been caught up in a war between the king of Sodom and three other kings and had been taken prisoner. Abram gathered 318 fighters and rescued his nephew. God then gave Abram a prophesy, or a foretelling of the future. He told Abram that the land between the Nile River and the Euphrates would belong to his descendants, but that they would be enslaved and mistreated for four centuries before such things came to pass. God also promised Abram that he would have as many heirs (children) as there were stars in the sky.

Fulfilling God's promise

In Egypt Sarai had acquired a maid named Hagar. Sarai was unable to bear children, so she gave Abram this maid to provide him with heirs. When Abram was eighty-six, Hagar gave birth to his son, Ishmael. Sarai soon grew jealous of her maid and drove her away, but God sent Hagar back. When Abram was ninety-nine, God again appeared to him and told him that he would be the father of many nations. God also declared that he was no longer to be known as Abram, but as Abraham.

Abraham's wife's name was changed to Sarah, and God said that she would bear a male child who would carry on Abraham's line and the covenant, or agreement, with God that promised that Abraham and his heirs would be blessed. The child would be called Isaac, meaning "he laughs," because Abraham laughed at the idea of having a son at the age of one hundred. Ishmael, the first-born son, would be blessed as the father of twelve rulers, which both Jews and Arabs believe to be the twelve Arab tribes.

Bargaining with God

A short time later, God appeared again, disguised as a visitor with two companions, and Abraham proved himself a generous host to these

The Birth of the Jews

God's blessing of Abraham was passed on to Abraham's son, Isaac. Isaac had two children, Esau and Jacob. Esau, as the oldest, was chosen to receive the blessing after his father. Jacob, however, tricked his brother out of his birthright by offering the hungry Esau a bowl of soup in exchange for his inheritance. Jacob, who later became known as Israel, had a dozen sons, and these sons formed the twelve tribes of Israel. Judah, Issachar, and Zebulun settled in the north of Canaan, while Ruben, Simeon, and Gad settled in the south. Benjamin made his home in the west, as did Ephriam and Menassah, the children of Joseph, Jacob's favorite son. Dan, Asher, and Naphtali moved to districts in the east. The tribe of Jacob's third son, Levi, was set apart to serve the Holy Temple in Jerusalem. The Bible refers to Abraham and his descendants as Hebrews, and later, after Jacob's change of name to Israel, as Israelites. The term *Jew* is a shortened version of Judahites, which is what the inhabitants of Judah's northern tribe were called.

strangers. God let Abraham know that he was going to destroy the cities of Sodom and Gomorrah because of their wickedness. Abraham bargained with God in order to save Lot, who still lived in Sodom. God agreed that if He could find ten righteous people in Sodom, He would spare the city. Although He failed to find ten good people, God did warn Lot and his family to leave the city before He destroyed it. Lot's wife, however, was turned into a column of salt because, although she was told not to, she glanced back to look at the city as they ran away.

After the destruction of Sodom, Abraham and his household moved to Gerar, located in the western Negev desert, about nine miles southeast of Gaza and fifteen miles northwest of Beersheba. Again fearing for his life because of his beautiful wife, Abraham introduced Sarah as his sister. The local king, Abimelech, was attracted to her and took her into his house, but once again God intervened. The king returned Abraham's wife untouched and gave Abraham sheep, cattle, slaves, and money as a form of apology.

Accepting God's will

As promised, Isaac was born to Abraham and Sarah while they were living in Gerar. Sarah still wished to get rid of Hagar and Hagar's son, Ishmael, and Abraham allowed her to send them away. God saved them, however, and, according to the Qur'an, mother and son traveled to Mecca, where Abraham often went to visit them.

God had one more test for Abraham. He wanted him to sacrifice his son, Isaac. (In Islamic tradition, it was believed that Ishmael was to have been the sacrifice.) Abraham obeyed this command and took his son, who was then probably an adult, to the appointed place, tied him down, and was about to kill him when God called out for Abraham to stop. As recounted in Genesis 22:12, God said, "Do not lay a hand on the boy. . . . Do not do anything to him. Now I know that you fear God, because you have not withheld from me your son, your only son." Then God renewed his promise to Abraham, saying, "I will surely bless you and make your descendants as numerous as the stars in the sky and as the sand on the seashore. Your descendants will take possession of the cities of their enemies and through your offspring all the nations on earth will be blessed, because you have obeyed me" (Genesis 22:17–18).

Abraham's wife Sarah reportedly lived to be 127 years old. When she died, Abraham buried her in the cave of Machpelah near Hebron and eventually took another wife, Keturah, who bore him many children. Abraham left all his possessions to his son Isaac, who married Rebekah. They became the parents of Jacob and Esau. Jacob, in turn, had a dozen sons who later formed the twelve tribes of Israel. Abraham is said to have lived to the age of 175, although this has never been confirmed. He was buried next to Sarah.

The importance of Abraham

The life of Abraham has had a profound influence on Hebrew (Jewish) culture right up to the modern day. It was Abraham who refused to follow polytheism and pursued the belief in one god, and it was to Abraham that God promised the lands between the Nile and the Euphrates rivers. Such a promise is important even in the modern-day state of Israel, as many Israelis believe it gives authority to their claim to the lands in this region. Jews trace their ancestry back to Abraham, his son Isaac, and grandson Jacob. Many Jews also see Abraham as a role model of faith, obedience, and success.

Abraham and the Old Testament story of Abraham's blessing also figures prominently in Christianity. Christians claim that God blessed all nations on Earth through Abraham, therefore showing that Judaism is not the one and true religion. In the orthodox, or conservative, Christian view, this interpretation is taken even further. Conservative Christians believe that Jesus Christ was the fulfillment of God's blessing and that Christianity is the true religion of God. In Islam, Abraham is considered to be a prophet. The Qur'an states that he was in fact the first Muslim. Christians also point out that Abraham's willingness to sacrifice Isaac was similar to God's later sacrifice of his only son, Jesus. As a test of his faith, Abraham was required to show his love for God by sacrificing his son, Isaac, as a burnt offering. Just as Isaac carried wood for his own sacrifice up the mountain and did not fight being sacrificed, so did Jesus carry his own cross and allowed himself to be crucified.

Similarly, Muslims also look to Abraham, whom they call Ibrahim, as one of the fathers of their faith. The Prophet **Muhammad** (c. 570–632; see entry) claimed Abraham was the first messenger or prophet of God, while he, Muhammad, was the final prophet. Arabs also see Abraham's first-born, Ishmael, or Ismail, as the ancestor of the Arab people. According to Muslim tradition, Ibrahim and Ismail built the Ka'aba inside the Great Mosque in Mecca, the holiest site in Islam. The Ka'aba is thought to be the shrine that Ibrahim built to God when he was traveling in the desert. The five repetitions of daily Muslim prayer also begin and end with a reference to Abraham.

For More Information

BOOKS

Feiler, Bruce. *Abraham: A Journey to the Heart of Three Faiths.* New York, NY: HarperCollins, 2005.

Schultz, Samuel J. *The Old Testament Speaks.* 2nd ed. New York, NY: Harper and Row, 1970.

Van Seters, John. "Abraham." *Encyclopedia of Religion.* Edited by Lindsay Jones. 2nd ed. Detroit, MI: Macmillan Reference USA, 2005, pp. 13–17.

Van Seters, John. *Abraham in History and Tradition.* New Haven, CT: Yale University Press, 1975.

Wilson, Marvin R. *Our Father Abraham: Jewish Roots of the Christian Faith.* Grand Rapids, MI: Eerdmans Publishing Co., 1989.

PERIODICALS

Baschet, Jerome. "Medieval Abraham." *MLN* (September 1993): 738.

Lerner, Michael. "Cruelty Is Not Destiny: Abraham and the Psychodynamics of Childhood." *Tikkun* (September–October 1994): 33.

Van Biema, David. "The Legacy of Abraham." *Time* (September 30, 2002): 64.

WEB SITES

"Abraham." *WebBible Encyclopedia.* http://www.christiananswers.net/dictionary/abraham.html (accessed on May 22, 2006).

Howlett, J. A. "Abraham." *Catholic Encyclopedia Online.* http://www.newadvent.org/cathen/01051a.htm (accessed on May 22, 2006).

Akhenaten

BORN: c. 1371 BCE • Egypt

DIED: c. 1334 BCE • Egypt

Egyptian pharaoh

"How numerous are your works, though hidden from sight. / Unique god, there is none beside him. / You mould the earth to your wish, you and you alone. . . ."

Akhenaten, which means "One useful to Aten," was the name taken by the pharaoh Amenhotep IV. He ruled Egypt from about 1350 to 1334 BCE. In the fourth year of his rule, he elevated a minor deity or god, Aten, to the position of state god of Egypt, and moved his capital from Thebes to Akhetaten, a deserted spot midway between Thebes and Memphis. He is often cited in history as one of the first leaders to direct religion toward monotheism, or belief in one god. Egypt had been a polytheistic society, or one that believes in many gods, before Akhenaten's reign. His switch to monotheism made him hated by many people in Egypt who did not like the change. A few years after his death the pharaoh Tutankhamen (reigned 1361–52 BCE) moved the capital back to Thebes and reestablished the power of the earlier gods. Attempts were later made to erase Akhenaten's name from historical records. This effort was successful until modern archaeology, which is the

Akhenaten.

scientific study of past human culture and behavior, established the identity of this mysterious ruler.

From Amenhotep IV to Akhenaten

Historical dating in ancient Egypt is a difficult matter because not all records survived or were accurately recorded. As a result, the exact date of the birth of Amenhotep IV is unclear, but most sources put his birth at 1371 BCE. He was the second son of Amenhotep III, a pharaoh, or king, during the Eighteenth Dynasty (c. 1540–c. 1307 BCE). He grew up in his father's court at Memphis, near modern-day Cairo, and then later at the court in Thebes, modern-day Luxor. After the early death of his older brother, Thutmose, Amenhotep IV became next in line to become pharaoh. It is believed that he served as coregent (co-pharaoh) with his father for a time, and when Amenhotep III died in about 1353 BCE, Amenhotep IV took the throne.

Amenhotep IV inherited a rich empire that stretched from North Africa to the Middle East. As pharaoh he was considered by his subjects to be both a ruler and a godlike person. Egypt had long been a theocracy, a government ruled by religious authority. Even though he was viewed as a god himself, the pharaoh still had to ask the most powerful gods for divine assistance. He prayed to the gods through the priests. During the time of Amenhotep IV, the primary god was Amen (also Amun or Amon), king of the gods. Next in importance was Ra (or Re), the sun god. These two were jointly worshipped by the powerful cult of Amen-Ra.

At the beginning of his reign Amenhotep IV appears to have followed the practices of previous Egyptian rulers. He worshipped the old gods, such as Amon and Re, and built temples in their honor at Thebes. There were some early hints, however, that he was not destined to be a completely traditional pharaoh. Like his father before him, Amenhotep IV married a commoner. This was noteworthy because Egyptian rulers were expected to marry only within the royal bloodline. Amenhotep IV took Nefertiti as his wife before he assumed the throne. Noted for her beauty, Nefertiti later shared divine status with her husband. She was the daughter of a military advisor, Ay, who may have been a brother of Amenhotep IV's mother, Queen Tiy. Amenhotep IV and Nefertiti had six daughters.

In the first year of his rule Amenhotep IV worshipped a minor god, Aten (also spelled Aton), a local variation of the sun god. Aten was the Egyptian word for the sun as seen in the sky, and Aten was portrayed as a disk with rays shining from it. The rays sometimes had human hands at the ends, holding out the *ankh,* or symbol of life, to the king and queen. It is unknown what drew Amenhotep IV to this minor deity. It may have been the idea of the sun as the source of all life. Some also believe that Amenhotep IV was sickly and the warmth of the sun eased his discomfort. Other historians say that there was a more practical reason for the pharaoh's attraction to this god. There was no powerful priest class built around Aten as there was around Amen-Ra. No great rituals were performed, and no temples had been erected. Therefore, by making Aten his god, Amenhotep IV may have been attempting to win more power for himself. He may have wanted to weaken the power of the priest class and centralize it in the office of pharaoh.

In his third year of power Amenhotep IV decided to celebrate what was known as a Sed-festival. The festival was a royal celebration usually held only in the thirtieth year of a pharaoh's rule. This made it apparent to many that Amenhotep IV was trying to increase his power. Around 1347 BCE he established Aten as the state god of Egypt. The following year he officially changed his name to Akhenaten. His wife changed hers to Neferneferuaten ("Exquisite Beauty of the Aten"). That same year Akhenaten decided to move the capital of Egypt from Thebes to a new location two hundred miles distant, on the east side of the Nile. This place is now called Tel el-Amarna or Amarna, and Amarna is the name given to the brief period of Akhenaten's rule from that capital.

Amarna Art

During the Amarna period, as Akhenaten's rule is known, the art of Egypt went through a revolution. Egyptian art traditionally portrayed people in a lifeless, dignified, and stiff manner. In profile, their faces appeared calm and almost expressionless. Emphasis was on angular lines. Realism became more common during Akhenaten's rule. In the visual arts there was more use of curved lines and roundness. Portraits showed motion and close relations between people. Vegetation and nature were added. Akhenaten and his wife, Neferneferuaten, were shown in formal poses making offerings to the sun god, Aten, but they were also seen in happy domestic scenes, playing with three of their daughters. This emphasis on realism and human qualities even translated to writing. The vernacular, or common spoken language, was introduced into the written language for the first time.

Realism was encouraged in paintings of Akhenaten. He was shown with a thin, drawn-out face, a pointed chin and thick lips, an elongated neck, and almost feminine breasts. He had a round belly with wide hips, fat thighs, thin legs, and long, spidery fingers. These portrayals have inspired many art and medical historians to consider the Akhenaten's physical condition. Many historians have speculated whether these depictions of him reflect a disease that affected his appearance, such as Marfan's syndrome, a disorder affecting the elastic tissue, skeleton, cardiovascular system, and eyes. There are many theories about Akhenaten and why he appears as he does in the artwork from the Amarna period. Until his mummy is found, however, no verification is available. Regardless of whether Akhenaten had such a disease, the art from his rule endures as a unique and curious period in Egyptian history.

The Amarna period

On this desert site Akhenaten created a new capital, called Akhetaten ("Horizon of Aten"). It stretched for five miles on a narrow band of desert between high cliffs and the Nile River. To the north and south were the homes of merchants and government officials. In the center of the city lay the royal palace, the granaries (grain storage buildings), and the Great Temple of Aten. Akhenaten's worship of the sun influenced a new style of architecture. His temples to Aten were not the usual massive, closed structures, but a series of open courts facing east, the direction in which the sun rises. Even the doorways in these temples had openings in the tops of their frames to allow the light of the sun to reach every corner. The city appears to have been created as a huge stage for Akhenaten. His daily journey from his palace through the city and back again was said to symbolize the passage of the sun from sunrise to sunset.

Just as Akhenaten and Neferneferuaten worshipped Aten, so did the Egyptian people in turn worship Akhenaten and his wife. They believed Aten gave life through the pharaoh, who they saw as his direct representative and son. In the ninth year of his rule Akhenaten announced that Aten was not just the supreme god of Egypt, but the only god. Therefore the power of Akhenaten, who was Aten's representative, was multiplied along with the god's increase in status. The word "gods" on public monuments was erased. The priest class the pharaoh established competed with the older priests who served Amen and Ra and had assembled enormous power for themselves. Temples to Amen and Ra were closed or destroyed. Akhenaten even declared that Aten would take over the work of Osiris, god of the underworld and the dead, and look after the souls of the departed. No longer would there be an underworld where such spirits dwelled. Instead the spirits, or *ba,* remained on Earth. At sunset, spirits that were found loyal to Akhenaten traveled to the temple of Aten at Akhetaten, where they received offerings.

These later stages of Atenism were a form of monotheism. Since the people actually worshipped Akhenaten and his wife rather than Aten directly, however, it was different from the strict monotheism practiced in religions developed later such as Judaism, Christianity, and Islam. Atenism had no apparent ethical system or code of conduct. Instead, it appears to have been more a form of nature worship. Hymns that were written to Aten praised nature and the power of the sun. Some historians have speculated that Akhenaten and his religion influenced the contemporary Hebrew lawgiver and religious leader **Moses** (c. 1392–c. 1272 BCE; see entry).

Akhenaten makes offerings to the god Aten, represented as a sun disk. The style of art during Akhenaten's reign was quite different from the traditional style and is often referred to as Amarna Art.

© ARCHIVO ICONOGRAFICO, S.A./ CORBIS.

For example, Sigmund Freud (1856–1939), the father of modern psychiatry (the study of the mind and its ills), wrote in his *Moses and Monotheism* that Moses was a priest of Aten forced to flee Egypt after the death of Akhenaten. The lack of moral guidelines in Atenism, however, is in striking contrast to the many laws of Judaism.

Another interesting aspect of Akhenaten's reign and of Atenism is the stronger role women played during this period. Akhenaten's mother, Tiy, continued to play an important role in the government. Some historians even say that she may have been a coregent until her death. Neferneferuaten is believed by many archaeologists and historians to have had a strong influential role over her husband. Akhenaten also had other royal wives, including Kiya. She was probably the mother of Tutankhamen, the child-pharaoh, whose tomb in Egypt's Valley of the Kings was discovered by Howard Carter in 1922. In addition, there was Meritaten, the primary royal wife later in Akhenaten's rule, and Ankhesenpaaten. These last two may also have been Akhenaten's own daughters.

Decline and fall

Akhenaten's focus on religion led to a decline in the economic power of Egypt. Great sums were spent on the building of Akhetaten and the construction of temples to Aten throughout the country. The property and wealth of other temples were transferred to those honoring Aten. This ultimately led to misuse of funds and corruption. Additionally, Akhenaten's focus on religion had harmful results on the politics of Egypt, both within the empire and internationally. Akhenaten made many political enemies when he destroyed the religious traditions of centuries in a few short years. He also neglected the army, and without a strong army, order could not be kept.

Akhenaten ignored the outposts of his empire in Syria and Palestine, as documented in the writings later called the Amarna Letters. These 380 clay tablets present letters between Akhenaten and the kings or princes of colonies all over the Middle East. They include requests for aid from the local princes, who were being invaded by other tribes. It appears Akhenaten did nothing to help these princes. The vast Egyptian empire he had inherited eventually began to fall apart. Foreign trade was lost, and new enemies threatened Egypt. There was also an outbreak of influenza (flu) or the plague during the later Amarna period. The sickness spread into the Middle East. The Egyptian people began to wonder if the old gods had turned against Akhenaten.

Toward the end of his seventeen-year reign, Akhenaten appears to have tried to strengthen his failing rule. His successor, Smenkhare, may have acted as coregent for a time. Historical documents do not note what happened to Neferneferuaten at the end of her husband's reign. Archaeologists suspect that she either took a stronger role in the government or died and was replaced by other wives. Akhenaten died peacefully at about thirty-five years of age. He was succeeded by Smenkhare, probably one of his sons by Kiya. When Smenkhare died suddenly, Tutankhaten took over the leadership. He soon changed his name to Tutankhamen, embracing the old god Amen and moving the capital back to Thebes.

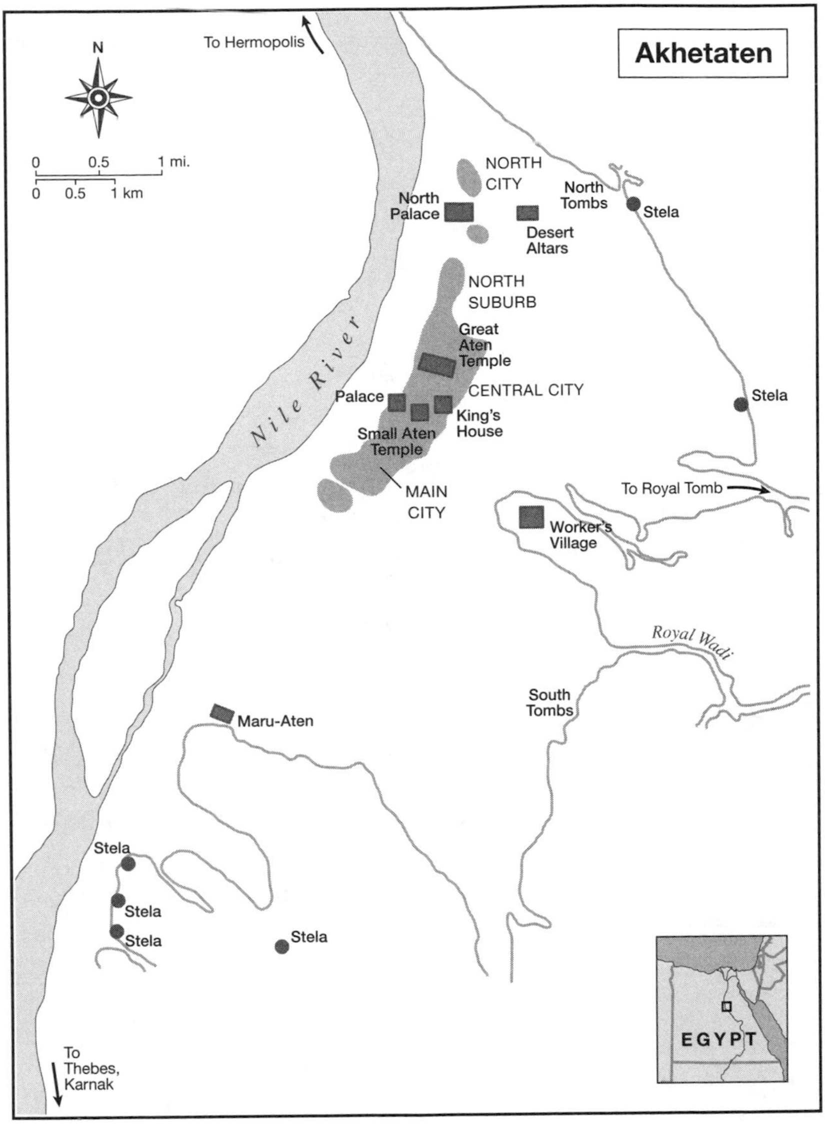

Akhenaten founded the city of Akhetaten, modern-day Tell el-Amarna, and moved Egypt's capital there. The city was dedicated to the worship of Akhenaten's one god, Aten THOMSON GALE.

The Amen-Ra priesthood once again came to power. After the death of the next pharaoh, Ay, and the takeover by the military leader Horemheb, all four pharaohs that were associated with the Amarna period were erased from the historical record of Egypt. The ruins of Akhenaten's once-glorious city eventually crumbled back into the desert. His experiment in monotheism was a forgotten part of history for three thousand years. It was not until the late nineteenth century that archaeologists uncovered the riches of this era in Egyptian history.

The site of Akhetaten was initially investigated by archaeologist John Gardner Wilkinson in 1824. Its story was then gradually revealed to the public.

For More Information

BOOKS

Aldred, Cyril. *Akhenaten: King of Egypt.* New York, NY: Thames and Hudson, 1991.

Assmann, Jan. *The Mind of Egypt: History and Meaning in the Time of the Pharaohs.* New York, NY: Metropolitan Books, 2002.

Johnson, Paul. *The Civilization of Ancient Egypt.* New York, NY: HarperCollins, 1998.

Montserrat, Dominic. *Akhenaten: History, Fantasy and Ancient Egypt.* London; New York: Routledge, 2000.

Redford, Donald. *Akhenaten, the Heretic King.* Princeton, NJ: Princeton University Press, 1984.

Reeves, Nicholas. *Akhenaten: Egypt's False Prophet.* London; New York: Thames & Hudson, 2001.

PERIODICALS

Ohayon, Stephen. "In Search of Akhenaten." *American Imago* (summer 1982): 165–179.

Ray, John. "Akhenaten: Ancient Egypt's Prodigal Son?" *History Today* (January 1990): 26–32.

Skurdenis, Julie. "Akhetaten: A Heretic Pharaoh's City." *International Travel News* (November 1992): 79–82.

Wassef, Ayyam. "Aket-aton, City of the Sun." *UNESCO Courier* (February 1991): 22–24.

WEB SITES

"Akhenaten." *Egyptology Online.* http://www.egyptologyonline.com/akhenaten1.htm (accessed on May 22, 2006).

"Amenhotep IV (Akhenaten)." *Egypt: Rulers, Kings, and Pharaohs of Ancient Egypt.* http://www.touregypt.net/18dyn10.htm/ (accessed on May 22, 2006).

"Great Hymn to the Aten." *Digital Egypt.* http://www.digitalegypt.ucl.ac.uk/amarna/belief.html (accessed on May 22, 2006).

Spence, Kate. "Akhenaten and the Amarna Period." *BBC Online.* http://www.bbc.co.uk/history/ancient/egyptians/akhenaten_01.shtml (accessed on May 22, 2006).

ʿAlī ibn Abī Tālib

BORN: c. 600 • Mecca, Saudi Arabia

DIED: January, 661 • Kufa, Iraq

Arabian religious leader

"Whoever is eager for Paradise will ignore temptations; whoever fears the fire of Hell will abstain from sins; whoever practices piety will easily bear the difficulties of life; and whoever anticipates death will hasten towards good deeds."

ʿAlī ibn Abī Tālib is considered the second most well-known Muslim after **Muhammad** (c. 570–632; see entry), the founder of the Islamic faith. ʿAli was one of the first converts (a person who changes his or her religion) to Islam, and he was a loyal follower of Muhammad, who was both his cousin and his father-in-law. A respected soldier and administrator, ʿAli became the fourth caliph, or leader, of the people of Islam in 656. Yet not all Muslims, or the faithful of Islam, accepted him. In fact, it was the disagreement over the legitimate succession to the position of caliph that caused the basic split in Islam that still exists in the early twenty-first century.

The followers of ʿAli were known as *Shiʾat ʿAli,* which became commonly shortened to Shiʾa. These people believe that the Muslim leader should come from the direct descendants of Muhammad. The opposite and larger branch of Islam is known as the Sunni. The Sunni do not want to accept the authority of the direct descendants of Muhammad and choose instead to follow the *sunna,* or practices of Muhammad himself.

The murder of ʿAli in 661 is one of the major events in Islamic history. Known as the Lion of God and Commander of the Faithful to both branches of Islam, ʿAli is honored by pilgrimages to his shrine

The Hand of Fatima, an Islamic symbol of good luck, is often used as a symbol to ward off evil spirits. Fatima was ʿAli's wife and the daughter of the prophet Muhammad. © JOHN AND LISA MERRILL/CORBIS.

in Najaf, Iraq. Muslims view ʿAli as a great man of learning. His speeches, letters, and sayings are gathered in his *Nahjul Belagha* ("Peak of Eloquence").

A youth in Muhammad's household

Ali was born in Mecca, part of modern-day Saudi Arabia, in about 600 CE. The Shiʾa Muslims say that his name comes from one of the ninety-nine names of God, Al-Ali, meaning the "exalted." He was the son of Abu Tālib, a member of the Banu Hashim clan. This was one of the twelve major clans of the Quraysh tribe, which was the most influential in Mecca. The Quraysh owned one of the most powerful trading businesses in central Arabia and also held custody of the Kaʾaba, the central shrine for pre-Islamic Arabs, since the fifth century. Many sacred idols, or statues to which people prayed, were housed in the Kaʾaba. The shrine was a major site of pilgrimage, or holy journey, for Arabs and thus was a great source of money for the Quraysh. Some Muslims say that ʿAli was actually born inside the Kaʾaba.

Abu Tālib was also uncle to a young businessman named Muhammad, who later became the founder of Islam. Abu Tālib had raised Muhammad after the death of the young man's parents. Now Muhammad repaid the favor, taking his cousin, ʿAli, into his household when the boy was about eight. When Muhammad later reported that he had a divine or spiritual revelation (message) from God, others doubted him, but ʿAli believed in him immediately. Some sources say that ʿAli was, in fact, the first male convert to Islam. Others give this title to Muhammad's friend, associate, and later father-in-law, Abu Bakr (573–634), who became ʿAli's primary rival for the leadership of Islam after the death of Muhammad.

ʿAli was a loyal helper to Muhammad during the years in Mecca when people first mocked and then tried to suppress the new religion of Islam. Despite the fact that Muhammad was a member of their tribe, the Quraysh were particularly hostile to Islam. Their largest objection to the new faith was that it taught that there was only one God. The Quraysh made a lot of money from pilgrims who came to worship the many deities (gods and goddesses) of Arabia, so they were not pleased with Muhammad claiming these deities were false. In 622 Muhammad learned of a plot to kill him and decided to leave Mecca and settle in Yathrib (modern-day Medina). Muhammad had to slip away in the night and ʿAli risked his own life for his cousin, sleeping in Muhammad's bed to make others think Muhammad was still there. Although ʿAli narrowly escaped the killers, he remained in Mecca until he had returned the money and property various people had left in safe-keeping with Muhammad. ʿAli then made his way to Yathrib to rejoin Muhammad and his small group of followers.

Building a religion

ʿAli and the others who had followed Muhammad to Yathrib had little money, and at first they lived on the charity of new converts to Islam. They eventually began working as laborers and raiding the trade caravans sent from Mecca. This angered the Quraysh, who raised an army to fight ʿAli and his forces. The Battle of Badr was fought in 624, and it was the first time ʿAli was identified as a warrior. Leading a smaller force with less equipment, ʿAli managed to defeat the army from Mecca. This victory became known throughout the region and helped to spread the word and fame of Islam. Muhammad publicly praised his younger cousin, and ʿAli was also honored with a marriage to Muhammad's daughter, Fatima. ʿAli and Fatima had many children, but only four survived to adulthood. Their two sons were Hasan and Husayn (also spelled Husein), and their daughters were called Zaynab and Umm Kulthum. ʿAli grew even closer to Muhammad with the birth of these children.

Until Muhammad's death in 632, ʿAli was his constant advisor, aide, and faithful lieutenant. He served in the many military campaigns that spread the power of Islam. He also became an important official in the theocracy, or government ruled by religious authority, that Muhammad established in Yathrib. By 630 Mecca had fallen to the forces of Muhammad and ʿAli, and all of Arabia was brought under the control of the Islamic state. According to legend, it was ʿAli who smashed the idols of the pre-Islamic deities at the Kaʾaba.

Fatima

Little actual information is known about Fatima bint Muhammad (or Fatima Zahra). She was the daughter of Muhammad and his first wife, Khadija (c. 555–619). Born in about 605, Fatima married Ali when she was seventeen and had four children with him. Her one son, Husayn (c. 626–680) had a strong impact on Islam.

Fatima, however, was more than the daughter, wife, and mother of famous Muslim men. She is viewed as a holy woman in Islam, and is sometimes referred to as the patron saint of fertility. Fatima is called *al-Azhar* (the Brilliant or Shining One) and is regarded as the female ideal in Islam. Muslims often appeal to Fatima as a mediator between themselves and God. As a source of blessing, her hand is often used as a symbol for protection.

During her life Fatima was very close to her father Muhammad. Although the exact day of her death is not known, historians agree that she died in 633, about six months after Muhammad's death. The later Fatimid Dynasty (909–1171) of North Africa and the Middle East claimed to be descended from Fatima.

When Muhammad died many Muslims assumed that ʿAli would take over leadership of the community and the religion. Some even said that Muhammad named ʿAli his successor just before he died. While ʿAli and Muhammad's family were busy preparing the body for burial, however, ʿAli learned that Abu Bakr had been chosen by the inner circle of the community to be the next leader. ʿAli had not even been told that this meeting was taking place. Abu Bakr took the title *khalifatu r-rasul,* or "deputy of the messenger." The "messenger" in this case was Muhammad, the prophet or messenger of God. In English this title has become "caliph."

ʿAli was disappointed, and not only because of the loss of the leadership position. There was also the matter of an inheritance from Muhammad. By the time of his death, Muhammad owned a great deal of property. Abu Bakr now said that this property belonged to the full community of Islam. Some money was given to the wives of Muhammad, including Aʾisha, who was Abu Bakr's daughter, but ʿAli and Fatima were denied any inheritance. Still ʿAli did not fight the election of Abu Bakr. He wanted there to be harmony within Islam and knew that a battle for succession would be bad for the religion.

The supporters of ʿAli, who formed a large part of the community in Yathrib, did not accept Abu Bakr at first. They were called *Rafidis,* or "refusers." This disagreement over the succession would later lead to the major division in Islam between the Shiʾa, followers of ʿAli, and the Sunni. Meanwhile, ʿAli spent the next several years doing religious work. He arranged the words of Muhammad chronologically, or in order of oldest to most recent, which became the content of the Muslim holy book, the Qurʾan. ʿAli was a scholar not only of the Qurʾan, but also of the Hadith, which contained the sayings and deeds of Muhammad. Because of this, he became a consultant to the caliphs in religious and legal matters.

The fourth caliph

ʿAli was passed over twice more for the leadership of Islam. After the death of Abu Bakr in 634, Umar (581–684), a former advisor to Muhammad, was chosen as the second caliph. Under Umar, Islam became an imperial power, and military conquests extended the empire out of Arabia and into Syria, Mesopotamia (modern-day Iraq), and Egypt. ʿAli again did not object to this choice, and even gave his daughter Umm Kulthum to Umar in marriage. Umar ruled for ten years before he was murdered in 644 by a slave. Umar was succeeded by Uthman (574–656), a member of the powerful Umayyad clan, one of the dominant families of the Quraysh tribe.

During his twelve years in power, Uthman replaced many of the generals and governors appointed by the earlier caliphs. He appointed members of the Umayyad clan to these positions. This earned the new caliph many enemies. It appeared to some critics that he was re-establishing the power of the nobles, the high-ranking families that Muhammad had originally fought against. Uthman was killed by Muslim troops in 656.

ʿAli served in many battles in the effort to spread Islam. By 630 CE *ʿAli and the Prophet Muhammad had brought all of the Arabian peninsula under the control of an Islamic state.* © ARCHIVO ICONOGRAFICO, S.A./CORBIS.

After Uthman's death the Muslims of Yathrib chose ʿAli to become the fourth caliph. He was at first reluctant to take the position, knowing that he would inherit the problems created by the three earlier caliphs. He also did not wish to be seen as profiting from the death of Uthman. Finally he accepted the leadership. ʿAli immediately angered the Quraysh nobility with his attempts to bring Islam back to the traditions created by Muhammad. He sought to base his rule on the Islamic ideals of equality and social justice. As a first step, he replaced many of those Uthman put in office with his own advisors. These were people from all levels of Arab and Muslim society, not just the higher classes, which displeased the Quraysh. Additionally, the murder of Uthman had caused great anger and a desire for revenge in the Muslim world. Uthman, like ʿAli, had been a son-in-law of Muhammad and an early convert to Islam. All these issues helped spark a five-year civil war among Muslims, called the First Civil War (656–661), or *fitnah,* which means "trial" in Arabic.

ʿAli had to battle various Muslim groups during his entire rule. The first of these was an army led by a group of Quraysh nobles, one of whom was Muhammad's widow, Aʾisha. ʿAli's troops defeated these warriors at the Battle of the Camel at Basra, Iraq (so named because Aʾisha rode a camel into battle). The male leaders were killed, and Aʾisha was escorted back to Yathrib. After the battle ʿAli moved his capital from Yathrib south to Kufa, in modern-day Iraq.

A new threat to ʿAli arose in Syria, which was ruled by Muawiya (c. 602–680), a relative of Uthman. Uthman's murder gave Muawiya the opportunity to challenge the rule of ʿAli. The two forces clashed at the Battle of Siffin in Syria in 657. ʿAli's forces were winning when the Syrian troops placed copies of the Qurʾan on the points of their spears and asked for arbitration (an agreement to be reached by a neutral party). ʿAli accepted this arbitration. In doing so he angered some of his followers, who became known as the Kharijites, an Arabic word meaning "those who split apart." These purists did not want any compromise with Muawiya.

While negotiations were underway, both ʿAli and Muawiya removed their troops to their own lands. In 658 ʿAli had to fight his former supporters, the Kharijites, and he killed most of them. Nothing was decided by all this bloodshed, and Muawiya continued to claim he was the rightful caliph. By 660 ʿAli had lost control of Egypt and of the northwestern region of Arabia known as the Hejaz, where both Mecca and Yathrib were located.

ʿAli's rule ended violently. While performing morning prayers at a mosque (Muslim house of worship) in Kufa, he was stabbed by a poisoned sword and died two days later. His killer was a Kharijite. The supporters of ʿAli in Kufa said that ʿAli's son Hasan should become the next caliph, but Muawiya also wanted the position. In the end, Hasan made an agreement with Muawiya and retired to Yathrib. Muawiya became the fifth caliph, moving the capital to Damascus and establishing the first dynasty, or rule by one family, in Islam. The Umayyads ruled from 661 to 750 and reinstated the power of the old pre-Islamic nobles.

With ʿAli's death, the first phase of the history of the Muslim people came to a close. The first four caliphs are called the *Rashidun,* or "rightly guided," by Muslims because they were true to the principles of their religion in the way they governed. Afterwards, the rule of the Islamic community became similar to a hereditary monarchy, or a kingdom in which rule is passed from father to son.

ʿAli's short reign did not accomplish the re-unification of Islam that he wanted. In fact, his greatest legacy was the split in Islam between the Shiʾa and the Sunnis. Although it began as a political disagreement over the succession of caliphs, this split later became religious when the Shiʾites claimed ʿAli was the first imam, or leader with divinely inspired powers. In the end, however, ʿAli is remembered by both Shiʾite and Sunni Muslims as a fair religious leader, a warrior, and a writer. The Mashad ʿAli mosque was built in ʿAli's honor at nearby Najaf, on the spot where he is supposedly buried.

For More Information

BOOKS

Armstrong, Karen. *Islam: A Short History.* New York, NY: Modern Library/ Random House, 2000.

Armstrong, Karen. *Muhammad: A Biography of the Prophet.* London, UK: V. Gollancz, 1995.

Clark, Charles. *Islam.* San Diego, CA: Lucent Books, Inc., 2001.

Dunn, John. *The Spread of Islam.* San Diego, CA: Lucent Books, Inc., 1996.

Elias, Jamal J. and Ninian Smart. *Religions of the World Series: Islam.* Englewood Cliffs, NJ: Prentice Hall, 1998.

Emerick, Yahiya. *The Complete Idiot's Guide to Understanding Islam.* New York, NY: Alpha Books, 2002.

Gordon, Matthew S. *Islam.* New York, NY: Facts On File, 2001.

Günther, Ursula. "Fatima (c. 605–633)." In *Encyclopedia of Islam and the Muslim World.* Edited by Richard C. Martin. Vol. 1. New York, NY: Macmillan Reference USA, 2004, 254–5.

Kheirabadi, Masoud. *Islam.* New York, NY: Chelsea House Publications, 2004.

Steigerwald, Diana. "ʿAli (600–661)." In *Encyclopedia of Islam and the Muslim World.* Edited by Richard C. Martin. Vol. 1. New York, NY: Macmillan Reference USA, 2004, 35–8.

PERIODICALS

Atkins, Corinne. "The Shrine of Islam's Tragic Divisions." *History Today* (November 2003): 6.

WEB SITES

"Ali ibn Abi Talib." *Anwary-Islam.com.* http://anwary-islam.com/companion/ali-bin-%20abi-%20talib.htm (accessed on May 22, 2006).

"Fatima." *Anwary-Islam.com.* http://anwary-islam.com/women/daughters-fatimah.htm (accessed on May 22, 2006).

"Infallibles: Sayings of Imam Ali." *Nahjul Belagha (Peak of Eloquence).* http://www.al-islam.org/nahjul/index.htm (accessed on May 22, 2006).

Anaxagoras

BORN: c. 500 BCE • Clazomenae, Greece

DIED: c. 428 BCE • Lampsacus, Greece

Greek philosopher

Anaxagoras. HULTON ARCHIVE/ GETTY IMAGES.

"Other things include a portion of everything, but mind is infinite and self-powerful and mixed with nothing ... over all that has life, both greater and less, mind rules."

Anaxagoras was one of the most famous of early Greek philosophers. He is credited with turning Athens into a center of ancient study and intellectual activity. Anaxagoras expanded on the work of earlier philosophers, especially those from the Milesian or Ionian School. These thinkers proposed that substances such as air, fire, water, or earth made up the universe. Anaxagoras, in contrast, proposed that the universe was made up of a substance that could be divided infinitely, or forever.

Anaxagoras, like many other philosophers of his time, sought to find an explanation for the source of motion by searching for an organizing principle. Anaxagoras believed this principle was what he called *nous* or "mind." His theory was that nous set unarranged matter in the universe into motion and created order from it. Because of his focus on this principle, Anaxagoras has been credited both with an advance towards theism, the concept of a personal creator-god involved in human affairs, and with the first steps toward atheism, or the total disbelief in god or gods. In placing nous as the beginning of creation, Anaxagorous paved the way for believing in a single creative force, God. Ironically, his philosophical concept of nous also helped lead to a rejection of all gods, for the beginning of the world and creation could now be explained in scientific terms rather than religious ones.

Early years

Anaxagoras was born in about 500 BCE, into a wealthy and noble family in the town of Clazomenae in Ionia in Asia Minor. This strip of land along the coast of what is modern-day western Turkey was part of Greece during Anaxagoras's lifetime. About fifty years before Anaxagoras's birth, Ionia had been conquered by the Persians under Cyrus the Great. The Persians were harsh rulers, and in 498 BCE the Greeks of Ionia rebelled against the current Persian ruler, Darius. The revolt was defeated in 492 BCE, but led to the later Persian Wars. In these wars, Persia attempted to punish Athens for having helped the Ionian citizens in their rebellion. Roughly fifty years of periodic warfare followed.

Anaxagoras was born into complex times. His focus, however, was on the mind rather than military and political affairs. Although little is known of these early years of Anaxagoras's life, it is believed that as a young man he gave up his noble position and wealth in order to concentrate on science. Most likely he was aware of the intellectual activity that was occurring in the nearby seaport of Miletus, which had no priesthood or king that ruled as God's representative on Earth. There early philosophers sought to describe the nature of the universe using reason and logic. They formed the Ionian or Milesian School of writers and thinkers, which was the birthplace of Greek philosophy.

Thinkers such as Thales (c. 636–c. 546 BCE), Anaximander (c. 611–c. 547 BCE), and Anaximenes (sixth century BCE) focused their attention on the study of nature. They were searching for an elemental building block of matter or for one primary substance or originating principle, the *archê.* The one primary substance or originating principle refers to the one substance that existed at the beginning of time. Anaximander defined the primary source of everything as *apeiron,* or the unlimited and infinite (forever). Anaximenes believed that everything was originally composed of air or vapor, the thinning and thickening of which gave substance to life. Heraclitus (c. 535–c. 475 BCE), from Ephesus on the coast of Asia Minor, credited fire as the original substance that formed everything and declared change was the only constant in the universe. Such change, according to Heraclitus, was guided by *logos,* or reason. Heraclitus, though not Ionian, advanced this search for the primary building blocks of the universe by saying that there were four unchanging elements: earth, water, fire, and air. These elements were combined and separated by Love and Strife, his organizing principles.

Anaxagoras was aware of the work of these Ionian philosophers. Even before the age of twenty, when he departed for Athens, he saw that their arguments failed to explain movement and change. He was determined to create a theory that accounted for all aspects of the universe. In Athens, Anaxagoras became friends with the young statesman Pericles (c. 495–429 BCE). Pericles rose to prominence in about 460 BCE, becoming a popular political and military leader of the city. Anaxagoras was also said to be friends with other important Athenians, and some say he was even a teacher of the famous philosopher Socrates (469–399 BCE), though this is unlikely.

Time in Athens

Anaxagoras's years in Athens were productive ones. By about 467 BCE he produced his major work of writing, *On Nature,* only fragments of which exist today. Many quotations from Anaxagoras come from the works of later philosophers. In *On Nature,* Anaxagoras attempted to further the work of the earlier Ionian School thinkers. Instead of air, fire, water, and earth as the four elements of creation, Anaxagoras said that there were an infinite number of particles or "seeds" (*spermata*) that combined to create everything in the universe. These seeds, or building blocks, could be divided into smaller parts, or combined to form larger items. Anaxagoras claimed that this ability of matter to be divided or combined together accounted for the vast variety of forms in the universe.

Anaxagoras's creation of the cosmos Anaxagoras held that these seeds were eternal and have always been in existence. For Anaxagoras, there was no such thing as a void or empty space. At the beginning of the cosmos (universe), such seeds were initially in one huge mass without shape or form. Through nous, or organizing principle, this mass was set in rotary motion. This motion caused the mass to separate out into smaller elements.

Anaxagors believed the creation of the world was due to this separating of the seeds and by the effect of the spinning motion on these seeds. The formation of the universe or cosmos took place in two stages. First was the revolving process, which separated and then remixed the particles. In this stage, all the dark particles came together to form night, and the fluid seeds joined to make the oceans. The friction in this rotary motion in turn caused heat, which set the stars and sun on fire.

The development of all living things came in the second stage, when the same types of seeds or particles attracted others like them. The separation of the seeds by the rotary motion was imperfect, as Anaxagoras noted, and therefore, according to his theory, there are a few seeds of everything in everything else. What makes something what we believe it to be is that it has a majority of seeds of one type. For example, white is white because it has a majority of white seeds, but it also contains black seeds. Hair is hair, because most of its seeds are of the hair type, but it also has parts of everything else in creation in it.

Ordering the universe and studying it An important factor of Anaxagoras's theory is the action he claimed nous had upon the organization of the universe. This approach was popular with later philosophers such as Socrates (469–399 BCE), Plato (428–348 BCE), and Aristotle (384–322 BCE), all of whom were highly concerned with ethical problems and how to live a good life. For them, the concept of an ordering principle to the universe, such as nous, was appealing. They criticized Anaxagoras, however, for not taking his theory further and explaining the purpose of such an ordering principle. Anaxagoras simply explained his theory of matter and motion but did not ask why it happened as it did.

Anaxagoras was also known for his work in astronomy (the study of the sun, moon, planets, stars, and objects found in space), which may have been inspired by the fall of a large meteorite, or mass of matter that falls to Earth from space, near Aegypotomi in 467 BCE. He believed that the sun was a blazing ball of metal about the size of the Peloponessus, the major island of southern Greece. Anaxagoras went further, however, and said that the moon was made of similar matter as Earth and shone because it reflected light from the sun. From this, he went on to describe how Earth moves between the sun and moon, blocking the light and causing lunar eclipses. He also explained how the moon sometimes moves between Earth and sun, causing a solar eclipse.

Anaxagoras accused

Anaxagoras's theories of the universe angered some citizens of Athens because they challenged the accepted beliefs of the time. His friendship with Pericles may also have caused Anaxagoras trouble. Pericles had enemies, and these enemies ultimately targeted his friends. Some time around 450 BCE Anaxagoras was imprisoned and charged with impiety, or disbelief in the gods. The reason for his imprisonment was his claim that the sun was only a huge mass of hot metal and not a god, as was commonly believed at the time. He was also accused of maintaining secret communications with the Persians, the enemy of Athens, and was sentenced to death. Pericles used his influence and had the death sentence changed to one of exile, which meant Anaxagoras's life was spared, but he was forced to live outside of Athens.

Exile in Lampsacus Anaxagoras left Athens for Lampsacus, an ancient Greek city in northwestern Asia Minor. Many young Greeks came to study with him until his death in 429 BCE. Few specifics are known of Anaxagoras's work in exile. However, a much later Roman author and architect mentioned that Anaxagoras created theater designs that allowed viewers to better see objects in the front and back of the stage. This suggests that Anaxagoras also may have done some philosophical work on perspective, perhaps the earliest of its kind. Perspective is the appearance to the eye of objects in respect to their relative distance and position.

Anaxagoras was not the last of the great philosophers of ancient Greece to be accused of not believing in the gods. Socrates was also tried for this offense and put to death. Aristotle was accused of the same crime, but fled from Athens, saying he refused to allow the Athenians to sin against philosophy a third time.

Pericles

Pericles, a well-known speaker and patron of learning and the arts, was born around 493 BCE in Athens. Although for much of his early life he was concerned with the theatre, in 461 BCE he became involved in politics. He helped organize a vote in the popular assembly that took power away from the Areopagus, the ancient aristocratic council that ruled Athens. The vote left the Areopagus basically a legal court rather than a ruling council.

Pericles then initiated a number of democratic reforms in Athens, including the payment of salaries to state officials and the opening of such offices to commoners. He introduced laws that limited the power of the Athenian aristocrats, although this won him many enemies. He also established a truce with Athens's longtime rival, Sparta, which created a golden age of peace in the city.

During his involvement in politics, Pericles continued to support the arts. Around 447 BCE he also began to show a strong interest in building and architecture. He oversaw the construction of the Parthenon, which he envisioned as a monument to the power of Athens. The Parthenon was built on the central fortified hill of the city, the Acropolis.

Pericles was eventually driven from office by political enemies, but was reelected the city's military commander in 428 BCE. He died shortly thereafter.

Effects on thought

Anaxagoras's work had a significant effect on philosophy and thought. His theory of nous proved an inspiration for Socrates, though the latter was sorry Anaxagoras had not taken his argument further. For Socrates, nous seemed to be simply a mechanical means of organizing the universe, a force without morality or goal. Socrates believed there was more than this to the universe. Nevertheless, Anaxagoras's theory of creation is historically important because some of its aspects were adopted by later scientists. These include his theory of the rotating cosmic mass at the beginning of time and his idea that the basic building blocks of life could be divided.

More importantly, by attempting to explain the process of creation without relying on gods as the driving factor, Anaxagoras helped to pave the way for criticism of religious ideas about the origin of the universe. His explanation of the formation of heavenly bodies such as the sun, stars, and the moon ultimately led to doubts in God's existence (agnosticism) or possibly even a complete lack of belief in God or gods (atheism). Some historians, however, call Anaxagoras the father of theism, the belief in a personal god that created the universe, or even of monotheism, the belief in one supreme being. Although it was never referred to as a god, the nous Anaxagoras believed in was the thing that set the early cosmos in motion and organized life. This was taken by some to mean that Anaxagoras's theory focused on one power or force in the universe, rather than a pantheon, or group, of gods as the Greeks had believed. Therefore, the father of agnosticism or atheism is sometimes also called the father of monotheism.

For More Information

BOOKS

Fairbanks, Arthur, ed. and trans. *The First Philosophers of Greece.* London, England: K. Paul, Trench, Trubner, 1898.

Gershenson, Daniel E., and Daniel E. Greenberg. *Anaxagoras and the Birth of Physics.* Waltham, MA: Blaisdell Publishing Co., 1964.

Kirk, G. S., and J. E. Raven. *The Presocratic Philosophers: A Critical History with a Selection of Texts.* Cambridge, England: Cambridge University Press, 1983.

Schofield, Malcolm. *An Essay on Anaxagoras.* New York, NY: Cambridge University Press, 1980.

PERIODICALS

Davison, J. A. "Protagoras, Democritus, and Anaxagoras." *Classical Quarterly* (July-September 1953): 33–45.

Kingsley, Peter. "Notes on Air: Four Questions of Meaning in Empedocles and Anaxagoras." *Classical Quarterly* (January-June 1995): 26–29.

WEB SITES

"Anaxagoras." *Atlantic Baptist University.* http://www.abu.nb.ca/Courses/GrPhil/Anaxagoras.htm (accessed on May 24, 2006).

"Anaxagoras of Clazomenae." *Turnbull School of Mathematical and Computational Sciences.* http://www-groups.dcs.st-and.ac.uk/~history/Mathematicians/Anaxagoras.html (accessed on May 24, 2006).

Fairbanks, Arthur. "Anaxagoras Fragments and Commentary." *Hanover Historical Texts Project.* http://history.hanover.edu/texts/presoc/anaxagor.htm (accessed on May 24, 2006).

"Pericles." *PBS.org.* http://www.pbs.org/empires/thegreeks/htmlver/characters/f_pericles.html (accessed on May 24, 2006).

Aristotle

BORN: 384 BCE • Stagira, Chalcidice, Greece

DIED: March 7, 322 BCE • Chalcis, Euboea, Greece

Greek philosopher; biologist; scientist; educator; writer

Aristotle.

"The whole is more than the sum of its parts."

Aristotle, and his teacher **Plato** (c. 427–347 BCE; see entry) were the most famous of the classic Greek philosophers. The word *philosophia* means "love of wisdom," a concept embraced with great energy by men such as these. Aristotle wrote not only on philosophical and logical matters, but also on biology, the natural sciences, ethics, politics, poetry, drama, economics, meteorology (the study of weather), astronomy (the study of the planets and stars), theology (the study of religion), and psychology (the study of the mind). Most significantly, he was the first to treat many of these areas of knowledge as subjects worthy of individual study. His existing writings fill more than two thousand pages, and that is thought to be only a small portion of his total work.

Plato searched for the ultimate reality behind existence. Aristotle found such a reality in existence itself and set out with excitement to organize and categorize it all. His classification system for animals was the model used for almost two thousand years. The same desire for order influenced Aristotle's approach to human conduct. He felt that achieving happiness was humanity's chief goal, and he organized all human behavior into a pyramid detailing the actions that led to this supreme goal for the individual.

Aristotle, perhaps more than any other great thinker, paved the way for the development of Western intellectual study. Though many of his conclusions on natural sciences—for example, the sun revolves around the earth—have been proved false, his ideas and methods are still used by modern-day thinkers. His greatest accomplishments were the formation of a system for studying formal logic and the establishment of the study of zoology, the branch of biology dealing with animals. His work in ethics, or proper behavior, was also significant. Many of his ideas were later adapted by the Arab philosopher Averroës (1126–1198); the Jewish scholar **Maimonides** (1135–1204; see entry); the Scholastics, or medieval church scholars, such as Thomas Aquinas (1224–1274); and by rationalist thinkers (those who believe in reason over experience) such as Thomas Jefferson (1743–1826), who drafted the United States Constitution and served as the country's third president.

The doctor's son

Aristotle was born in the small town of Stagira, in the northern Greek province of Chalcidice, in 384 BCE. His mother's name was Phaestis, and she came from Chalcis in the province of Euboea. His father, Nicomachus, was a doctor. Nicomachus probably intended to hand down his medical skills to his son, as was the tradition of the time, so as a young boy Aristotle most likely studied biology and anatomy. The family later moved to the neighboring province of Macedonia, a powerful district in Greece, and Nicomachus soon won an appointment as court physician to the king, Amyntas III. It is not known if Aristotle accompanied his father to Pella, the capital city of Macedonia, but it is clear from historical records that he became friends as a youth with the king's son, Philip (382–336 BCE), who later became King Philip II of Macedon.

Aristotle's life changed greatly when he was ten. His father died, and his mother passed away not long after. He was put into the care of his uncle, Proxenus, who saw to the youngster's further education in the humanities. Aristotle studied Greek, rhetoric (the study of the use of language), and poetry. He had already been taught the sciences by his father. At about the age of seventeen, in 367 BCE, Aristotle was sent to Athens, where he became a student in the Academy, the educational institution established by Plato about two decades earlier. Aristotle remained at the Academy for twenty years, as both student and teacher, lecturing and writing on rhetoric.

With the death of Plato in 347 BCE, Aristotle finally left the Academy. There are several explanations for this move. Some say it is because he was passed over for head of the Academy in favor of Plato's nephew, with whom Aristotle had philosophical differences. Aristotle's connections to the Macedonian court may also have been a factor in his decision to leave. Phillip II came to the throne in 359 BCE, and his kingdom was a challenge to the power of Athens. Anti-Macedonia sentiment was strong in Athens as a result, and some thought that Aristotle left the city because of it.

The wandering scholar

Aristotle found a more welcoming environment on the coast of Asia Minor at Assus, where the ruler, Hermias of Atarneus, a former soldier, wanted to establish the system of Greek learning. Hermias not only offered Aristotle a school to head, but also provided a bride for him. Aristotle married Hermias's niece and adopted daughter, Pythias. The couple was married for ten years and had a daughter.

Aristotle worked on part of his book, *Politics,* in Assus, sketching out his ideas about the purpose of the city-state, which he believed was to provide an atmosphere where philosophy could thrive. Aristotle was in favor of rule by an enlightened oligarchy, or a small and dominant class of well-educated rulers, who had the best interests of the people at heart. He said the kings of such an oligarchy should, however, be willing to take the advice of wise philosophers.

Aristotle and his followers also began to collect observations on the physical structures of animals that helped lay the foundations of biological sciences. Aristotle continued these studies when he left Assus for the neighboring island of Lesbos (modern-day Mytilene). His move was the result of political events; an uprising had led to the execution of Assus's ruler and Aristotle's protector, Hermias. Aristotle stayed on Lesbos for a year, gathering a group of scholars around him. He continued his studies in animal life, developing his theory that all plants and animals have goals or natural ends. To Aristotle, such ends must be understood in order to comprehend the animal's physical structures fully. Such belief is called teleology, and it assumes there is some sort of organizing principle at work in the cosmos. It was during this time that Aristotle also formed

A manucript illumination of Greek philosopher Aristotle tutoring Alexander the Great. Aristotle is said to have tutored Alexander when he was a boy in Pella, Macedonia. © ARCHIVO ICONOGRAFICO, S.A./CORBIS.

his idea that the soul was the most important part of an individual, and that it joined with the body to form the whole. This differed from Plato's belief in a more universal soul that was only a temporary part of an individual.

By 343 BCE Aristotle had returned to the Macedonian capital, Pella, where he remained for several years. Some accounts have Aristotle tutoring the thirteen-year-old son of Philip II, Alexander (356–323 BCE). Later this boy became known as Alexander the Great, and he conquered much of Asia, bringing it under Greek rule. Other historians note, however, that these stories of Aristotle and Alexander only arose much later in history. In fact, the two were very much opposites. Aristotle loved the concept of the city-state, but Alexander later destroyed such localized governments in order to rule over them.

Aristotle assembled a group of followers in Pella and took them with him when he left the capital for his hometown, Stagira, in 340 BCE. After the death of his wife, Aristotle formed a lifelong relationship with a woman named Herpyllis, and they had a son together, Nicomachus, named after Aristotle's father. He remained in Stagira until 335 BCE, when he returned to Athens. He was nearly fifty, which was considered quite old as the life expectancy of most Greeks at the time was around twenty.

Founds the Lyceum

In Aristotle's absence from Athens, the leadership of the Academy had passed to an old friend, Xenocrates of Chalcedony. Aristotle began teaching at a location near the temple of Apollo Lyceus, just outside Athens in a grove of olive trees. The school was called the Lyceum, after its temple location. A shaded walkway, the *peripatos,* was a favored place of instruction for Aristotle, who liked to walk as he lectured. Because of this, the school also became known as the Peripatetic School, as *peripatoi* means "to walk." Aristotle believed that a person could not really claim to know a subject until he could teach it to another. For the next twelve years, he lectured at the school while he continued his research.

The wide variety of subject matter offered for study made Aristotle's Lyceum different from the Academy founded by Plato. Indeed, because of the many subjects Aristotle taught, and also because of his emphasis on observation and research, many consider the Lyceum to be the first true university in history. Aristotle also founded a library and museum at the Lyceum, further enhancing its reputation.

It was during his years at the Lyceum that Aristotle composed most of his writings. Many of these works are in the form of dialogues, a model Plato had originated, in which theories and ideas are presented and explained in popular language in the form of a conversation between two people. He also wrote many treatises, or systematic explanations of a subject, in more formal and technical language.

After the death of Alexander the Great in 323 BCE, anti-Macedonian sentiment again became high in Athens. The people of Athens blamed Macedonians like Alexander and his father for taking away their power as a city-state. Aristotle again became the focus for some of this negative sentiment. Like another well-known philosopher before him, Socrates (470–399 BCE), Aristotle was charged with impiety, or disbelief in the

Aristotle the Man

It is difficult to get an accurate picture of Aristotle as a normal human being, rather than as a giant of thought. The busts and engravings that still exist show a rather handsome and elegant individual. Some writings, however, describe Aristotle in less flattering terms. According to these descriptions, he had very thin legs, small eyes, suffered from poor digestion, and spoke with a lisp. These reports also say he wore fashionable clothing to compensate for his physical defects. His cloak and sandals were always of the finest materials. He wore finger rings and kept his hair cut short. Whether or not he lisped, he was known as a fine public speaker, and was clear, witty, and persuasive in his lectures and in conversation. It is believed that he was comfortable financially, and his family's holdings in Stagira allowed him to indulge his passion for collecting books. Aristotle appears to have been devoted to his family, and he made continual references to them in his will.

gods. Instead of facing his accusers, Aristotle left Athens, saying that he would not give the Athenians a chance to sin against philosophy again, for Socrates had been put to death as a result of his trial. Aristotle went to his mother's estate in Chalcis on the island of Euboea. The next year, 322 BCE, Aristotle developed stomach problems and died.

The works

Historians think it likely that Aristotle authored more than 170 books. Of these, only about thirty are still in existence. These works cover Aristotle's wide range of interests, but it is uncertain if they were ever meant to be published, as they resemble working papers and lecture notes rather than perfected pieces. The polished works meant for publication have largely been lost. No real chronology or timeline can be established for Aristotle's works, so they are usually organized by subject or discipline. Although Aristotle wrote about many different theories, a central theme in his work is his belief that reality and the fundamentals of existence can only be understood by careful observation and categorization.

Aristotle was essentially an empiricist, or someone who believes knowledge should be gained through experience and experimentation. He not only used observation to learn about an object or being, but also studied what others had said about it. He was an advocate of two different types of reasoning. In deductive reasoning, he would take a general idea, such as "all birds can fly" and conclude that, based on this, if he saw a bird, it could fly. In inductive reasoning, he approached the argument in reverse order, going from a specific statement to a general idea. "This particular bird can fly," Aristotle might have said, "therefore all birds can fly."

Logic and the sciences Aristotle published six discussions on logic collected in the *Organon* ("a tool or instrument of thought"). He intended this work to provide his readers with a universal method of reasoning whose use would make it possible to learn everything there was to know about reality. Aristotle's primary work in philosophy is the *Metaphysics.* In the twelve books of *Metaphysics* Aristotle rejects Plato's idea of abstract and universal forms. He lays out his reasoning for the eternal existence of substance.

In *Physics,* Aristotle details one of his most important ideas, the Four Causes, which forms the core of modern Western scientific thought. Aristotle said that in order understand an object, a person must be able to answer four questions about it. The first cause, or descriptive trait, is the material out of which the thing is made. Next is the formal cause, or the pattern, structure, or model of the thing. The efficient cause is how the thing came into being, or was created. The final cause is the goal, function, or purpose of the object. Aristotle also addressed social issues and politics in *Politics,* literary art in *Poetics,* and the use of persuasive language in *Rhetoric.*

Ethics Two of Aristotle's works, *Eudemian Ethics* and *Nicomachean Ethics,* deal with moral behavior. In these works, Aristotle discussed how moral responsibility is assumed by individuals, the ways such moral responsibility was evaluated, the nature of friendship, and how to achieve happiness in human life. The major question Aristotle sought to answer was what was necessary for an individual to be a good person. Aristotle concluded that ethics are man-made rather than passed down by a supernatural being or god. He also felt that whether an action was right or wrong varied according to the situation, which was a new concept at the time. This belief made him suspicious of strict and unchanging principles. (An example of a strict, unchanging principle is the Christian commandment "Thou shall not kill.")

Aristotle called his belief that all actions needed to be judged according to the situation "equity." This has become a guiding principle in the modern-day legal system and is also integral to parts of Christianity. In the modern legal system and in Christianity, the condition of guilt or of committing a sin depends in part on a person's intent. For example, in law, murdering someone with intent and not in self defense is called homicide and is punished more severely than causing a death accidentally, which is called manslaughter. Aristotle believed that happiness was the primary goal of mankind. He claimed that such happiness could be found in doing good deeds, because virtuous activity, rather than a focus on mindless amusement, led to a life of real value. For Aristotle, intellectual thought was the highest form of moral activity because it was what human beings were best suited for. He believed it was the ultimate cause or reason for being. This system of thought has formed the core of Western intellectual study for more than two thousand years.

For More Information

BOOKS

Aristotle. The Basic Works of Aristotle. Edited by Richard McKeon. New York, NY: Modern Library Classics, 2001.

Barnes, Jonathan. *Aristotle.* New York, NY: Oxford University Press, 1982.

Ferguson, John. *Aristotle.* Boston, MA: Twayne, 1972.

Grene, Marjorie. *A Portrait of Aristotle.* London, UK: Faber & Faber, 1963.

Parker, Steve. *Aristotle and Scientific Thought.* New York, NY: Chelsea House, 1995.

WEB SITES

"Aristotle." *Philosophy Pages.* http://www.philosophypages.com/ph/aris.htm (accessed on May 25, 2006).

Cohen, Marc. "Introduction to Aristotle." *Department of Philosophy, University of Washington.* http://faculty.washington.edu/smcohen/433/arintro.htm (accessed on May 25, 2006).

Hooker, Richard. "Aristotle." *Greek Philosophy.* http://www.wsu.edu/~dee/GREECE/ARIST.HTM (accessed on May 25, 2006).

O'Connor, J. John, and Edmund F. Robertson. "Aristotle." *School of Mathematics and Statistics, University of St. Andrews, Scotland.* http://www-groups.dcs.st-and.ac.uk/~history/Mathematicians/Aristotle.html (accessed on May 25, 2006).

Bahá'u'lláh

BORN: November 12, 1817 • Tehran, Persia

DIED: May 29, 1892 • Acre, Palestine, Persia

Persian religious leader; writer

"The earth is but one country, and mankind its citizens.... The well-being of mankind, its peace and security, are unattainable unless and until its unity is firmly established."

Bahá'u'lláh, a Persian noble by birth, was the founder of the Bahá'í faith. Bahá'u'lláh was a writer as well as a religious leader, and he produced hundreds of books, speeches, and essays during his lifetime. The most important of these works is the Kitab-i-Aqdas, or "Book of Laws," which is the primary sacred text for Bahá'ís. Bahá'u'lláh called himself the Messenger of God, claiming he was a prophet like the **Buddha** (563–483 BCE; see entry), **Jesus Christ** (c. 4 BCE–c. 30 CE; see entry), and **Muhammad** (c. 570–632; see entry).

A privileged childhood

Mirza Husayn ʿAli Nuri, later known as Bahá'u'lláh, was born on November 12, 1817, in Tehran, Persia (modern-day Iran). He was the son of a well-respected nobleman who held a position at the court of the shah (ruler) of Persia, Fath-ʿAli Shah (1762–1834). His father was Mirza Abbas Nuri, better known as Mirza Buzurg, and his mother's name was Khadijih Khanum. The Nuri family traced its heritage back to a ruling family of Persia in the seventh century.

Nuri grew up in a wealthy household and was a sensitive and well-educated youth. According to his biographers, he began demonstrating an interest in spiritual matters at an early age. One story relates that while viewing a puppet show he was struck by how temporary and

The Bahá'í temple in Wilmette, Illinois, was the first Bahá'í temple constructed in the West. Its foundation was laid under the oversight of Bahá'u'lláh's son and successor, Abdu'l-Baha.

short life is, because when the show came to an end, all the puppets were quickly packed into a trunk and taken away. Like other young men of the Persian upper class, Nuri was trained in horsemanship, swordsmanship, calligraphy (fine writing), and classic poetry. He was brought up in the Muslim faith and belonged to the Shi'ite branch of that religion, one of the two main sects of Islam. Some sources report that by the age of thirteen, Nuri was already having complex discussions with Muslim religious officials regarding spiritual issues and details in the Qur'an, the Muslim holy book.

Nuri's father was a favorite at court and was appointed governor of two provinces in the late 1820s. When the old *shah,* or leader, died in 1834, however, one of his sons took over and wanted to show his independence from his father and all his old advisors. Mirza Buzurg was no longer a royal favorite and lost his positions and salary. He did manage to keep his family's lands near the village of Takur in the district of Nur, which was located in the province of Mazandaran.

Joins the Babis

Nuri married his first wife, Asiyih Navvab, in 1835. She was the daughter of another noble family, and together they had three children. Muslim law permitted polygamy, or having more than one spouse, so Nuri also wed two other women. He was the father of fourteen children in total, only seven of whom survived to adulthood. Despite the fact that his father was not liked by the new shah, Nuri was offered a post in the government. He turned it down and instead chose to work for the good of humanity by organizing various charities with his first wife. By the early 1840s his kind deeds had earned him the name "Father of the Poor," and he became highly respected in Tehran.

During this time Nuri was also becoming involved in the more mystical teachings of the Shi'ite Muslim religion. Shi'ites believe that there are divine successors to the Prophet Muhammad. Such a person is called an *imam.* Shi'ites are waiting for the return of the twelfth and final imam, who they believe went into hiding in the ninth century to avoid being killed by rivals. His return, according to the Shi'ites, will usher in a new golden age for the world, a belief similar to that held by Christians regarding the second coming of God's son, Jesus Christ. Indeed, during the first half of the nineteenth century, there were several movements throughout the world that claimed a new spiritual age was close to arrival. In the United States and Europe, many groups declared that Christ was about to return, while in the Muslim world some predicted a new messiah, or savior, would soon come to save the world. Some called this savior the Twelfth Imam while others referred to him as the *mahdi,* which translates as "he who is divinely guided."

The Twelve Principles of Bahá'í

The Bahá'í faith is guided by twelve main principles or laws:

1. The oneness of the entire human race.
2. The independent investigation and search for truth.
3. The harmony between religion and science.
4. The idea that religion is unfolding, always growing, and that the gods of all religions are representatives of the one true God.
5. All religions have the same divine foundation and are thus part of each other and not separate from or better than others.
6. The equality of men and women.
7. The removal of all prejudice regarding race, religion, and class.
8. The creation of universal peace through a world government.
9. The creation of universal compulsory (required) education.
10. The need for a universal language shared by all humankind.
11. The solution of economic problems through spirituality.
12. The creation of a Universal House of Justice with a divinely inspired president.

By following these guiding principles laid out by Bahá'u'lláh, Bahá'ís believe they will create the kingdom of heaven on Earth.

In 1844 a holy man from Shiraz, Persia, announced that he was the *Bab,* or "gateway" to the Twelfth Imam. This man, named Siyyid ʿAli Muhammad (1819–1850), claimed to be the spokesperson for the purer spiritual age to come and criticized what he saw as the intellectual dishonesty of the Muslim religious leaders. He also promised that within twenty years a Messenger of God would appear and teach humanity the principles for this new spiritual age. The Bab won followers throughout Persia, one of whom was Nuri, who converted to Babism, as the religion became known, in 1844. Nuri's half-brother, Mirza Yahya (1830–1912), also converted to the new faith. Due to his impressive speaking ability and the high standing of his family, Nuri quickly became one of the movement's most successful speakers in spreading the word of the new faith.

The Babi movement was greatly distrusted by the Muslim religious leaders, or *mullahs,* who felt threatened by the Bab. The mullahs encouraged the government to attempt to stop the movement, and the Bab was imprisoned. In 1848 the Babi leadership, including Nuri and Mirza Yahya, met to discuss how they might get the Bab out of prison. The Babis decided to make a final break with the laws and principles of Islam. At this point Nuri took the name Bahá'u'lláh, which means "Glory of God." His half-brother assumed the title Subh-i Azal, or "Morning of Eternity." Bahá'u'lláh, as one of the leaders of the Babis, was closely watched by the mullahs and the government. When the Bab was put to death in 1850, Bahá'u'lláh, who still had friends in powerful positions, was advised to leave Tehran.

When Bahá'u'lláh returned to Tehran in 1852, he discovered that a plot had been formed by several Babis to kill the shah in revenge for the execution of the Bab. Although Bahá'u'lláh rejected this plan, it was carried out, unsuccessfully, in August 1852. Bahá'u'lláh was one of many Babis arrested after the incident. Thousands were executed, and Bahá'u'lláh was imprisoned in a huge jail in Tehran known as the *Siyah-Chal,* or the "black pit." There he received what he called a visitation from a "Maiden from God" who told him that he was the Messenger of God of whom the Bab had spoken. When Bahá'u'lláh was found innocent of the attempted crime and released several months later, he did not tell anyone of the visitation. He and his family, along with many other Babis, were banished from Persia by the authorities and decided to settle in Baghdad, in present-day Iraq. The city at that time was ruled by the Ottoman Empire, a dynastic (ruled by the same family or line) state that was based mostly in modern-day Turkey.

Into exile

Though Bahá'u'lláh felt that he was the messenger the Bab said would come, the leadership of the Babi religion passed to his half-brother, Subh-i Azal. Some historians believe that Subh-i Azal was actually a false leader set up to protect the real authority of the Babis from government harassment. Subh-i Azal took his position seriously, however, and tensions grew between the two men. Many new followers to the religion and those visiting Baghdad saw Bahá'u'lláh as the spiritual leader and not Subh-i Azal. In order to avoid conflict and to take some time to consider the mission that he had been given by the Maiden of God, Bahá'u'lláh went alone into the mountains of Kurdistan, far to the north of Baghdad. He stayed there for two years, during which he wrote one of his first books, Four Valleys.

In 1856 Subh-i Azal discovered the whereabouts of Bahá'u'lláh and wrote his half-brother, asking him to come back to Baghdad. When Bahá'u'lláh returned to the city, he discovered that twenty-five people had already claimed to be the Messenger of God that the Bab spoke of. He also learned that Subh-i Azal had had several of his opponents killed.

Bahá'u'lláh's became even more well-known in Baghdad during the next seven years, and he continued writing texts of his teachings and spiritual discoveries. A couple of the most important of these were the Kitab-i-Iqan, or the Book of Certitude, and the Hidden Words. In 1862 Bahá'u'lláh completed the Bab's Bayan, a book of laws for the Babis, which had been left unfinished with only eleven of its proposed nineteen chapters written. Bahá'u'lláh used his authorship of these works to argue that he should be the leader of the Babis, but he still did not reveal that he was the Messenger of God. Subh-i Azal also claimed to have completed the Bab's work with his Motammem Al-Bayan, and relations between the two half-brothers grew worse.

Bahá'u'lláh's influence began to reach beyond Baghdad to his native Persia. This rebirth of the popularity of the Babi movement again upset the mullahs and the Persian government. They convinced the Ottoman government, which controlled Baghdad, to banish Bahá'u'lláh from the city. In 1863, just before he was exiled to the city of Constantinople (modern-day Istanbul, Turkey), Bahá'u'lláh finally told a small group of followers about his visitation in prison eleven years earlier, announcing for the first time that he was the Messenger of God. This took place in the Garden of Ridvan near Baghdad, between April 21 and May 2. These dates later became an important Bahá'í holy celebration, the twelve-day Festival of Ridvan.

Splits from Babis to form the Bahá'í faith

Bahá'u'lláh, his family, and a small group of followers moved from Baghdad to Constantinople and then on to Adrianople (modern-day Edirne, Turkey). In 1866 Bahá'u'lláh publicly declared that he was the Messenger of God and a prophet, as Muhammad and Christ had been before him. He wrote official letters to political and religious leaders of the world, such as Pope Pius IX and Queen Victoria of England, announcing his presence and mission. Bahá'u'lláh declared in these letters that he was the promised one of whom all religions spoke, the Messenger of God. He also spoke out against war and the purchasing of weapons, telling these leaders that their budgets would be better spent taking care of the poor and establishing a world government that could provide security for all citizens.

These actions led to a complete break with the Babis who still followed Subh-i Azal. Those who sided with Bahá'u'lláh called themselves Bahá'ís, while followers of Subh-i Azal called themselves Azalis for a time and then Bayanis. The Bayan religion still existed as of the early twenty-first century, though with only a few thousand believers located mainly in Iran. The Bahá'ís, in contrast, went on to create one of the major world religions.

Shortly after the break, Bahá'u'lláh was poisoned, possibly on the orders of Subh-i Azal. Though he survived, the poison left a permanent

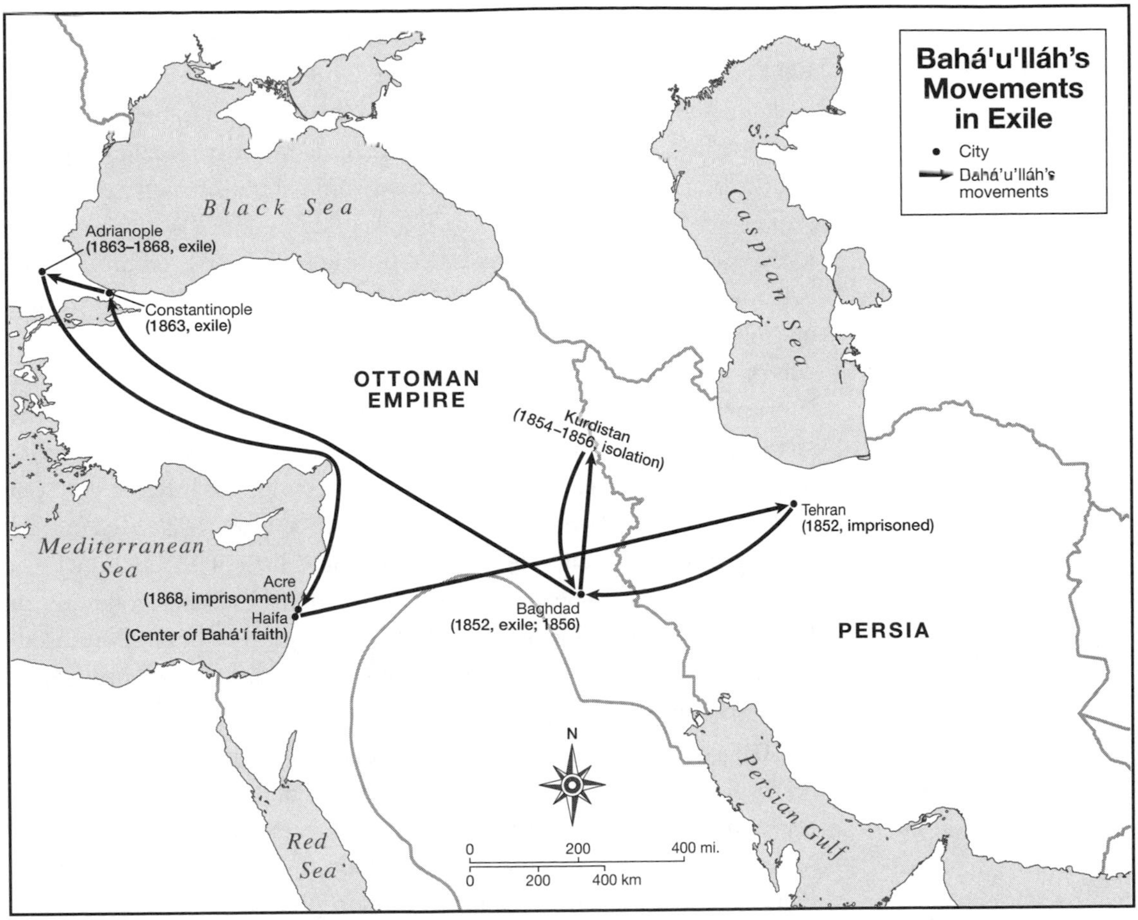

Bahá'u'lláh was forced into exile or imprisonment several times in his life as he sought to spread the word of God as it was revealed to him. He spent the last years of his life in Palestine, modern-day Israel. THOMSON GALE.

tremor, or shaking motion, in his hand. In 1868 Bahá'u'lláh and his followers were transported to the prison city of Acre in Palestine (modern-day Akko, Israel). This walled city was the final destination for some of the worst criminals and for political and religious trouble-makers. According to legend, the air was so bad in Acre that birds flying over would die. Bahá'u'lláh and his family were held for nine years, at first in the general prison population, and then in a small house inside the city walls. It was here that Bahá'u'lláh wrote the book that is central to the Bahá'í religion, Kitab-i-Aqdas, or the Book of Laws, also known as the Most Holy Book of Bahá'ís. In this work he laid out the main beliefs and principles of the Bahá'í faith.

The central belief of the Bahá'í faith is the concept of oneness. Bahá'ís believe that there is only one God and that all religions are built on the messages of that God. Similarly, Bahá'ís believe in the unity of humankind and that all humans should be treated equally. Bahá'u'lláh wrote that it is the duty of a spiritual person to try to understand God, and that the more one is able to do this, the closer one will be to the idea of heaven. He also laid out daily laws for the faithful. Members must pray at least once a day; avoid alcohol and drugs; fast (go without food and water) for nineteen days before the Bahá'í New Year, which falls on the first day of spring; do good works; and reject prejudice. There is no priesthood in the Bahá'í faith. Any member can read from the sacred texts during the monthly meetings. Bahá'u'lláh also made a covenant, or solemn agreement, with his followers. He said that if they put their faith in Bahá'í, he would lead them to a new age and guarantee the continuity of their religion by creating a line of succession, or a line of people who would lead the religion after his death. Followers of Bahá'í believe that although Bahá'u'lláh was not the last of God's messengers, he is the one who created the spiritual foundation from which global peace and unification will one day arise.

Bahá'u'lláh was finally permitted to depart Acre in 1877 to live in the nearby town of Bahji. He found an abandoned mansion and lived out the rest of his life there, continuing to write and teach. He died of a fever on May 29, 1892, after naming his oldest son, Abdu'l-Baha ("Servant of Baha" in Arabic; 1844–1921), his successor. A shrine built to Bahá'u'lláh in Bahji is the main pilgrimage site of the Bahá'í religion.

Since the death of Bahá'u'lláh, the Bahá'í faith has spread around the globe to 247 countries and has more than seven million members. Although it is one of the world's youngest religions, it had already grown to be the thirteenth largest by the early twenty-first century. The center of the Bahá'í faith is in Haifa, Israel, where the Universal House of Justice, the main administration of the Bahá'í faith, is located. The Bab and Abdu'l-Baha are also buried in this city.

For More Information

BOOKS

Bahá'u'lláh. *Gleanings from the Writings of Bahá'u'lláh.* Wilmette, IL: Bahá'í Publishing Trust, 1976.

Bahá'u'lláh. *Kitab-i-Aqdas, the Most Holy Book.* Haifa, Israel: Bahá'í World Centre, 1992.

Balyuzi, Hasan. *Bahá'u'lláh: The King of Glory*. Oxford, UK: George Ronald, 1980.

Rabbani, Shoghi Effendi. *God Passes By*. Wilmette, IL: Bahá'í Publishing Trust, 1987.

Smith, Peter. *The Bahá'í Faith: A Short History*. Oxford, UK: Oneworld Publications, 1996.

WEB SITES

"Bahá'u'lláh." *Bahá'í Faith*. http://www.bahai.com/Bahaullah/Bahaullah1.htm (accessed on May 25, 2006).

"Bahá'u'lláh." *Bahá'í Topics*. http://info.bahai.org (accessed on May 25, 2006).

Black Elk

BORN: December, 1863 • Little Powder River, Wyoming

DIED: August 19, 1950 • Manderson, South Dakota

Native American shaman; writer

Black Elk.
DEPARTMENT OF SPECIAL COLLECTIONS AND UNIVERSITY ARCHIVES, MARQUETTE UNIVERSITY LIBRARIES.

"The first peace . . . is that which comes within the souls of people when they realize their relationship, their oneness, with the universe and all its powers, and when they realize that at the center of the universe dwells Wakan-Tanka (the Great Spirit), and that this center is really everywhere, it is within each of us."

Black Elk, a medicine man and spiritual leader of the Lakota, one of the three branches of the Sioux nation, was among the most influential Native Americans of his generation. During his lifetime, the lands of his people in the modern-day U.S. states of South Dakota, Montana, and Wyoming were opened to white settlement. The Indians who lived in these areas were moved to reservations or limited territories. Other Native Americans during the late nineteenth century, such as Sitting Bull (1831–1890) and Crazy Horse (1849–1877), battled against the settlers and gold miners and were killed by soldiers. Black Elk also fought as a young man and was present at two of the most important battles in the closing chapter of Indian independence: the defeat of George

Armstrong Custer (1839–1879) at the Battle of the Little Big Horn in Montana, and the 1890 massacre of Indians at Wounded Knee in South Dakota.

Ultimately, however, Black Elk turned to the spiritual world to help his people recover from the loss of their lands. Said to experience powerful visions as a boy, he became a *wicasa wakan,* or holy man. He was also a strong supporter of the preservation, or saving, of traditional Indian religious practices. When his healing and spiritual work were limited by the whites, who the Native Americans referred to as *Wasichu,* Black Elk became a Catholic and spread his beliefs through that religion. These beliefs were documented in two important works, *Black Elk Speaks: Being the Life Story of a Holy Man of the Oglala Sioux as Told to John G. Neihardt (Flaming Rainbow)* and *The Sacred Pipe: Black Elk's Account of the Seven Rites of the Oglala Sioux.* Both whites and Native Americans have used these books to understand Indian traditions and spirituality.

Born to medicine men

Black Elk was born in December 1863, on the Little Powder River in what is modern-day Wyoming in the United States. He was the son of Sees the White Crow and of Black Elk, who was a medicine man for the Big Road band of Oglalas (one of the seven tribes of the Lakotas). At the time of Black Elk's birth, the United States government was beginning to take over large parts of what were traditionally Native American lands and encouraging white settlers to move to these lands. The discovery of gold in the Black Hills of South Dakota added to the crush of new settlers, and the construction of the Transcontinental Railroad also displaced many Native Americans. (The Transcontintental Railraod was the first railroad to span the entire continent, from the east coast to the west coast. It was completed in 1869.) Several treaties (agreements) promising land rights were made with the Indians, but they were often broken by the U.S. government. The Native Americans began to lose their traditional way of life, which involved following the herds of buffalo on the Great Plains and moving from camp to camp across hundreds of miles of open land.

Black Elk began having visions as a very young boy, with one of the most important occurring when he was nine years old. In this vision a voice came to him, saying that the Grandfathers were waiting for him. Suddenly, Black Elk fell ill and went into a coma for many days. During this time, he experienced visions of being taken to a cloud world where he met six Grandfathers. These men represented the central spirit or mystery of Lakota belief. Each Grandfather gave him some special gift, such as a wooden cup of water that represented the life force, a sacred pipe to cure sick people, or a red stick which sprouted blooming branches and represented rebirth.

The Grandfathers told Black Elk that he had the spirit of an eagle and would make his nation live once again. Black Elk also experienced tests of strength and endurance in the vision. Horses ran at him from the four directions of the compass. He saw a village of tepees arranged in a circle, but the village seemed to be dying until he rode through it and planted the red stick. The stick quickly grew into a tree at the center of the village, giving fresh life to the Native American people. More tests followed. He saw the rise and fall of his people, and he saw the sacred hoop (representing the harmony and oneness of being) broken and finally repaired again. When Black Elk woke, his parents told him that he had been sick for many days. Black Elk did not tell them of his great vision, but he knew that somehow he must work to help his people.

The shrinking world of the Lakota

In 1866 the Lakota chief Red Cloud (1822–1909) fought and defeated the soldiers of Lieutenant Colonel William Fetterman at Fort Phil Kearny in Wyoming. Almost one hundred U.S. soldiers were killed, and Black Elk's father was injured in the battle. Red Cloud later signed the Treaty of 1868, which was supposed to save the Lakota territory from white settlement. By the terms of the treaty, the Lakota were promised the western part of modern-day South Dakota. This area included the sacred Black Hills, where Lakota tradition says man first emerged from underground to live in the world.

Despite this treaty the whites continued to push into the western lands. Custer led an patrol in 1874 and 1875 that discovered gold in the Black Hills, and the area was taken from the Lakota. By late spring of 1876, Black Elk's father had lost faith in his chief, Red Cloud, for accepting this white injustice. He took his family to join with the band led by Crazy Horse, his cousin and a chief who was still eager to fight the whites. Many other tribes gathered that summer at Greasy Grass, the Indian name for the Little Big Horn in Montana. They held a ritual Sun Dance, with the chief Sitting Bull as the leader. The next day the bands were attacked by soldiers of the Seventh Cavalry, led by Custer.

The Pine Ridge Reservation in South Dakota. Black Elk was forced to move to the reservation in 1880. It was there that he experienced his visions for his people. THE ART ARCHIVE/ NATIONAL ARCHIVES WASHINGTON DC.

The cavalry, however, was hugely outnumbered by the four thousand warriors it faced, and the Native Americans defeated the U.S. soldiers, killing Custer in the process. Black Elk, only twelve at the time, killed a soldier and took his first scalp at this battle.

This defeat of Custer's forces, however, did nothing to strengthen the Native Americans' claims to their land. In fact, the U.S. defeat brought more soldiers into their territory. When Crazy Horse was killed by soldiers in 1877, Black Elk's clan headed north to Canada, where they joined Sitting Bull outside the reach of the U.S. Army. In Canada, Black Elk continued to have visions, and he began to feel he should go back to his people and use the power his visions told him he had.

Black Elk returned to the United States in 1879, where he found most of the Native Americans gone and the buffalo herds destroyed by the whites. At age seventeen, Black Elk finally told an old medicine man, Black Road, about his visions, and this man became his teacher. Black Road trained Black Elk, telling him how he could use his visions and powers to create a ritual dance to educate his people. The next year Black Elk was forced to move to the Pine Ridge Reservation in South Dakota. On the reservation he began to practice as a healer, or medicine man.

From Europe to the Ghost Dance

In 1886 Black Elk joined many other Native Americans, including Sitting Bull, in Buffalo Bill's Wild West Show. Buffalo Bill (1846–1917) was a scout and promoter who gathered a cast of hundreds and toured throughout the East Coast and Europe. Black Elk traveled with the show in an effort to learn the secrets of the Wasichu. He was disappointed, however, to learn that the whites did not have any special knowledge or powers, and that in fact they were less civilized in many ways than the Native Americans. Black Elk left Buffalo Bill after the show toured England. He joined another western show and traveled through Italy, Germany, and France. He stayed for two years in Paris, settling down with a French woman.

Black Elk had more visions while in Paris, and in 1889 he returned to Pine Ridge, where he found his family and his band suffering. The soldiers had taken their rifles and horses from them, and they were dying from diseases passed to them from the whites. Black Elk began working as a healer once again. He soon heard of a Paiute Indian named Wovoka who claimed to have had a vision for the renewal of the Native American way of life. Wovoka was leading the people in a movement called the Ghost Dance. This movement became a rallying cry for Indians across the Great Plains who thought that by dancing they could bring the buffalo back and get rid of the white settlers. Black Elk saw similarities in the vision of Wovoka and his own, and joined the Ghost Dancers. He developed colorful Ghost Shirts, which were thought to be able to protect the wearers even from bullets.

The Ghost Dance movement soon earned the suspicion of the soldiers and administrators running the reservations. They were afraid of renewed Indian wars and decided to put a stop to the practice. On December 29, 1890, soldiers rode into an Indian camp at Wounded Knee, not far from the Pine Ridge Reservation where Black Elk was living. They killed 153 men, women, and children in an effort to take their weapons away, and another 150 were missing after the attack. Black Elk rode to Pine Ridge and managed to save a baby from the massacre, but was too late to stop the rest of the slaughter. For him, this was the end of the dream of Indian independence.

Converts to Catholicism

Black Elk continued to work as a healer and holy man for the Indians on the reservation. He was married in 1892 to Katie War Bonnet. After she died in 1903 he converted to the Roman Catholic faith, taking Nicholas as his Christian name. This conversion was partly a practical measure, as the traditional Lakota spiritual practices and societies

Lakota Religion

For the Lakota people and most other Native Americans, religious practice provided a basic way of observing the world and interacting with it. The Lakota rhythm of life was determined by the movement of the sun and moon. They believed the universe was a whole, and saw the circle, or hoop, as the symbol for that unity. Another Lakota symbol of unity was the buffalo skull. The buffalo was a sacred animal to the Lakota because it provided food and skins to make clothing. At the very center of this unity was the supreme god of the Sioux religion, *Wakan Tanka,* who was called the Grandfather or the Great Mystery. According to Lakota tradition, their lives passed through four stages: childhood, adolescence, maturity, and old age. At death, a person's spirit went to meet an old woman who would determine if the person was ready to pass on to the spirit world or would be reborn on earth to learn to live peacefully and in harmony. Values such as a sense of community, bravery, wisdom, and generosity were highly valued.

Holy men, or *wicasa wakan,* were responsible for conducting seven sacred rites or rituals given to the Lakota by the legendary White Buffalo Calf Woman. Along with instructions for these holy rituals, she also gave the Lakota *Cannupa Wakan,* or the sacred pipe. By smoking it during ceremonies, the Lakota could send their prayers upward in the smoke to Wakan Tanka. The first of the seven rites was *Inikagapi,* or life renewal. During this the Lakota cleansed their bodies in a sweat lodge, a dome-shaped sauna. The second was a vision quest in which young men would be isolated on a hill for days without food or water until they experienced a vision. A third rite involved grieving for a year for dead relatives. The fourth rite, the Sun Dance, was one of the most important of all. It was a yearly gathering of tribes and bands during the summer in which participants sacrificed bits of their skin and tied them to a sacred tree at the center of the dance. Other rites included a young person taking an adopted family, prayers for a young girl just entering maturity, and a game in which a girl threw a ball up and many young men attempted to catch it. The winner was thought to be more fortunate than other participants.

were not allowed on the reservation. Although his eyesight was beginning to fail, Black Elk committed himself to his new religion with great energy and made a thorough study of the Bible, the sacred book of Christianity. He became a catechist, or assistant to the priests. Sometimes, if no priest were available, he would even perform the church services. In 1905 Black Elk took a second wife, Anne Brings White, and they were together until her death in 1941. He had four sons and a daughter from his two marriages. Black Elk became an important elder in the Oglala Lakota band. He kept their traditional practices alive by organizing dances for tourists visiting the Black Hills.

In the early 1930s, poet John G. Neihardt (1881–1973) interviewed Black Elk to get information on the Ghost Dance for a cycle of poems he was writing. Black Elk did not speak English, so he told his stories to his son Benjamin, who then translated them for Neihardt. The Lakota holy man was impressed by Neihardt's interest in Native American affairs. He decided to entrust him with his life's story and the lessons he had learned and wished to pass on to others before he died. Working together, the two men created *Black Elk Speaks,* which follows the story of Black Elk's life up to the massacre at Wounded Knee. When the book was published in 1932, it was a critical success. The book's descriptions of visions and traditional Lakota values, however, were disliked by the Jesuit priests Black Elk worked with.

Black Elk Speaks has become a classic and a favorite on school reading lists. Since its publication scholars have disagreed about how much of the work is Black Elk's and how much is Neihardt's. Regardless, as the Native American author N. Scott Momaday (1934–) noted in *A Sender of Words: Essays in Memory of John G. Neihardt,* the Black Elk–Neihardt team "is one of the truly fortunate collaborations in our American heritage, bridging times, places, and cultures." Momaday also calls the work "an extraordinary human document."

Other authors came to talk with Black Elk after *Black Elk Speaks* was published. One of these was Joseph Epes Brown (1920–2000), who interviewed Black Elk during the winter of 1947–48. Brown focused on recording the rituals of the Lakota Sioux. His book, *The Sacred Pipe,* was published in 1953, three years after Black Elk's death at eighty-six.

Black Elk is an important figure in both his own culture and the culture of whites. He contributed to the renewal of his people through his role as a holy man. He was able to blend the cultures of Native American and white by serving in both traditional Lakota spirituality and the Catholic Church. His sayings have become part of a revival in native wisdom and faith. For non-Native Americans, his words have helped inspire interest in traditional and alternative religions. Though at the end of *Black Elk Speaks* the medicine man appears saddened that he was unable to save his people, others believe that Black Elk accomplished his mission. Gretchen M. Battaile, an American critic and educator, for example, noted in an essay for *A Sender of Words,* "By keeping their traditions alive, the [Lakota] people continue to live. Through the telling of his story, Black Elk fulfilled his vision."

For More Information

BOOKS

Black Elk. *Black Elk Speaks: Being the Life Story of a Holy Man of the Oglala Sioux as Told to John G. Neihardt (Flaming Rainbow) Illustrated by Standing Bear.* New York: Morrow, 1932. Reprint. Lincoln: University of Nebraska Press, 1979.

Black Elk. *The Sacred Pipe: Black Elk's Account of the Seven Rites of the Oglala Sioux.* Edited by Joseph Epes Brown. Norman, OK: University of Oklahoma Press, 1953.

Black Elk. *The Sixth Grandfather: Black Elk's Teachings Given to John G. Neihardt.* Edited by Raymond J. DeMallie. Lincoln, NE: University of Nebraska Press, 1984.

Deloria, Vine, Jr., ed. *A Sender of Words: Essays in Memory of John G. Neihardt.* Salt Lake City, UT: Howe Brothers, 1984.

Rice, Julian. *Black Elk's Story: Distinguishing Its Lakota Purpose.* Albuquerque, NM: University of New Mexico Press, 1991.

Steltenkamp, Michael F. *Black Elk: Holy Man of the Oglala.* Norman, OK: University of Oklahoma Press, 1993.

PERIODICALS

Neihardt, John. "The Book That Would Not Die." *Western American Literature (February 1972): 227–30.*

WEB SITES

Lorenz, Caroline and Rod. "Nicholas Black Elk, Cathecist." *Olive Leaf.* http://www.peace.mb.ca/00.Native/nlrnz02.htm (accessed on June 2, 2006).

The Buddha

BORN: April 8, 563 BCE • Lumbini, Nepal

DIED: February 25, 483 BCE • Kushinagar, India

Indian philosopher; spiritual teacher

"Hold fast to the dharma as your lamp, hold fast to the dharma as your refuge, and you shall surely reach nirvana."

The Buddha.
© EDIFICE/CORBIS.

Siddhartha Gautama was a prince who sought to eliminate the sufferings of life. He abandoned the luxuries of the palace for the difficulties of life as a poor ascetic, or one who shuns worldly pleasures in pursuit of spiritual truth. After years of seeking, Siddhartha became enlightened and took the name of the Buddha, or the "Awakened One." To become enlightened means one has come to understand the realities of the world and how to end its suffering. The Buddha shared his wisdom with others throughout the rest of his life. His teachings evolved into the religion of Buddhism, the fourth largest religion in the world in the twenty-first century.

Early life

The Buddha was born Siddhartha Gautama on April 8, 563 BCE, in Lumbini in modern-day Nepal. His father, Suddhodana, was the king of a local tribe called the Shakyas. For this reason one of the Buddha's traditional names is Shakyamuni, meaning "wise man of the Shakyas." His mother was Queen Maha Maya. At the time of his birth, a holy man predicted that Siddhartha would grow to become a great ruler or a great spiritual man. In fact, *Siddhartha* means "He whose purpose in life has already been attained."

Siddhartha's mother died shortly after his birth. Siddhartha's father did not want his son to fulfill a spiritual destiny. He wanted Siddhartha to succeed him as king. Suddhodana did all in his power to protect Siddhartha from the tragedies of life and made sure that Siddhartha's every desire was met. Siddhartha grew up in the palace, where he received the best education and became very skilled at archery. He was so protected that he knew nothing of life's suffering.

By the time he was twenty-nine years old, Siddhartha was married to Yasodhara and had a son, Rahula. He had everything he wanted, and yet the young prince was not satisfied. He began to question whether there was no greater purpose to life. At the time of Siddhartha's life, many people were asking the same type of questions. The religion of Hinduism was established but still developing in the region, and disagreements existed over religious beliefs and practices and the best way to achieve a better existence.

Siddhartha received his father's permission to travel beyond the palace gates. His father tried to make sure that Siddhartha would not be exposed to any suffering or tragedy in town. Nevertheless, Siddhartha saw four things he had never seen before: a man with disease, a person bent and slow with age, a dead body, and an ascetic. At each sight, he asked his servant, Channa, to explain what he was seeing. Siddhartha came to realize that people grew old, suffered, and died. He also came to understand that there were people, such as the ascetic, who looked for ways to escape from this suffering.

He returned to the palace, his thoughts troubled by what he had learned. Siddhartha felt compelled to find the answers to this suffering. That evening Siddhartha left his wife and son in the palace and renounced the only life he had known. Outside the palace gates, he changed into a simple robe, cut off his hair, and took a bowl for the food he would beg. Siddhartha then walked off into the forest to become an ascetic.

Enlightenment

Siddhartha devoted himself to attaining spiritual understanding. He learned yoga and meditation. Yoga is an intense physical and spiritual discipline meant to focus and train the mind to receive spiritual truths. Meditation is the practice of tuning out distractions in the world to focus inward and achieve spiritual knowledge. Siddhartha even subjected his body to great deprivation, such as going without food, in an effort to deny the material world and focus solely on the spiritual. His intense dedication impressed other ascetics and he gained followers. Siddhartha eventually realized, however, that neglecting his body weakened his mind and made it difficult for him to focus on his spiritual pursuits.

The Buddha is tempted by the devil Mara while meditating. It was after resisting all of Mara's temptations that the Buddha achieved enlightenment. © BETTMANN/CORBIS.

With this realization, Siddhartha began to eat regular meals again. His followers were upset, believing he had abandoned his search for enlightenment. They left him. His body satisfied, Siddhartha sat under a *bodhi,* or fig, tree near the city of Gaya, India, and fell into a deep meditation. He became completely unaware of the outside world as his senses focused increasingly inward. Mara, the tempter, soon appeared to Siddhartha and tried to distract him from his goal. He did not want anyone to know how to end suffering. Mara sent his beautiful daughters to Siddhartha, and tried to encourage passion, desire, and doubt. For weeks as he meditated, Siddhartha faced these temptations. Eventually, Mara himself appeared before Siddhartha, but Siddhartha would not be deterred.

When he awoke from his meditation, he was the Buddha, the "Awakened One." The word *buddha* comes from the Sanskrit word *budh,* meaning "to wake up." During his long meditation under the bodhi tree, the Buddha found escape from life's suffering and death. This escape is called *nirvana.* The knowledge that life's suffering could be ended, and how to end it, is called enlightenment. The Buddha was enlightened, and he sought to share his knowledge with others. His former followers realized that the Buddha had gained new insight. They returned to learn from him the *dharma,* or the path to enlightenment and nirvana.

Teaches the dharma

The Buddha gave his first sermon on the dharma at Deer Park, near Benares, India. In this sermon the Buddha revealed the central teachings of what would become the religion of Buddhism. The first teaching is the Four Noble Truths. These are that life contains suffering, that desire causes suffering, that nirvana is the end of suffering, and that one can attain nirvana by following the Eightfold Path.

The Eightfold Path is the second teaching revealed by the Buddha at Deer Park. It contains the following steps:

1. Right understanding, being aware of the world the way it really is;
2. Right purpose, vowing to live life aware of its true nature rather than being deceived by illusion and desire;
3. Right speech, such as not lying or hurting others through one's words;
4. Right conduct, including not killing or harming other living beings;
5. Right occupation, including avoiding work that brings harm to others, such as hunting animals or selling weapons;
6. Right effort, trying to think, act, and speak in accordance with right understanding;
7. Right attention, keeping the mind in the present and always aware of the dharma; and
8. Right meditation, training the mind so that it can overcome its desires.

By following these eight steps, a person could attain enlightenment and achieve nirvana. The Buddha taught the Middle Way, meaning a path that avoided extreme indulgence and extreme denial. For instance, a Buddhist may abstain from alcohol by choice, but the Middle Way would allow for the drinking of alcohol so long as one did not become intoxicated. These teachings could be followed by anyone and did not rely on an authority structure, such as priests, or on ritual methods of worship. From Deer Park, the Buddha set forth to travel throughout northern India, teaching others about the dharma.

A religion for all

Indian society in the sixth century BCE was heavily divided by the caste system, a hereditary social structure that determined people's education, their jobs, who they could marry, and many other aspects of their lives.

The castes did not interact with one another beyond what may have been needed to carry out work. They did not even worship at the same temples. The Buddha, born a prince, was from the highest of the four castes. He did not, however, distinguish between castes as he spread his teachings and considered all people to be equally able to understand the dharma and achieve nirvana. This was very appealing to people, and the Buddha gained an increasing number of followers everywhere he went.

One day, five or seven years after he had left, the Buddha returned to the palace of his youth. He made converts of his family. His aunt, Maha-Pajapati Gautama, wanted to join him on his travels. The Buddha, however, would not let women join him. He told her that women could follow the dharma just as easily from home. He believed that it would be too difficult for men and women to focus on their spiritual pursuits if they had to also handle the challenges of living side-by-side. His aunt persisted, however, and became the first nun of the new religion.

In 483 BCE, after more than forty years of spreading the dharma, the Buddha's health began to fail. He had established no written teachings and no hierarchy of authority. He did not believe that these things were necessary. Shortly before his death, one of the Buddha's followers, Ananda, asked the Buddha about his successor. According to Eknath Easwaran in *The Dhammapada,* the Buddha replied, "Be a refuge unto yourselves, Ananda. Be a lamp unto yourselves. Rely on yourselves and on nothing else. Hold fast to the dharma as your lamp, hold fast to th dharma as your refuge, and you shall surely reach nirvana." A few days later, outside the town of Kusinara in modern-day Nepal, and before all of those who had followed him for so many years, the Buddha died.

Formalizing a religion

Although the Buddha himself did not believe his teachings needed to be recorded, his followers worried that without a written record, his words could be changed or reinterpreted. They did not want to lose the original meaning of the Buddha's teachings. A council of elders met a few weeks after the Buddha's death to discuss how to continue to spread the dharma to others. They agreed to write down some of the Buddha's words. This became the Dhammapada, a part of a larger collection of Buddhist sacred texts called the Tipitaka.

Buddhist Nuns

The first Buddhist nun was Siddhartha's aunt, Maha-Pajapati Gautama. When the Buddha returned to his hometown five years after gaining enlightenment, his aunt converted to his teachings. She approached him about joining his order of monks, wishing to devote her life to this spiritual path, but he refused her. Just as the Buddha would not be tempted by Mara, however, Maha-Pajapati would not be deterred. She gathered a large group of women and walked 150 miles (241 kilometers) to join the Buddha at his camp in Vesali, India.

It was not until the Buddha's follower, Ananda, asked the Buddha whether women could not attain *nirvana,* or the end of suffering, just as men could, that the Buddha relented. The *sangha,* or community, of nuns is called *bhikkhuni,* while the sangha of monks is called *bhikkhu.*

The women who would be nuns had to agree to eight conditions.

1. They must give deference, or high regard and respect, to monks.
2. They must spend their yearly retreat in a separate location from monks.
3. They must consult with monks on teaching the dharma.
4. Nuns must confess any wrongdoing before a community of both monks and nuns.
5. Any nun breaking a rule that governs monks and nuns will receive punishment before them.
6. Nuns must be ordained, or accepted into the bhikkhuni, before a gathering of both monks and nuns.
7. Nuns may not treat any monk badly or abuse him.
8. Buddhist nuns cannot teach monks.

The Buddha was among the first of religious leaders to grant women such a high status. In early years, he ordained monks and nuns himself. The potential monk or nun had to recite the Three Refuges: "I take refuge in the Buddha; I take refuge in the Dharma; I take refuge in the Sangha." As the sangha grew, however, the Buddha allowed trusted followers to carry out the ordinations. He also added more rules that a person needed to meet in order to be a monk or nun. These were primarily rules of conduct. They gradually increased from ten to more than two hundred.

Buddhist nuns live in monasteries. These are refuges away from worldly distractions where one can focus on following the dharma and attaining enlightenment. They have very few personal possessions, oftentimes just a robe or two and a bowl for food. Meals may be taken only once a day, when laypeople, or Buddhists within the community who have not taken vows to join the bhikkhuni, give alms to the nuns. Additionally, nuns shave their heads as a symbol of their giving up their former lives and of their membership in the sangha. Nuns take the spiritual knowledge they have learned at the monastery and share it with laypeople. A layperson may consult a nun for guidance on handling a difficult family matter or to hear teachings on the dharma. This is also true of monks.

The word *dhamma* is an alternate spelling of *dharma* and means "the path." The word *Dhammapada* is often translated as "Words of the Doctrine." It consists of hundreds of aphorisms, or short, concise statements that contain a truth, principle, or sentiment, usually in memorable language. The verses are divided into sections that follow a particular theme, such as "The Mind" or "The Wise." The Dhammapada has been translated into numerous languages and is consulted daily by many Buddhists.

Examples of the Buddha's sayings from the Dhammapada, as relayed in the translation by Eknath Easwaran, include:

"Do not give your attention to what others do or fail to do; give it to what you do or fail to do."

"Hasten to do good; refrain from evil. If you neglect the good, evil can enter your mind."

"Better than ruling this world, better than attaining the realm of the gods, better than being lord of all the worlds, is one step taken on the path to nirvana."

While the Buddha taught that anyone could follow the dharma and that one did not need to rely on a priest or any other authority figure, as well as on any formal instructional setting, such a system did not easily lend itself to the continued growth of his teachings. His followers created an organized structure for the religion in the years following his death. Monasteries arose as places to house Buddhist monks and nuns, and where laypeople, or Buddhists who were not monks and nuns, could seek refuge. Buddhist temples also developed, where people could gather to meditate and hear the Buddha's teachings together in a community, or *sangha.*

About a century after the Buddha's death, another council was held to formalize Buddhist doctrine, or the principles of the religion. During this council a major split emerged in the faith and two main schools of Buddhism emerged: Theravada and Mahayana. The Theravada school is the most traditional. It follows the Buddha's early teachings as recorded in what is called the Pali Canon, which it believes to be the most accurate documentation. Theravada also gives great attention to the final step on the Eightfold Path, right meditation. The Mahayana branch accepts later writings as part of the Buddha's teachings, particularly those representing the later part of his life. Mahayana also contains numerous *bodhisattvas,* or enlightened individuals who exist on another level. They have turned back from nirvana so that they may help others attain enlightenment.

Mahayana Buddhists may direct their worship to these bodhisattvas, which are similar to gods. Theravada Buddhists, however, recognize no gods.

The nirvana described by the Buddha can be compared to the heaven detailed in religions such as Judaism and Christianity, a place where there is no suffering, a reward for a good life lived with kindness and compassion. While heaven is a reward from God in these other faiths, however, the Buddha did not discuss the existence of a god, nor did he claim to be one. He believed that everything in existence had an opposite, such as happy and sad and fear and hope, and he believed that suffering must also have non-suffering. He discovered that in order to attain non-suffering, one must train the mind to see through illusion and desire so that one can recognize and live within the unity and harmony of all things in creation. The Buddha believed that the divine truth of existence is everywhere and is available to everyone.

For More Information

BOOKS

Armstrong, Karen. *Buddha.* New York, NY: Viking Penguin, 2001.

"The Buddha." In *Encyclopedia of World Biography.* 2nd ed. 17 vols. Farmington Hills, MI: Thomson Gale, 2005.

The Dhammapada. Eknath Easwaran, trans. Tomales, CA: Nilgiri Press, 2004.

Fouchet, Alfred. *Life of the Buddha According to the Ancient Texts and Monuments of India.* Translated by Simone Boas. New Delhi, India: Munshirm Manoharlal Publishing, 2003.

Netzley, Patricia D. *Religions of the World: Buddhism.* San Diego: Lucent Books, 2002.

Phangcham, C. *Buddhism for Young Students.* 5th ed. Centereach, NY: Council of Thai Bhikkhus in the U.S.A., 2001.

Strong, John S. *The Buddha.* Oxford, UK: Oneworld Publications, 2001.

Watts, Alan. *Buddhism: The Religion of No-Religion.* Boston, MA: Tuttle Publishing, 1995.

WEB SITES

"Buddhist Monks and Nuns." *BuddhaNet.* http://www.buddhanet.net/e-learning/buddhism/pbs2_unit08a.htm (accessed June 5, 2006).

"Dharma Data: Nuns." *BuddhaNet.* http://www.buddhanet.net/e-learning/dharmadata/fdd38.htm (accessed June 5, 2006).

"Life of the Buddha." *BuddhaNet.* http://www.buddhanet.net/e-learning/buddhism/lifebuddha/contents1.htm (accessed June 1, 2006).

Caitanya Mahaprabhu

BORN: February 4, 1485 • Navadvipa, West Bengal, India

DIED: June 14, 1533 • Puri, Orissa, India

Indian religious leader

"One should chant the holy name of the Lord in a humble state of mind, thinking oneself lower than the straw in the street; one should be more tolerant than a tree, devoid of all sense of false prestige and should be ready to offer all respect to others."

Caitanya (also spelled Chaitanya) Mahaprabhu was an Indian Hindu ascetic and mystic who lived during the sixteenth century. An ascetic is someone who gives up the pleasure and comforts of the world to lead a life of self-denial and religious devotion A mystic is a person who claims to have direct knowledge of God and of spiritual truth. Caitanya was the founder of a sect, or division, of Hinduism called Gaudiya Vaishnavism. Vaishnavas, or those who practice Vaishnavism, regard Krishna as the supreme, original God. In this respect they differ from members of other schools of Hinduism who see Krishna as an *avatar* of Vishnu. Vishnu is one of the major Hindu gods and is regarded as the preserver of the universe. An avatar is an incarnation, or birth in human form, of a Hindu god. All Hindu gods are considered to be representations of the one God, Brahma.

The movement Caitanya founded declined after his death, but in the late nineteenth and early twentieth centuries it experienced a rebirth.

Caitanya, a Hindu holy man, founded a new branch of Hinduism called Gaudiya Vaishnavism, and worshipped Krishna as the supreme God. He is shown here with a follower, Nityananda. © THE BRITISH LIBRARY/ TOPHAM-HIP/THE IMAGE WORKS.

In the twenty-first century, the teachings of Caitanya are followed by many Hindu communities throughout the world. His most readily recognized followers are members of the Hare Krishna movement.

Birth and early life

Caitanya was born on February 4, 1485. His father, Jagannath Mishra (or Misra), was a Brahmin, meaning he belonged to the highest caste, or social class, in India. His mother was Sachi Devi. The couple had had eight daughters, all of whom died soon after they were born. The couple's ninth child, a son named Viswarup, survived. Caitanya was their tenth child.

Caitanya was born in the town of Navadvipa in West Bengal, India. Caitanya's name at birth was Visvambhar (also spelled Viswambar) Mishra, but in his youth he acquired two nicknames. One was Nimai, taken from the name of the Neem tree under which he was supposed to have been born. The other was Gaura, meaning "the fair," or "the golden one," referring to his fair skin.

Many of the details recorded by biographers about Visvambhar's early life may or may not be true. He became such a mythical figure among his followers that some of what was later written about him may have been exaggerated. According to his early biographers, the young Visvambhar was an extremely intelligent student. At a school founded by a famous guru, or teacher, named Vasudev Sarvabhauma, he studied logic, grammar, literature, rhetoric (language), philosophy, and theology (religion). He was a student of Nyaya, a school of logic dating back to the second century. According to legend, one of the teachers at Visvambhar's school had written a book on Nyaya and sought to become the world's leading authority on the subject. While still in his teens Visvambhar also wrote a book on Nyaya. When Visvambhar shared what he had written with the teacher, the teacher wept because he recognized that Visvambhar's book was the better of the two. As an act of humility and kindness, Visvambhar dismissed his own book as nothing but dry philosophy and threw it into the river.

At the age of sixteen Visvambhar started his own school. He married Lakshmi, the daughter of a highly respected teacher named Vallabha. While Visvambhar was traveling, his wife was bitten by a snake and died. He later remarried, to a woman named Vishnupriya. He continued to accept students and gained a reputation as an accomplished teacher. Up until this time he had not shown any particular interest in religious concepts, although he was a devout Hindu. That changed, however, after the death of his father. In 1509 Visvambhar went on a pilgrimage to the northeastern Indian city of Gaya in honor of his father. In Gaya he met another famed guru, Ishvar Puri. Under the guru's instruction Visvambhar became a follower of the god Krishna. He then returned to West Bengal, where the local Vaishnavas saw that a major change had come over him. They recognized him as the leader of their sect.

The life of a sannyasi

Visvambhar spent the rest of his relatively short life as a *sannyasi.* A sannyasi is an ascetic, a person who has given up worldly pleasures in favor of a life of religious devotion. It was at this point in his life that Visvambhar took the name Caitanya Mahaprabhu. During his final years he traveled throughout India, preaching to people and attracting followers to his sect. He finally settled in the town of Puri. He often forgot to eat or drink and he slept naked on the ground. He constantly chanted the name of Krishna.

During this period Caitanya attracted the attention of Maharaja Prataparudra, the king of Orissa, a region of India. (India was a collection of separate kingdoms in the sixteenth century. Orissa is now a modern-day Indian state.) The king saw Caitanya as an incarnation of Krishna and gave him considerable support, allowing the sect to grow in numbers and influence. At one point Caitanya and a well-known scholar named Sarvabhauma Bhattacharya held a debate about the meaning of a verse from Hindu scripture. According to legend, Sarvabhauma was able to explain nine different meanings of the verse. Caitanya was able to explain sixty-one meanings. The scholar was overcome with humility, knowing that Caitanya had bested him. Sarvabhauma realized that he had lost his devotion to God. Under Caitanya's influence, he converted to the Gaudiya Vaishnavism sect and became a more devoted follower of Krishna.

Caitanya spent much of his time in deep meditation, or focused thought with the goal of attaining greater spiritual understanding.

Caitanya's Writings

Caitanya left behind little in the way of written materials. In fact only eight of his verses have survived. These verses, called Sikshashtaka, are regarded as prayers by his followers. Below are some excerpts from these verse-prayers, as found on the *Divine Life Society* Web site.:

• • •

Glory to the Shri Krishna Sankirtana [chanting of God's names by worshippers], which cleanses the heart of all the dust accumulated for years and extinguishes the fire of conditional life, of repeated birth and death. This Sankirtana movement is the prime benediction [blessing] for humanity at large because it spreads the rays of the benediction moon.... It increases the ocean of transcendental [beyond the universe or material existence] bliss, and it enables us to fully taste the nectar for which we are always anxious.

O my Lord, Your holy name alone can render all benediction to living beings, and thus You have hundreds and millions of names.... There are not even hard and fast rules for chanting these names. O my Lord, out of kindness You enable us to easily approach You by Your holy names, but I am so unfortunate that I have no attraction for them.

One should chant the holy name of the Lord in a humble state of mind, thinking oneself lower than the straw in the street; one should be more tolerant than a tree, devoid of all sense of false prestige and should be ready to offer all respect to others. In such a state of mind one can chant the holy name of the Lord constantly.

O Almighty Lord, I have no desire to accumulate wealth, nor do I desire beautiful women, nor do I want any number of followers. I only want Your causeless devotional service birth after birth.

He was also given to outbursts of ecstasy, or periods of uncontrolled emotion, and often fell into a trance. Modern-day scholars believe that Caitanya may have suffered from epilepsy, a disorder of the nervous system, and that his trances were actually seizures. Believers, however, insist that his periods of ecstatic chanting and dancing, as well as his trances, resulted from his deep religious faith.

Accomplishes miracles

A number of miracles have been attributed to Caitanya. One concerned two brothers, Jagai and Madhai, who were well-known drunkards, robbers, and murderers. Caitanya took upon himself the task of converting them into members of his sect. He and a group of his followers went to the brothers' camp, chanting the name of Krishna. Madhai assaulted one of Caitanya's followers, wounding him severely, and was about to kill the man when Jagai stopped him. Caitanya pushed to the front of the group, tended to his follower's injuries, and embraced Jagai for his act of kindness. According to legend Jagai then fell to the ground in a trance. When he awoke, he confessed that he was a sinner and asked Krishna for forgiveness. Madhai, too, fell into a trance and was converted. The two brothers went on to become saints.

Caitanya made converts of many people in much the same way. One story tells how Caitanya encountered a man washing clothes in a river. Caitanya approached the man, who believed that Caitanya was simply a beggar. Caitanya first persuaded the man to repeat the name of Krishna, then he embraced him, and the man immediately began dancing and chanting in a state of ecstasy. The man's wife called the villagers to help her husband, thinking he had gone mad. As the villagers approached the man, he embraced each one. At that point they too began to dance and chant. In this way, the entire village was converted. Another legend claims that Caitanya healed and converted a leper by embracing him. Leprosy is a disease that causes deformities and rotting of the flesh. Lepers were outcasts, and at that time one would never touch a leper for fear of getting the disease.

In another story Caitanya leapt into the sea in a fit of devotional ecstasy. He was very thin and frail because of his constant fasting (not eating), so he was soon lost in the waters. His followers searched frantically up and down the seacoast but were unable to find him. Meanwhile, a fisherman had cast his net into the sea and pulled up what appeared to be a human body. He was frightened because the body was making noises. He left his boat and walked along the shore, not knowing what to do. He encountered a pair of Caitanya's followers and told them the story. They rushed to the fisherman's boat, freed Caitanya from the net, and brought him back to consciousness.

Regardless of whether any of these legends are true, they show how highly Caitanya's followers respected him. Indeed, followers of Gaudiya Vaishnavism believe that Caitanya was the latest avatar of Krishna. As he neared his death, Caitanya selected six of these followers to spread his principles of devotion. These six formalized the teachings of Gaudiya Vaishnavism and spread them throughout eastern India, primarily in Bengal and Orissa. In fact some historians of religion believe that Hinduism in Bengal might not have survived if not for Caitanya's influence. To keep Gaudiya Vaishnavism alive, Caitanya's followers established lineages, or family lines, that passed the traditions of the

Krishna is pictured with the goddess Radha. Some of the miracles attributed to Caitanya occurred after Krishna's name was repeated several times.

sect down from generation to generation. These lineages still exist in the early twenty-first century, and many of the members have become noted Hindu scholars and teachers.

The tradition of Gaudiya Vaishnavism spread farther in the twentieth century due to the teachings of Swami Prabhupada (1896–1977), who established temples in the West (the countries in Europe and the Americas). Swami Prabhupada is also generally regarded as the founder of the Hare Krishna movement. Members of this group can often be seen in public places chanting "Hare Krishna, Hare Krishna, Krishna, Krishna, Hare Hare; Hare Rama, Hare Rama, Rama Rama, Hare Hare." *Hare* means something like "the devotional energy of God," although it is often translated simply as

"O," as in "O Lord." *Rama* means loosely "the supreme personality of God," so it is another name for Krishna. Followers of the Hare Krishna movement believe that people have to awaken their "Krishna consciousness," or love for God, by repeating this mantra, called the "maha-mantra," or "great chant," repeatedly.

Caitanya died on June 14, 1533. Although no firm evidence supports the theory, he may have been murdered by priests of the temple of Jagannath in Puri. The priests disagreed with Caitanya regarding whether Muslims and "Untouchables" could be accepted at the temple as disciples of Gaudiya Vaishnavism. Caitanya once commented on the caste system, according to Srila Vrindavan das Thakur, saying: "Only the most wretched sinner will discriminate a Vaisnava's caste, race or nationality, and for doing so he suffers the pangs of repeated birth in the lower species of life." As noted in "Lord Gauranga (Sri Krishna Chaitanya Mahaprabhu)," he spoke the following words before dying: "Oh Lord, I ask not for wealth or followers, or for poetic genius. May my motiveless devotion to Thee continue in me whenever I take birth." This was a reference to the Hindu belief in reincarnation, or being born into a new life.

For More Information

BOOKS

Thakur, Bhaktivinode. *Sri Chaitanya: His Life & Precepts.* San Rafael, CA: Mandala Publishing, 2002.

Tirtha, B. V. *Chaitanya: His Life and Associates.* San Rafael, CA: Mandala Publishing, 2001.

WEB SITES

das Thakur, Srila Vrindavan. *Chaitanya Bhagavat.* http://www.acbspn.com/books/cb/cb_madhya10.htm (accessed on June 2, 2006).

Sivananda, Swami. "Lord Gauranga (Sri Krishna Chaitanya Mahaprabhu)." *The Divine Life Society.* http://www.dlshq.org/saints/gauranga.htm (accessed on June 2, 2006).

"Sri Caitanya Mahaprabhu: His Life and Precepts." *Lord Caitanya, Prabhupada Hare Krishna News Network.* http://caitanya.krishna.org/Articles/2000/06/00016.html (accessed on June 2, 2006).

John Calvin

BORN: July 10, 1509 • Noyon, Picardy, France

DIED: May 27, 1564 • Geneva, Switzerland

French religious leader

John Calvin.

"Our minds ought to come to a halt at the point where we learn in Scripture to know Jesus Christ and him alone, so that we may be directly led by him to the Father who contains in himself all perfection."

John Calvin had a powerful influence on Western religion and thought. Calvin was a French theologian, or religious scholar, who developed a system of belief called Calvinism. Calvin taught that the Bible, the sacred text of Christianity, was the ultimate word on all religious matters, including the organization of the church itself. He also developed the idea of predestination. Predestination teaches that God chooses certain people for spiritual salvation, and this choice does not change regardless of a person's actions. These chosen people, called the "elect," form the core of the Calvinist Church.

The Calvinist belief in a strict interpretation of the Bible led to a strong and rigid moral position on matters of faith. These principles eventually had a direct influence on the Puritans, those Protestants who fled England and helped settle North America. Consequently, Calvinism had a significant influence on early culture and thought in the United States.

French origins

John Calvin, originally named Jean Cauvin, was born to Gérard Cauvin and Jeanne Lefranc in Noyon, Picardy, France, in 1509. Gérard was a lawyer and the secretary to the bishop of Noyon, and he used his influence to ensure his son would have a suitable professional career. Gérard decided that his son should work in the church, and at age twelve Jean secured the minor position of chaplain in the Cathedral of Noyon. Two years later he was sent to Paris for schooling. While in college he changed his name to its Latin version, John Calvin.

Calvin first studied Latin at the Collège de la Marche, at the University of Paris. He then took classes in scholastic debate at the Collège de Montaigu, where the famous scholar and theologian Erasmus (1466–1536) had studied. In 1528 Calvin earned his Master of Arts degree. Around this time Calvin's father had a disagreement with the bishop of Noyon, leading to his excommunication, or exclusion from the church community. Because of this, Gérard Cauvin suggested his son change his studies from theology to law. Calvin obeyed and moved to Orléans to study law, despite the fact that he had already developed a passion for theology and the study of the Bible. He then transferred to Brouges in 1529 and earned his law degree in 1531, which was also the year of his father's death. Historians believe that the difficulties Calvin had in securing a Christian burial for his excommunicated father may have partly turned him against the Catholic faith.

Following his father's death, Calvin returned to Paris to study humanism and classical literature. He published his first book in 1532, a commentary on the work of the Roman philosopher Seneca. Around this time Calvin became interested in the ideas of German theologian **Martin Luther** (1483–1546; see entry). Luther was gaining popularity in France by calling for church reform and promoting faith as a means to salvation. Calvin was attracted to these Protestant teachings, which led him to become a friend of Nicholas Cop, the rector of the University of Paris. In 1533 Calvin converted from Catholicism to Protestantism and pursued religious studies with renewed passion.

Later that year Calvin's friend, Cop, gave an address at the university that called for a return to a simpler, more biblical Christianity, rather than one focused on the showy ceremonies of the Catholic Church. The king of France, Frances I (1494–1547; ruled 1515–47), did not approve of such Protestant ideas, so he arrested many of those involved in the speech. Cop himself escaped to Switzerland. As some believed that Calvin had actually written the speech, he also left Paris for a time, settling first at the court of the king's Protestant sister, Marguerite of Navarre. After briefly returning to Paris in 1534, he decided to leave France permanently to escape the king's anger. He moved to Switzerland, where about half the population was Protestant.

A life in exile

Traveling under the false name Martianus Lucianus, Calvin first took refuge in Basel, Switzerland, where Protestants from other European countries had settled to avoid harassment. In 1536 he published the first edition of what would become a lifelong work, *Institutes of the Christian Religion,* a manual on Christian theology. Later editions appeared in 1541, 1559, and 1560. In this book Calvin explained his main religious ideas, such as his belief that God was glorious and magnificent far beyond humanity's ability to understand. Calvin said that all humans were sinful and had no free will, a belief similar to Luther's. He also said humans could not seek their own salvation, because only the grace of God determined who was saved and who was damned. So while strong faith and good works are important to Calvinists, they do not automatically lead to salvation. Calvin also stated that the authority of the pope should be rejected.

Calvin organized his basic thoughts into the Five Points of Calvinism, which were later developed further by his followers. These are often referred to by the acronym TULIP:

- "Total depravity" refers to the sin into which humans are born.
- "Unconditional election" refers to selection by God for salvation.
- "Limited atonement" is the concept that God's son Jesus Christ was crucified (nailed to a cross until dead) to erase the sins not of all people but of the elect.
- "Irresistible grace" is the principle that God's mercy and grace apply to those He elects for salvation.
- "Perseverance of the saints" holds that those who have been elected cannot later be condemned.

In creating his new religious system, Calvin based all his principles on a literal reading of the Bible. He called for a simple church ceremony, with the sermon (discussion of the Bible readings) being the central part. There are only two sacraments, or holy rituals, in the Calvinist Church. One is baptism, a symbolic use of water resulting in admission to the Christian community. The second is the Lord's Supper, or the reenactment of the Last Supper, which took place between Christ and his closest followers before Christ was crucified. In many congregations, the faithful stand during the entire service. In Calvinism the "visible church" includes all those who worship Christ, and the "invisible church" includes those chosen by God for salvation. Belonging to the visible church and having faith are requirements for being saved, but do not themselves guarantee salvation. Also, in Calvinism church and state are not considered separate but are both God's creations. The church teaches morality and faith, while the state preserves order and carries out the laws of the church.

In 1536 Calvin traveled to Geneva, Switzerland, where he met the Protestant reformer Guillaume Farel (1489–1565), who persuaded him to make the city his home. Farel, who was also a Frenchman in exile, had led Protestant reform in Geneva for several years. At Farel's insistence, Calvin took a position as a minister and began playing a major role in the establishment of a set of principles for Geneva's faithful.

Calvin was largely responsible for the passage of a set of laws that greatly reduced Catholic influence in Geneva. These laws prohibited numerous activities Calvin believed were immoral, including adultery (sexual intercourse with someone other than a person's spouse), gambling, and even the wearing of expensive clothing. A new city council with leanings toward Catholicism came to power, however, and both Calvin and Farel were forced to leave Geneva. Calvin then went to Strasbourg, France, where he became the minister for a small congregation of Protestants. In France he married Idelette de Bure, and the couple had one child who died in infancy.

Return to Geneva

Calvin's stay in Strasbourg did not last long. In 1541 he was summoned back to Geneva, where he was promised the freedom to set up a reform church according to the principles outlined in his *Institutes*. This

Ulrich Zwingli

The Protestant religion was introduced to Switzerland by Swiss native Ulrich Zwingli (1484–1531). Zwingli was born to a prominent family in Wildhaus. His father was the chief magistrate (a civil officer with the power to administer and enforce law) and his uncle was a church leader. Zwingli studied religion in various cities—including Vienna, Austria, and Basel—and earned his degree in 1506. After his graduation he served as a pastor in Glarus for ten years, at times accompanying Swiss mercenaries, or hired soldiers, into battle as their chaplain. In 1518 he became the priest at Zurich's Great Minster church.

Until his appointment in Zurich, Zwingli had been a strong believer in Catholicism and the pope. During his time at Great Minster, however, he began to question the Catholic Church, especially its ceremonies and excesses. He soon began preaching against practices such as enforced celibacy (not having sexual intercourse) for priests and the selling of indulgences, which are special favors from God. Martin Luther had recently opposed the same practices in Germany, although the two had no contact with each other. Zwingli himself married and had four children, thereby taking a personal stand against Catholic priesthood celibacy.

Zwingli was popular in Zurich, having done much for the population during an epidemic of the plague, a deadly disease caused by bacteria, and his new practices were welcomed by most of the faithful. Zwingli looked for inspiration and information in the Bible. In 1523 Zwingli introduced his sixty-seven articles calling for reform of the church. The city fathers of Zurich decided that these principles should apply throughout the entire canton, or province, effectively creating a state church. His denomination was called Reformed, and it was very similar to the Lutheranism that was developing in Germany.

The reform movement swept through Switzerland, and Zwingli became the virtual ruler of Zurich. His Reformed Church was not without its critics and opponents, however, and Catholic territories began banding together against Zurich and Zwingli's increasing power there. In 1531 a civil war broke out between Protestants and Catholics, and Zwingli was killed in battle. His death ended the period of theocracy in Zurich, as his successor became a religious leader only, rather than a ruler of both church and state. The leadership of Swiss Protestantism then passed to a French immigrant named John Calvin.

opportunity gave him the chance to put his theories into action and create a society where church and state worked together. Calvinists believe the correct structure of any Christian state is laid out in the Bible: the clergy, or the body of people authorized to perform religious service, must teach and interpret the laws, and the state must enforce them. Such an arrangement is referred to as a theocracy, and Calvin helped form such a government in Geneva. He wrote the *Ecclesiastical Ordinances* in 1542, and these rules were accepted by the city council. They gave the clergy a great deal of control in terms of disciplinary powers, including that of excommunication.

Calvin's laws set up four levels of the ministry: pastors, deacons, teachers, and lay elders. The pastors had authority over all religious matters, such as deciding whether or not a person could preach in the city. The deacons cared for the sick and elderly. The individual behavior of all citizens was reviewed regularly by a group of lay elders and pastors known as the Consistory. These people had the power to make unscheduled visits and search people's homes. Attendance at weekly services was required. Drunkenness and gambling were not allowed. Even clothing color, hairstyles, and amounts of food eaten were closely regulated. There was no freedom of the press, and criticism of Calvin or of the clergy was forbidden. Typical punishments for offenses included fines, religion classes, whippings, torture, and exile (being forced to leave a place). Death sentences were given to people who committed adultery and blasphemers, or those who took the name of God in vain. In 1553 Calvin was personally responsible for the burning of a Spanish physician who denied the concept of the Trinity, which is the union of the Father (God), Son (Christ), and Holy Spirit. Education was controlled by the church, as were social services such as charities. Begging was not allowed. In short, Geneva was ruled by very strict and rigid laws. Calvin remained the head of, and force behind, this theocracy from 1541 until his death in 1564.

Calvin's intention was to turn Geneva into a model Christian city. All who visited were impressed by the order and cleanliness of the city, but the costs were high. During Calvin's years of control, fifty-eight people were put to death and seventy-six banished for failing to obey moral laws and church discipline. Calvin used his Consistory to help strengthen his power. When he was criticized for ordaining, or making pastors of, French immigrants before Swiss natives, he had his critics first humiliated and then murdered. He had the city council, which he controlled, find such people guilty of offenses from treason (crimes against the state) to heresy (crimes against the faith). These people were tortured and sometimes killed by the Consistory as punishment. Meanwhile, in addition to attending to his administrative tasks, Calvin continued to revise and expand his *Institutes* and wrote many lengthy commentaries on the Bible.

Calvin became famous throughout Europe, and translations and new editions of *Institutes of the Christian Religion* were printed. Calvinism became the dominant form of Protestantism throughout Switzerland, France, the Netherlands, and Scotland. Calvin also wrote letters to powerful

John Calvin speaks of reform at the Council of Geneva in 1542. Calvin's reforms stemmed from guidelines that he believed were laid out in the Bible. The city of Geneva accepted his proposals. HULTON/ARCHIVE/GETTY IMAGES.

Protestants throughout Europe and the British Isles and strongly affected the development of Protestantism in Germany and Scandinavia. In addition, Calvin claimed that the Church of England had been weakened by political struggles and was not focusing enough on spiritual matters. His writings on this subject inspired a group in England called the Puritans who were also discontented with the Church. These Puritans eventually left England to colonize North America.

Calvin's health began to fail late in his life, and he eventually needed to be carried to the pulpit at times. He suffered from kidney stones, lung problems, swollen joints, and severe headaches. He died on May 27, 1564, and was buried, as requested, under a simple tombstone bearing only the initials "J. C." His followers continued to spread Calvinism throughout the Christian world, and his writings helped make him one of the most influential Protestant theologians. His *Institutes of the Christian Religion* has had a deep and lasting effect on the development of Protestantism.

For More Information

BOOKS

Armstrong, Brian. "John Calvin." In *Encyclopedia of Religion.* 2nd ed. Edited by Lindsay Jones. Detroit, MI: Macmillan Reference USA, 2005, 1374–77.

Bouwsma, William J. *John Calvin: A Sixteenth-Century Portrait.* New York, NY: Oxford University Press, 1988.

Calvin, John. *Calvin: Commentaries.* Grand Rapids, MI: Christian Classics Ethereal Library, 1958.

McGrath, Alister. *A Life of John Calvin: A Study of the Shaping of Western Culture.* Oxford, UK; Cambridge, MA: Blackwell, 1990.

McNeil, John T. *The History and Character of Calvinism.* New York, NY: Oxford University Press, 1954.

Mullet, Michael A. *Calvin.* New York, NY: Routledge, 1989.

Parker, T. H. L. *John Calvin: A Biography.* Philadelphia, PA: Westminster Press, 1975.

PERIODICALS

Allen, W. Lloyd. "John Calvin." *Great Thinkers of the Western World* (1999): 155–58.

Pellerin, Daniel. "Calvin: Militant or Man of Peace?" *Review of Politics* (winter 2003): 35–59.

WEB SITES

Barry, William. "John Calvin." *Catholic Encyclopedia Online.* http://www.newadvent.org/cathen/03195b.htm (accessed on May 29, 2006).

"Calvin, John (1509–1564)." *Christian Classics Ethereal Library.* http://www.ccel.org/c/calvin (accessed on May 29, 2006).

Hooker, Richard. "Reformation: John Calvin." *World Civilizations.* http://www.wsu.edu/~dee/REFORM/CALVIN.HTM? (accessed on May 29, 2006).

"John Calvin." *History Learning Site.* http://www.historylearningsite.co.uk/John_Calvin.htm (accessed on May 29, 2006).

"John Calvin." *Reformation Guide.* http://www.educ.msu.edu/homepages/laurence/reformation/Calvin/Calvin.Htm (accessed on May 29, 2006).

Confucius

BORN: September 28, c. 551 BCE • Qufu, Lu, China

DIED: c. 479 BCE • Qufu, Lu, China

Chinese philosopher; teacher; writer

Confucius.

"Do not do to others what you do not want others to do to you."

Confucius was ancient China's most famous philosopher and is believed by many to be one of the most influential in history. His system of thought and behavior has been followed by more people for a longer period of time than any other set of ethical principles. Confucian ideas spread throughout Chinese and east Asian society so thoroughly that in the early twenty-first century, most Chinese still lived by some of his principles. Chief among these are a focus on family and respect for ancestors, elders, and paternal (fatherly) authority. Confucius founded what is known as *Ru Jia* (*Ju Chia*), or the School of the Scholars, which in the West is referred to as Confucianism. Although Confucianism is termed a religion in Western tradition, in China it is simply seen as a way of confronting the world and living appropriately.

The main principle of Confucian philosophy holds that a natural social order revolves around five basic family and social relationships. The strongest of these is filial devotion, or the love and respect shown by a child for a parent. Also central to Confucian thought is the importance of *ren* (*jen*), a focus on social virtue and empathy, or understanding another person's feelings and situation. Confucians believe that if certain manners or society rituals, called *li,* are observed, then these relationships will remain in order, and society as a whole will also remain in order.

Early life

The philosophical work of Confucius can only be properly understood by studying the time period in which he lived. He was born Kong Qui around 551 BCE, in the small town of Qufu (Ch'u-fu) in the state of Lu, or the modern-day Chinese province of Shandong (Shan-tung). He is most often referred to in Chinese as Kongzi (K'ung-tzu), which means "Master Kong," and also sometimes as Kong Fuzi (K'ung Fu-tzu). China already had a long history of intellectual and cultural advances by the time of Confucius's birth. During the Shang Dynasty (c. 1766–c. 1112 BCE), the Chinese had established an administrative system, a complex agricultural system, and defined social classes. A method of writing and the first Chinese calendar had also been developed. This era was followed by the Zhou (Chou) Dynasty (c. 1025–256 BCE), China's classical age. This period featured written laws, a monetary economy, tools made from iron, and ox-drawn plows.

During the Zhou Dynasty, the kings began gradually losing their hold on the people, and large areas of China fell under the control of local princes. By 800 BCE these princes began fighting not only the Zhou leaders but also each other for control of the lands. The next several hundred years were ones of great chaos and disorder. In Lu, the state where Confucius lived, the three leading families fought bitterly for powerful positions. Assassinations (political killings) and dishonesty within the government were common, and the people lived under the constant threat of invasion by neighboring states. An almost continual state of war existed, maintained by roving bands of mercenaries (soldiers who fought for money) hired by the various princes. Additionally, the aristocracy, or ruling class, expanded until not enough government positions remained to accommodate everyone. Due to this, the class of *shi* (*shih*), the lower aristocracy trained for public service into which Confucius was born, began to experience the same poor living conditions as the peasants. Perhaps because of the effects these conflicts had on people's lives, the period gave rise to some of the greatest thinkers in Chinese history, Confucius among them, and is called the Hundred Schools of Thought period.

Confucius was the son of Shuliang He (Shu-liang Ho) and Yan Zhensai (Yen Chen-sai). Historians disagree on his family's status. Many hold that his father was a soldier and a government official, perhaps even governor of the town of Zou (Tsou). Others believe Confucius was a direct descendant of the royal house of the Shang dynasty. According to these accounts, about three to five generations before Confucius's birth, his ancestors moved from the state of Song (Sung) to Lu. Confucius himself later wrote in his Analects (Lun Yu) that he was "without rank and in humble circumstances" at the time of his birth. Later legends speak of strange occurrences at Confucius's birth, such as dragons and a unicorn appearing.

Shuliang He died when Confucius was three years old. Confucius was then educated by his mother and also perhaps at a school for nobles. He learned the basics of the Six Arts, also known as the Six Disciplines: ritual, music, archery, chariot riding, calligraphy (fine handwriting), and computation (mathematics). For Confucius, the arts of music, dance, painting, and poetry, which he classified as *wen,* were the highest forms of culture. He would later emphasize these in his teachings. He was skilled, as were most nobles of the day, in fishing and hunting, though he reportedly did not fish with a net and never shot a bird at rest. As a young child, his favorite pastime was arranging the various objects used in traditional sacrifices and offerings and then playacting through the entire rituals. Confucius determined by age fifteen that he would be a scholar, and as a young man he held various minor offices in the state of Lu, such as keeping accounts of sheep and cattle. At the age of nineteen he married Qiguan Shi (Ch'i-kuan Shih), and they had, by some accounts, both a son and a daughter. In 528 BCE Confucius's mother died, and he left his government post to perform the traditional three years of mourning.

The Confucian ethical system

Confucius remained busy during his years of mourning. He concentrated on the study of li, classical music, and poetry. He focused on the ancient Shang Dynasty and its well-defined social classes, court and family etiquette (manners) and rituals, and orderly bureaucracy. He also studied the early Zhou dynasty, in particular one of its founders, the Duke of Zhou, who became for Confucius the model of the virtuous (good and fair) ruler. According to tradition, such rulers were given their power through a *Tianming* (*t'ien-ming*), or "mandate of Heaven," a concept that Confucius accepted. Confucius held that rulers should still behave well,

Temples such as this one in Nanjing, China, were built in honor of Confucius and his teachings. © LIU LIQUN/CORBIS.

however. He believed their strength lay in *de* (*te*), or virtue, rather than in force. Like other thinkers of his age, Confucius sought a way through which society could be renewed, and he saw the traditions of the past as an answer. He also believed that a new individualism had taken over Chinese society as a result of the lack of strong central power. This led Confucius to assemble a set of principles based on traditional Chinese culture and its heavy reliance on the family as the basis of all society.

Confucius's goal was the development of a *junzi* (*chun-tzu*), a superior person or gentleman, both as leader and as citizen. Such a gentleman would have a strong sense of humanity and empathy, or *ren,* which would in turn be developed through li. Confucius specified three different types of li: making sacrifices to gods and ancestors, following the rituals of social and political institutions, and obeying the rules of society in daily behavior. Before Confucius, the rules surrounding li were assumed to come from Heaven, *Tian.* Though he claimed to be a transmitter of knowledge rather than a creator, Confucius in fact redefined li as a law of humankind rather than of Heaven.

Confucius held that propriety, or following the rituals of society, should become part of one's every action. Self-interest was always to be balanced by the needs of family and society. Confucius applied his concept of li to the basic five relationships, which he defined as those between father and son, elder brother and junior brother, husband and wife, elder friend and junior friend, and ruler and subject. For example, a father should act lovingly towards his child, and a son should be deeply respectful to his father. Similar conditions were put on friendships and sibling relationships, with age being the deciding factor in terms of who received the most respect. Confucius said that between husband and wife, the wife is to be respectful and supportive. When a ruler is benevolent, or kindly, the subject should be loyal. The two aspects of these relationships that most deeply and continually affected the Chinese were filial piety, or the devotion and honor children give to their parents, and respect for those who are older.

Teacher and politician

Following his period of mourning, Confucius hoped to put his new theories about the family and leadership into practice, first by teaching and then by achieving high government office. He felt that by teaching young men the correct way to live, he could improve society as a whole. He is known as the first such teacher in China who attempted to make education available to all men. Prior to his efforts, education was generally obtained in the home through a hired tutor or not at all. Confucius was a key figure in the establishment of teaching as a profession. His supposed birthday, September 28, is still celebrated as Teachers' Day in Taiwan.

Confucius taught by example and by telling stories from his life and the lives of others. He also taught through conversation, asking questions that challenged the beliefs of his pupils. In addition to Confucian philosophy, his students also learned to master the Six Arts, just as Confucius had. He took groups of twenty to twenty-five pupils at a time and was said never to have turned away a hopeful student because the student could not pay. He attempted to inspire a sense of empathy in these young men and also to prepare them for government service. Chinese civil service examinations were later based on Confucian philosophy.

> ### Naming Confucius
>
> In the late 1500s, the Jesuits, a Roman Catholic religious order, chose to perform missionary work in China. One of the first Jesuits in China was Matteo Ricci (1552–1610), who came from Italy in 1578. He had to keep his missionary work secret, for the Chinese government was highly suspicious of foreign influence. In order to understand and communicate with the Chinese people, Ricci immersed himself in the nation's history and customs and learned its language and traditions. He worked in China for more than thirty years. In order to share his work with Jesuits in Europe, he transformed Chinese words and names into Latin, the language of the Catholic Church at the time. Kong Fuzi thus became Confucius, the name by which the West has known the Chinese philosopher ever since.

Confucius was the first to make merit more important than family connections in the awarding of government positions.

Many of Confucius's teachings were later gathered by his followers and compiled in a work called the Analects. This book is considered the most reliable source of information about the life and teachings of Confucius. Analects is also the most important volume of what are known as the Four Books, four collections of Confucius's wisdom. The others are The Great Learning, The Doctrine of the Mean, and Mencius.

Confucius left Lu for the neighboring state of Qi (Ch'i), hoping to advise the Duke of Qi in how to establish a more fair and reasonable government. He remained there for one year, but the duke did not listen to Confucius, so he returned to Lu and continued teaching there. When he was about fifty years old, Confucius became a minister of public works and then minister of crime, or chief magistrate, under Duke Ling. For a number of years, he attempted to reduce the influence of the three most powerful families in Lu and restore more power to the duke. However, his efforts were not successful, and the duke continued to lose power to these powerful families, who in turn became enemies of Confucius. Finally, around age fifty-five, he was forced into exile (made to leave his home city).

Years of exile, years of contemplation

Confucius traveled throughout China for thirteen years with a small group of followers, teaching his principles of proper etiquette and ritual. He sought administrative positions from various rulers, but few listened to him. At times his life was in danger. He was once mistaken for an infamous bandit and thrown in a dungeon. He escaped assassins and near-starvation and, in time, began to miss his home in Lu. A chance to return came with the death of Duke Ling and his replacement by Duke Ai. When Ai's primary minister died, he appointed one of Confucius's students to the position. After a number of years this student was able to arrange for Confucius's safe return to Lu.

Confucius then moved away from politics and focused on teaching and writing. He took a minor government position, edited and wrote comments on classical Chinese texts, and continued to teach his followers, who came from all social and economic classes. He wrote a history of Lu's rulers, Spring and Autumn Annals, which he felt would be his greatest contribution to learning. In his final years, Confucius saw the deaths of his son, Bo Ye (Po Yeh), and his most beloved pupil, Yan Hui (Yen Hui). Confucius died in 479 BCE, never having achieved his ambition to become a great political leader but having gained a reputation as a hugely successful teacher and philosopher.

In the Analects, Confucius summed up his life this way: "At fifteen I set my heart on learning; at thirty I took my stand; at forty I came to be free from doubts; at fifty I understood the Decree of Heaven; at sixty my ear was attuned; at seventy I followed my heart's desire without overstepping the line." Confucius's life was an example of a virtuous existence, and he became the *junzi,* or superior man, that he had encouraged others to be for the good of society. Although he was a simple man who never claimed divine status, Confucius was the creator of an ethical system that would regulate the daily lives of people in China and east Asia for thousands of years to come.

For More Information

BOOKS

Ching, Julia. "Confucius." In *Encyclopedia of Religion.* 2nd ed. Edited by Lindsay Jones. Detroit, MI: Macmillan Reference USA, 2005, 1933–37.

Confucius. *Analects.* Translated by D. C. Lau. New York, NY: Penguin Classics, 1998.

Creel, H. G. *Confucius: The Man and the Myth.* New York, NY: John Day Company, 1949.

Dawson, Raymond Stanley. *Confucius.* New York, NY: Hill and Wang, 1982.

Legge, James, ed. *The Analects of Confucius, the Great Learning & the Doctrine of the Mean.* Mineola, NY: Dover Publications, 1971.

Liu, Wu-chi. *Confucius, His Life and Times.* Westport, CT: Greenwood Publishing Group, 1972.

Oldstone-Moore, Jennifer. *Confucianism: Origins, Beliefs, Practices, Holy Texts, Sacred Places.* New York, NY: Oxford University Press, 2002.

PERIODICALS

Adil, Janeen R. "The Early Years." *Calliope* (October 1999): 4–19.

WEB SITES

Aaronson, Jeffrey. "The Way of Confucius." *Smithsonian.* http://www.smithsonianmag.com/issues/2001/november/confucious.php (accessed on May 29, 2006).

"Confucius." *The Proceedings of the Friesian School.* http://www.friesian.com/confuci.htm (accessed on May 29, 2006).

Riegel, Jeffrey. "Confucius." *Stanford Encyclopedia of Philosophy.* http://plato.stanford.edu/entries/confucius/(accessed on May 29, 2006).

Dalai Lama

BORN: July 6, 1935 • Taktser, Amdo, Tibet

Tibetan religious leader; writer

"I am just a simple Buddhist monk—no more, nor less."

Tenzin Gyatso is the name that was given to the fourteenth *dalai lama,* or spiritual and temporal (civil) leader of Tibet. Part of a lineage that stretches back to the fourteenth century, the dalai lama has been referred to as "the Buddhist pope." Unlike the Catholic pope, however, the dalai lama does not speak for all Buddhists. Rather, he is the representative of one distinct branch of Tibetan Buddhism, known as Geluk (also Gelug). Since the Chinese invasion of Tibet in 1950 and his subsequent exile, the Dalai Lama has become an important spokesperson for an independent Tibet. His tireless efforts on behalf of his homeland and his search for a nonviolent end to Tibet's struggle for independence won him the 1989 Nobel Peace Prize and made him a well-known figure in the international community.

Dalai means "ocean," or "all-embracing," while *lama* means "teacher," or "wisdom." The title is therefore loosely translated as "ocean of wisdom." In his role as religious leader, the Dalai Lama travels worldwide and speaks extensively on his belief in religious tolerance and the need for dialogue between religions. He has also written nearly eighty books.

Dalai Lama. JUNKO KIMURA/ GETTY IMAGES.

These include works of autobiography, such as *My Land and My People* and *Freedom in Exile,* as well as numerous texts explaining Buddhist principles.

Humble origins

Tenzin Gyatso was born on July 6, 1935, in the village of Taktser in northeastern Tibet. He was the fifth of nine children born to the relatively well-off peasants Sonam Isomo and his wife, Diki Tsering. The future dalai lama was given the birth name of Lhamo Dhondup, which translates as "wish-fulfilling goddess." According to his mother, his birth was preceded by strange happenings, including the death of the family's small herd of horses, years of drought and famine, and the mysterious illness of his father. When Lhamo Dhondup was born, his father was suddenly cured of his sickness and rains once again returned. Lhamo Dhondup's mother knew that he was different from her other children while he was still young. She often found him packing his clothes and his belongings. When she asked where he was going, he would reply that he was going to Lhasa.

Lhasa was the capital of Tibet and home to the religious and political head of the country, the dalai lama. Two years before Lhamo Dhondup's birth, the thirteenth dalai lama had died. Since that time monks had been searching for the child they believed to be his reincarnation, or the body into which his soul had been reborn. Each of Tibet's dalai lamas is believed to be the reincarnation of the previous dalai lama, a line that stretches back to Gedun Drub (1391–1474). The dalai lamas are also believed to be representations of Avalokitesvara, also known as Chenrezig, Bodhisattva of Compassion, a near-divine *bodhisattva*, or enlightened one, who is considered by many in Tibet to be the patron god of the country. It would seem by his actions that, from a very early age, the child Lhamo Dhondup thought of himself as the next reincarnated dalai lama.

The family of Sonam Isomo already had one important member. The oldest son, Thupten Jigme Norbu, had been designated a *tulku,* or reincarnation of a famous lama, or Tibetan monk and teacher. With one tulku in the house, the appearance of another was thought highly unlikely. Nonetheless, when Lhamo Dhondup was barely three years old, an official search party reached the area near his home. Several signs had led them to this location. First, the head of the deceased thirteenth dalai lama had turned to the northeast. Additionally, the lama who was then temporarily acting as ruler of the faith had experienced a vision. While looking into the waters of the sacred lake of Lhamoi Lhatso, he noticed the Tibetan letters "ah," "ka," and "ma" float into view. These in turn were followed by the visions first of a monastery with three floors and a turquoise and gold roof, then of a small house with very distinctive gutters. The regent became convinced that the letter "ah" referred to Amdo, the northeastern province of Tibet, the direction toward which the previous dalai lama's head had turned. A search party was sent to the monastery there, Kumbum, which began with the letter "ka" and had three floors and the properly colored roof. All that remained for the search party to find was the small dwelling with the distinctive gutters, which led them to the home of Lhamo Dhondup. When they arrived, the lamas did not reveal the reason for their visit, instead merely asking for lodging for the night in hopes of observing the child. Lhamo Dhondup, however, recognized the leader of the party and called out the name of his monastery. The lamas were impressed and returned the next day with further tests, bringing some of the previous dalai lama's possessions, which the boy was asked to pick out from among an assortment of objects. Lhamo Dhondup passed all the tests, and the lamas were convinced that he was the new dalai lama.

The training of the Dalai Lama

The boy was taken to the nearby Kumbum monastery, where he began his religious training. In 1939, in the company of his parents, his brother, Lobsang Samten, and the original search party, he set off for Lhasa, a journey that took three months. On February 2, 1940, he was officially installed as the spiritual leader of Tibet and given the name Jetsun Jamphel Ngawang Lobsang Yeshe Tenzin Gyatso ("holy lord, gentle glory, compassionate, defender of the faith, ocean of wisdom") and the title of fourteenth dalai lama. At this point Gyatso was only confirmed as the spiritual leader of Tibet; political power remained in the hands of elder monks until he reached the proper age. He lived in the Potala and Norbulinka palaces in Lhasa and had as his chief tutors two important high spiritual leaders who were themselves tulku lamas. In addition to his Buddhist studies, Gyatso was given some training in history and literature. He also studied English, and from an early age he demonstrated a love of machines of all sorts. During World War II (1939–45; a war in which Great Britain, France, the United States, and their allies defeated

The Tradition of The Dalai Lama

Tibetan Buddhism contains a mixture of many Buddhist traditions and teachings. It developed from one of the two main branches of Buddhism, Mahayana, and combines some of the sorcery of the native religion of Tibet, Bön, and the mystical beliefs of Tantrism, a system of meditation and chanting used in both Hinduism and Buddhism to bring rapid enlightenment. Tibetan Buddhism, also sometimes referred to as Vajrayana, or "vehicle of the thunderbolt," was introduced into Tibet in the seventh century CE. By about 750 the first Tibetan Buddhist monastery had been built near Lhasa.

Four major sects (religious divisions) of Tibetan Buddhism ultimately formed: *Nyingmapa*, or "ancient ones"; *Kagyupa*, or "oral lineage"; *Sakyapa*, or "grey earth"; and *Gelukpa*, or "way of virtue." The Dalai Lama is a member of this last sect. The Gelukpa originated in a fourteenth-century reform movement that sought to restore discipline in monastic life. The leader of the Gelukpa is not the dalai lama but the Ganden Tripa, or "holder of the throne of Ganden." The tradition of the dalai lama began in 1391, with the first to hold the office, Gedun Drub (1391–1474). The second, Gendun Gyatso (1475–1541), established a permanent seat for the lineage at the monastery of Drepung, near Lhasa. Each dalai lama is believed to be the reincarnation of the previous one, so upon the death of the dalai lama, monks set out on a search for signs of the new leader. Sometimes, as with Tenzin Gyatso, the search takes several years, leaving gaps in the dalai lama lineage.

By the seventeenth century, Lobsang Gyatso (1617–1682), the fifth dalai lama, was able (with the help of a Mongol ruler) to use force to extend his power over most of Tibet and unify the country. It was this dalai lama who built the huge winter palace, Potala, in Lhasa. Also supposedly during the time of Lobsang Gyatso, new texts were discovered showing that the dalai lama was not merely the reincarnation of the previous holder of the office but also the incarnation of the bodhisattva of compassion, Avalokitesvara. This discovery helped to give the holder of the title real authority. The dalai lamas maintained rule in Tibet until 1951, when the country came under the direct control of the People's Republic of China. Though still the primary spiritual leader of Tibetan Buddhism, the dalai lama does not speak for all Tibetan sects, merely for the dominant Geluk school.

Germany, Italy, and Japan) the Austrian mountaineer Heinrich Harrer, who later wrote the book *Seven Years in Tibet,* escaped a British prison camp and became friends with the young Dalai Lama, introducing him to events in the rest of the world.

Such events quickly began affecting Tibet. Although it had long been considered a protectorate (a region under the protection and partial control of another) of China, Tibet was invaded by the newly established Chinese communists in 1950. On November 17 of this year, after the invasion began, Gyatso finally assumed political control of Tibet. The communists quickly overran the country, reaching Lhasa in late 1951.

The Dalai Lama then played a dangerous diplomatic game with the Chinese for nearly ten years in an attempt to preserve Tibetan traditions. The Chinese demanded that the country be modernized, specifically through the termination of its age-old feudal society. In fact, even into the twentieth century Tibet closely resembled a medieval European land, with a few nobles and the clergy controlling the wealth while the peasants worked the land. Such a system was not always fair to the lower classes. The Chinese advance, however, accompanied as it was by violence and threats of violence against peasants and Buddhist monks and nuns alike, did not present an agreeable alternative. In an effort to work with the Chinese, the Dalai Lama visited Beijing in 1954 to speak personally with Chinese leaders. His efforts failed, and the Chinese continued to employ force in governing Tibet and even tried to enlist the second spiritual leader of the country, the Panchen Lama, to act as an opponent of the Dalai Lama and to reduce his influence with the people. This move by the Chinese was not successful, and war broke out by the late 1950s.

Throughout these difficult years the Dalai Lama continued his studies, and by the age of twenty-five he was ready to take his exams at the Jokhang Temple in Lhasa, where he earned a Lharampa degree, the highest level degree in Buddhist studies. There was little time for rejoicing, however. In March 1959 the Dalai Lama was invited to a Chinese theatrical performance, a deception that had been used previously to kidnap Tibetan leaders. Accordingly, he stayed in his palace, surrounded by thousands of his followers, while the Chinese sent in troops. On March 17, disguised as a simple soldier, the Dalai Lama escaped from the palace, accompanied by his mother, sister, and a small group of followers, and headed over the Himalaya Mountains on horseback toward India. After two weeks the group reached the mountain village of Dharamsala, where the Dalai Lama set up a government in exile.

Life outside of Tibet

Ultimately, more than one hundred thousand Tibetan refugees joined the Dalai Lama in exile, and Dharamsala came to be known as "Little Lhasa." From Dharamsala, the Dalai Lama has continued to put pressure on China, through the international community, to provide Tibet with some form of autonomy, or self-rule. He has also attempted to create a piece of Tibet in a foreign land, thereby preserving his nation's cultural traditions. The Dalai Lama has helped refugees settle on agricultural land in northern India and established an educational system to teach his

Potala Palace in Lhasa, Tibet, in China, was home to the Dalai Lama before he was exiled. © KEREN SU/CORBIS.

fellow countrymen Tibetan language, history, and culture. Two institutions have helped further these goals: the Tibetan Institute of Performing Arts and the Central Institute of Higher Tibetan Studies, an Indian university for Tibetan refugees. Also, in order to preserve religious traditions, the Dalai Lama has overseen the construction of about two hundred Tibetan monasteries in India.

The Indian government, fearful of angering their powerful neighbor, China, at first refused to allow the Dalai Lama to travel outside of the country. Nevertheless, he was able to inspire United Nations resolutions in 1959, 1961, and 1965 that called on China to respect human rights in Tibet and to allow for free choice by the people. In response to criticism of Tibet's impractical political system, the Dalai Lama helped draw up a democratic Tibetan constitution in 1963 which provided for a parliament elected directly by the people. He has also declared that if Tibet regains its independence, he will forgo holding public office and act solely as a spiritual leader.

In 1967 the Indian government finally permitted the Dalai Lama to travel, and since then he has visited almost fifty countries, including the United States. On his journeys he speaks of conditions in his homeland under the continued rule of the Chinese and addresses spiritual questions. He discusses the bridges that can be built between different faiths and the emphasis in Tibetan Buddhism on compassion and nonviolence, ideas he feels could be of use to people in Western religions.

As the first dalai lama to travel to the West, Gyatso has become the symbol of Buddhism for many. He has met with numerous world leaders, from U.S. presidents to popes, and has called for a "zone of peace" in his native Tibet. For his efforts, he won the Albert Schweitzer Humanitarian Award in 1987 and the Nobel Peace Prize in 1989. As noted on the *Nobelprize.org* Web site, the Nobel committee wanted to recognize the fact that the Dalai Lama opposed the use of violence in efforts to liberate Tibet: "He has instead advocated peaceful solutions based upon tolerance and mutual respect in order to preserve the historical and cultural heritage of his people." For his part, Gyatso, as reported on the Web site *His Holiness the Dalai Lama,* is said to have often observed, "I am just a simple Buddhist monk—no more, nor less."

In the late twentieth and early twenty-first centuries, the Dalai Lama continued to press for an independent Tibet, free of Chinese control. In 1995, partly due to his influence, the European parliament issued a statement noting Tibet's unique religious and cultural heritage and reaffirming the illegality of the Chinese occupation. In 2001, after a meeting between the Dalai Lama and President George W. Bush (1946–), the White House announced its support of the preservation of Tibetan culture, language, and religion. Eventually, the Dalai Lama began to lessen his demands for a totally independent Tibet, noting that the state could remain part of China if the Chinese showed due respect for the people's culture and religion.

In addition to addressing the needs of his people, the Dalai Lama has spoken out on a wide range of other issues, including the importance of creating world peace and ending world hunger, and has promoted these goals through the Dalai Lama Foundation. He has also continued to advocate discussions between different faiths. His many books deal with that subject as well as with Buddhist concepts, and many are based on his talks around the world. Particularly notable are such works as *Buddha Heart, Buddha Mind: Living the Four Noble Truths* and *An Open Heart: Practicing Compassion in Everyday Life*. The Dalai Lama has also written on the intersection of faith and science in *The Universe in a Single Atom: The Convergence of Science and Spirituality.*

Because of his high profile and the fact that he leads his life by the principles of compassion, the Dalai Lama is partly responsible for the spreading popularity of Tibetan Buddhism. Westerners from movie stars to politicians have been embracing Buddhist principles and meditation (deep and concentrated thinking) practices. Speaking with Robert Thurman of *Mother Jones,* the Dalai Lama explained why he thought his faith was becoming so popular in Western countries, including the United States:

> I feel that Americans are interested because they are open-minded. They have an education system that teaches them to find out for themselves why things are the way they are. . . . Also, your education tends to develop the brain while it neglects the heart, so you have a longing for teachings that develop and strengthen the good heart.

In 2005 the Dalai Lama celebrated his seventieth birthday. More than ten thousand Tibetan refugees, monks, and followers from around the world gathered outside his home in Dharamsala. There, he has continued to live the simple life of a Buddhist monk, rising at four o'clock every morning to say prayers.

For More Information

BOOKS

Friese, Kai. *Tenzin Gyatso, the Dalai Lama.* New York, NY: Chelsea House, 1989.

Goldstein, Melvyn C. *The Snow Lion and the Dragon: China, Tibet, and the Dalai Lama.* Berkeley, CA: University of California Press, 1997.

Gyatso, Tenzin. *Freedom in Exile: The Autobiography of the Dalai Lama.* New York, NY: HarperCollins, 1990.

Gyatso, Tenzin. *My Land and My People: The Original Autobiography of His Holiness the Dalai Lama of Tibet.* New York, NY: Warner Books, 1997.

Hicks, Roger, and Ngakpa Chogyma. *Great Ocean: An Authorized Biography of the Buddhist Monk Tenzin Gyatso, His Holiness the Fourteenth Dalai Lama.* New York, NY: Penguin, 1990.

Marcello, Patricia Cronin. *The Dalai Lama: A Biography.* Westport, CT: Greenwood Press, 2003.

PERIODICALS

Bilski, Andrew. "A God-King in Exile." *Maclean's* (October 15, 1990): 49.

Clifton, Tony. "A Life in Exile." *Newsweek* (October 13, 1997): 48.

Gere, Richard. "Dalai Lama: He Belongs to the World." *Time* (April 18, 2005): 92.

Gyatso, Tenzin. "A Conversation with the Dalai Lama." Interview with Alex Perry. *Time International* (October 25, 2004): 36.

Gyatso, Tenzin. "Dalai Lama: A Truly 'Far-Sighted' Person." Interview with Sudip Mazumdar. *Newsweek International* (December 27, 2004): 102.

Iyer, Pico. "The God in Exile." *Time* (December 22, 1997): 72.

Seaman, Donna. Review of *The Universe in a Single Atom: The Convergence of Science and Spirituality,* by Tenzin Gyatso. *Booklist* (September 15, 2005): 9.

WEB SITES

"Dalai Lama: A Spiritual Leader in Exile." *CNN.com.* http://www.cnn.com/SPECIALS/2001/dalai.lama/ (accessed on June 2, 2006).

"The Fourteenth Dalai Lama—Biography." *Nobelprize.org.* http://nobelprize.org/peace/laureates/1989/lama-bio.html (accessed on June 2, 2006).

Gyatso, Tenzin. "The Dalai Lama." Interview with Robert Thurman. *Mother Jones.* http://www.motherjones.com/news/qa/1997/11/thurman.html (accessed on June 2, 2006).

His Holiness the Dalai Lama. http://www.tibet.com/DL/ (accessed on June 2, 2006).

"Tibet Overview: HH Dalai Lama." *TibetOverland.com.* http://www.tibetoverland.com/1_4a_biography1.asp (accessed on June 2, 2006).

Dayananda Sarasvati

BORN: 1824 • Tankara, India

DIED: October 30, 1883 • Ajmir, India

Indian religious reformer

"Every living being has a soul which deserves affection; in every human being there is a soul worthy of respect. Any one who does not know this basic principle cannot understand the true meaning of the Vedic religion."

Dayananda Sarasvati (often spelled Saraswati) was a leading Hindu ascetic, or person who gives up worldly comforts to live in poverty, in nineteenth-century India. He is best known as an aggressive reformer who urged Hindus to return to the traditions and principles in the Vedas, the Hindu sacred scripture. He was also the founder of the Arya Samaj, a Hindu reform movement. This organization played a major role in the growth of Indian nationalism. At the time of Dayananda Sarasvati's birth, India was a British colony, but his Arya Samaj and other organizations encouraged the desire among Indians to achieve independence from Great Britain.

Dayananda Sarasvati. K. L. KAMAT/KAMAT'S POTPOURRI.

Birth and early life

Sarasvati was born as Mula Sankara in 1824, in Tankara, a city in the modern-day Indian state of Gujarat. He came from a wealthy *Brahmin* family. Brahmins are the highest Indian caste, or social hereditary class, which consists of religious leaders, teachers, and intellectuals. Sankara received an education both in orthodox (traditional) Hinduism and in the Sanskrit language, the historical literary language of the religion.

Hindu religious practice often involves presenting a statue or other image, representing a Hindu god or goddess, with offerings such as fruit and water. (While Hinduism has many gods, all are considered to be manifestations, or forms, of the one God, Brahma.) According to one story, when Sankara was fourteen he made a visit with his father to a Hindu temple. During the night he saw mice running over the image of the Hindu god Shiva because they were attracted by the offerings of food placed before it. Sankara was disturbed by this and turned away from worship that involved images. Even as a youngster, then, he began to question Hindu practices that he later came to believe they were not part of true, historical Hinduism.

Sankara had many doubts about his religion. When a beloved uncle died five years after the incident at the temple, he began to search for a path that humans could follow to overcome their mortality (death). Hindus believe in reincarnation, an ongoing cycle of birth, death, and rebirth that in effect traps the human soul in the material world. In an attempt to escape that trap, Sankara began to practice yoga, an intensely focused mental, spiritual, and physical discipline that some believe can lead to enlightenment and spiritual salvation, or release from the cycle of death and rebirth, called *samsara.* In 1843 Sankara fled his home, fearing that his family would arrange a marriage for him. He became a member of the wandering order of monks called the Sarasvatis, taking the name of the order as his own.

The wandering ascetic and crusader

Dayananda Sarasvati spent nearly twenty-five years, from 1845 to 1869, as a wandering ascetic, searching for religious truth. An ascetic is someone who gives up material goods and lives a life of self-denial, devoted to spiritual matters. He lived in jungles, in retreats in the Himalayan Mountains, and at a number of pilgrimage sites in northern India. During these years Dayananda Sarasvati practiced various forms of yoga. He became a disciple, or follower, of a well-known religious teacher, Swami Birajananda (sometimes spelled Virajananda). Birajananda believed that Hinduism had strayed from its historical roots and that many of its practices had become impure. Dayananda Sarasvati promised Birajananda that he would devote his life to restoring the rightful place of the Vedas in the Hindu faith.

He kept his vow to Birajananda and became a religious crusader. Leaving behind the quiet, private existence he had led up to this time, Dayananda Sarasvati entered public life and began to develop his views about reforming Hinduism. His goal was to urge Hindus to turn away from worship involving images and to place their entire faith in the truth of the Vedas. He began to gain some recognition after he took part in a public debate with traditional Hindu scholars in the city of Benares. The subject of the debate was the authority of the Vedas. This debate was conducted by the *maharaja,* or ruler, of Benares, who came to share Dayananda Sarasvati's views. Through the support of the influential maharaja, Dayananda Sarasvati and his views became more widely known throughout the region.

The early 1870s were an important period in Dayananda Sarasvati's life. By this time he had abandoned the life of a wandering ascetic. He lived among and had close contact with many of the Hindu Brahmins in the city of Calcutta (now Kolkata). Prior to his arrival in the city, he had worn only a loincloth (a cloth covering just the middle portion of his body) and had preached in the Sanskrit language. His supporters in Calcutta urged him to go about fully clothed. They also recommended he preach and lecture in Hindi rather than Sanskrit, since Hindi was the language of the majority of the population, while Sanskrit was spoken only by the educated few. Dayananda Sarasvati followed their advice and was able to reach a much wider audience. In the years that followed, he continued to lecture and hold public debates not only with Hindus but with Christians and Muslims as well.

The Light of Truth

Two important events in Dayananda Sarasvati's life occurred in 1875. The first of these was the publication of his book *Sathyartha Prakasha* (Light of Truth). This was Dayananda Sarasvati's most important published work. In the book, he outlined his beliefs in a very brief and direct way. For example, he wrote, "I hold that the four Vedas . . . are the Word of God. . . . They are absolutely free from error, and are an authority unto themselves."

Dayananda Sarasvati argued that the commentaries on and additions to the Vedas over the centuries were not true Hindu teachings. To find the truth of Hinduism, he claimed, one had only to read the original Vedas.

The Vedas

The Vedas, Hinduism's sacred scripture, consist principally of a large number of hymns or songs. These hymns were composed by early Hindu wise men who, according to traditional belief, heard them in ecstatic (highly emotional and trancelike) visions. Most scholars date the Vedas at about 1500 to 1200 BCE, although some claim they are even older and were written around 5000 or 7000 BCE. One of the Vedas, called the Rig Veda, may date from as far back as 12,000 BCE.

The Vedas were transmitted orally from teachers to students. They are often referred to as *sruti,* a word that means "that which is heard." Many of these teachers and students were able to memorize thousands of lines of text. The Vedas encompass all spiritual knowledge and detail rituals, philosophies, and other practices. Devout Hindus see the Vedas as timeless and authorless. According to this belief, they did not come from the hand of humans. They represent an eternal wisdom that appears anew with each new cycle of history.

He also restated his belief in such principles as the eternal nature of God, rebirth, and *moksha,* the liberation of the soul from the cycle of reincarnation.

Arya Samaj

In 1875 Sarasvati also formed the Arya Samaj, which can be translated into English as "Society of Aryans." The Aryans were speakers of an original, unrecorded Indo-European language from which many of the languages spoken in Europe and Central Asia are descended. Thousands of years ago the Aryans moved eastward into the Indian subcontinent. The Arya Samaj is a sect of Hinduism that preaches Dayananda Sarasvati's view that the Vedas are the only real source of God's truth and that all other developments in the faith since the time the Vedas were revealed are false.

The Arya Samaj opposes ancestor worship, the sacrifice of animals, religious beliefs and practices that do not originate in the Vedas, and the caste, or social class, system. It also rejects the notion of "untouchability," which refers to the lowest caste of Indian society, the Untouchables, who perform such tasks as disposing of waste and dead animals. The sect is also against child marriage, offerings made to the gods in temples, pilgrimages, and the belief that priests hold some sort of secret wisdom. The Arya Samaj upholds belief in karma (the idea that a person's actions affect his or her destiny), reincarnation, and the important role of *samskaras,* or individual sacraments (rites or rituals). There are sixteen such sacraments marking important stages in a person's life, ending with the final funeral rites.

The group was, and continues to be, a force for social change in Indian society. The Arya Samaj has supported many programs of reform. It opposes discrimination against women and supports education for both men and women. To that end, it has built a network of schools and institutions of higher learning. It also defends marriages between members of different castes, a practice discouraged by traditional Indians.

In addition, the Arya Samaj has built missions, orphanages, and homes for widows, and has carried out medical work and famine relief (help for those suffering from a severe food shortage).

In the late nineteenth and early twentieth centuries the Arya Samaj also supported Indian independence from Great Britain. During the remainder of his life Dayananda Sarasvati challenged Indians to be more aggressive against British rule. He called for armed revolution against the British, as well as against Christian missionaries in India. At the same time he expressed admiration for European civilization. He believed that the nations of Europe were advanced because they had representative governments, a system of education, and networks of trade. Dayananda Sarasvati's goal for India was realized when the country became independent from Great Britain in 1947.

An image of the Hindu god Shiva. Dayananda Sarasvati was disturbed when mice ran over an image of the god in a temple. This experience helped form his beliefs about how Hinduism should be practiced. © ROYALTY-FREE/CORBIS.

Death

Dayananda Sarasvati continued to preach his views for the remainder of his life. He engaged Christians and Muslims in debate and gained a reputation for being an opponent of those religions. He also offended orthodox, or traditional, Hindus because he challenged their views. Several attempts were made on his life.

In 1883 Dayananda Sarasvati was a guest of the maharaja of Jodhpur. The maharaja led a life of worldly pleasure, and Dayananda Sarasvati advised him to change his ways and seek purity and discipline in his life. Some of the members of the maharaja's court were offended by Dayananda Sarasvati's boldness. It is believed that they poisoned him on the night of October 30, 1883. The accusation, however, was never proven, and the cause of Dayananda Sarasvati's death remains a mystery.

For More Information

BOOKS

"Dayananda Saraswati, Swami." In *Encyclopedia of World Biography.* 2nd ed. 17 vols. Farmington Hills, MI: Gale Research, 1998.

Jordens, J. T. F. *Dayananda Sarasvati: His Life and Ideas.* Delhi, India: Oxford University Press, 1978.

Salmond, Noel A. *Hindu Iconoclasts: Rammohun Roy, Dayananda Sarasvati, and Nineteenth-Century Polemics against Idolatry.* Waterloo, Ontario, Canada: Wilfrid Laurier University Press, 2004.

WEB SITES

Sarasvati, Dayananda. *The Light of Truth.* http://www.victoriaaryasamaj.org/lotruth.pdf (accessed on June 2, 2006).

Sundaram, V. "A Great Harbinger of Hindu Renaissance." *News Today.* http://newstodaynet.com/12oct/ss1.htm (accessed on June 2, 2006).

Anagarika Dharmapala

BORN: September 9, 1864 • Colombo, Ceylon

DIED: April 29, 1933 • Sarnath, India

Ceylonese religious leader; writer

"The tendency of enlightened thought of the day all over the world is not toward theology, but philosophy and psychology. Indeed, the [ship] of theology drifts into danger."

Anagarika Dharmapala was a religious leader who is credited with introducing Buddhism to the United States and Europe. He also helped to restore Buddhism in his native Ceylon (modern-day Sri Lanka) after centuries of foreign invaders had forced their religions on its citizens. He gave new energy to the religion through a reform movement that emphasized its moral and ethical aspects. Anagarika Dharmapala preached his ideas in many countries and was the Buddhist representative to the World Parliament of Religions in Chicago, Illinois, in 1893. He made several other trips to the United States and Europe and wrote widely on Buddhist topics before dying in India in 1933.

The making of a Buddhist

Anagarika Dharmapala was born David Hewavitarne in Colombo, Ceylon, on September 17, 1864. His father, H. Don Carolis, was the wealthy founder of a furniture manufacturing business. His mother was Mallika Hewavitarne, whose surname comes from a famous queen in Buddhist literature. The family was of Sinhalese origin. The Sinhalese people arrived in Ceylon from northern India around the fifth century BCE. They conquered the native forest-dwelling Veddas and quickly formed the majority of the nation's population. Buddhism was adopted as the national religion in the third century BCE, and the island became one of its leading world centers.

Several centuries of foreign intervention began when the Tamil people of south India invaded Ceylon in the late third century. Then the Portuguese conquered much of the island by the late sixteenth century and introduced Roman Catholicism to the inhabitants. Slightly more than a century later, the Dutch overthrew the Portuguese and occupied Ceylon. They were in turn defeated by the British, who made most of Ceylon a crown colony in 1798 and installed the Anglican religion. In 1815 the entire country was brought under British rule, and the ancient line of Sinhalese kings ended. The British established rubber, tea, and coffee plantations and created an educational system in the form of missionary schools and a university. The native population attempted to regain its independence several times, but the British remained in power until 1948.

When Hewavitarne was born in 1864, the country had been under British control for many years. Christianity had replaced Buddhism as the religion of much of the population, and the Sinhalese culture was largely lost as a result of the three hundred years of foreign occupation. Most of the middle and upper-middle class population, especially in the coastal areas, had taken Christian names, including Hewavitarne's family. Young David was sent to missionary schools for primary and secondary education, as was the practice at the time. At Saint Benedict's Anglican School and then later at Saint Thomas's Collegiate School, Christian values were emphasized, and church attendance and Christian religious instruction were required.

Throughout his education, however, Hewavitarne did not lose his belief in Buddhism, his ancestors' faith. He became influenced by two of the most well-known Buddhist leaders of the period, Venerable Hikkaduwe Sri Sumangala Thera and Migettuwatte Sri Gunananda Thera. Hewavitarne found he much preferred the two Buddhists' simple lifestyles over those of the missionary teachers for whom he had little respect. After witnessing a riot that broke out after Christians attacked a peaceful Buddhist procession, Hewavitarne became disgusted with the hypocrisy (the claiming of beliefs one does not actually hold or follow) of the British and their religion. He dropped out of school to study on his own.

Around this time Ceylon received a pair of interesting guests. One of these, Helena Blavatsky (1831–1891), was a founder of the Theosophical

Buddhists light lamps in a temple during the Wesak Festival, which celebrates the Buddha's birthday and enlightenment. Dharmapala was able to celebrate the first Wesak Festival in the United States in 1896. © ANURUDDHA LOKUHAPUARACHICHI/REUTERS/CORBIS.

Society, a mystical religious and philosophical movement that combines Buddhist and Hindu beliefs. The society is aimed at helping a Western audience investigate the universe and humanity's place in it by becoming closer to the divine. Blavatsky was accompanied by the society's cofounder, Colonel Henry Steel Olcott (1832–1907). The two had come to Ceylon to learn more about Buddhist principles. Soon after their arrival they began studies with a *bhikkhu,* an ordained Buddhist monk, and declared themselves Buddhists. After he dropped out of school, Hewavitarne met Blavatsky and Olcott and joined the Theosophical Society. He acted as a translator to aid Olcott in his efforts to open Buddhist schools throughout the country and revitalize Buddhism. Hewavitarne also became a good friend of Blavatsky, who encouraged him to learn Pali, an early Indian language in which much of the Buddhist canon, or body of literature, is written. Blavatsky also inspired him to work for his people and religion.

Hewavitarne gave up his family wealth and changed his name to Dharmapala, which means "guardian of the dharma." The dharma are the teachings of the Buddha, an Indian philosopher and the founder of Buddhism who revealed the path to enlightenment and nirvana. For a first name he took Anagarika, which means "one who has no home." This choice reflected his pledge to dedicate himself to a life following the rules of Buddhism, including celibacy, or refraining from sexual intercourse. He wore a yellow robe similar to those of Buddhist monks, although he was not one himself. He also counseled others to exchange their Western names for traditional native names. Dharmapala assisted Olcott in opening more than three hundred schools in Ceylon. This helped revive Buddhism's traditional branch of Theravada, which means "the way of the elders."

When he was twenty years old, Dharmapala began writing for a weekly paper, the *Saraasavi-Sandaresa.* This was the first of many writing jobs he held throughout his lifetime. He eventually took over the paper's entire operation, writing, printing, and distributing it twice a week. He argued for a revival of native Sinhalese traditions and a return to the country's Buddhist roots. Together with Olcott he toured Ceylon's villages to see the religious conditions across the country for himself. In 1888 he founded an English-language newspaper, the *Buddhist,* and used it to communicate his thoughts about the Buddhist revival and Sinhalese nationalism to the English-speaking community.

Missions abroad

In 1888 Dharmapala traveled with Olcott to Japan to visit Buddhist sites and to attempt to encourage good relations among the different branches of Buddhism. Three years later Dharmapala and Blavatsky toured India, the country of Buddhism's origins. The religion had nearly died out there, however. Dharmapala was distressed to find Buddhist shrines, such as the Mahabodhi Temple at Bodh Gaya, in poor condition. When he returned to Ceylon, Dharmapala founded the Maha Bodhi Society in order to restore the temple, which honors the site of Buddha's enlightenment. The aims of the society soon broadened to include teaching and promoting Buddhism in Ceylon

Buddhism in Sri Lanka

In the early twenty-first century, Sri Lanka was the home of the world's oldest ongoing Buddhist civilization. Though the religion began in India, it nearly ceased to exist there after it spread to other countries. The Indian emperor Ashoka Maurya, also called Asoka, who ruled from c. 273 to c. 232 BCE, converted to Buddhism after a bloody struggle to gain power and was determined to devote himself to peace. He attempted to achieve this by sending missionaries outside of India to spread the faith. One of these, his son, Mahinda, is credited with bringing Buddhism to Ceylon in the third century BCE.

The Sinhalese king accepted Buddhism, linking the religion with the line of Ceylon rulers. The civilization's magnificent central city of Anuradhapura became the center for Theraveda Buddhism. The city covered a relatively large amount of land, measuring about 30 square miles, and featured houses of two and three stories tall and temples up to nine stories tall. By the fifth century CE, eight thousand Buddhist monks lived there. A cutting from the *bodhi* tree, the sacred fig tree under which the Indian philosopher Buddha (563–483) was said to have been sitting when he gained enlightenment, was planted in the city. When the Tamil invaded in the eighth century, the Sinhalese moved farther south and the city was abandoned.

Despite occupations by three different foreign powers and the invasion of Christianity, Buddhism retained a hold on the people of Ceylon. The Sinhalese kings remained Buddhists until the British overthrew the last of their line in 1815. The efforts of Anagarika Dharmapala and other reformers helped to revive the religion in the nineteenth and twentieth centuries, restoring a belief system with roots more than two thousand years old. Due to their efforts, Sri Lanka eventually became the primary center of Theravada Buddhism in the world.

and India. In 1892 he founded the *Maha Bodhi Journal* to aid in this process.

Dharmapala became known outside Asia when he traveled to Chicago in 1893 as the Theravada Buddhist representative to the World Parliament of Religions. Though he was a young man of only twenty-nine among gray-haired elders, Dharmapala spoke emotionally and intelligently of his religion. He gained followers in the United States and opened a U.S. chapter of the Maha Bodhi Society.

A life of Buddhist service

Dharmapala continued to work for the revival of Buddhism in his native Ceylon and in India. He also spoke out for an independent Ceylon, free of British rule. When Blavatsky died Dharmapala stopped working with the Theosophical Society. A wealthy American patron, Mary E. Foster, helped finance further tours abroad for him. During an 1896 tour,

Dharmapala was able to celebrate the first Wesak Festival in the United States. The Wesak Festival is held in honor of the Buddha's birthday and enlightenment. In 1906 he founded a weekly publication, the *Sinhala Bauddhaya,* with financial support from Foster. In this paper he discussed his twin passions of Buddhism and Sinhalese nationalism and criticized the British administration in Ceylon. His also continued to travel around the world. He opened new branches of the Maha Bodhi Society in cities such as London, England; New Delhi, India; and New York in the United States. On a trip to England in 1926, he founded a publication called the *British Buddhist,* and the following year he led that nation's first Wesak Festival.

His efforts to promote Sinhalese nationalism and an independent Ceylon gained him many enemies. Because of this, towards the end of his life he decided to leave Ceylon and settle in India. On January 13, 1933, he was ordained (authorized to have priestly authority) a bhikkhu, or Buddhist monk, by Sinhalese monks. He died three months later.

Dharmapala is credited with establishing a code of ethics directed at the Buddhist worshippers rather than at the monks and nuns. This code is in many respects similar to Protestant Christianity with its emphasis on worldly, ethical actions. For example, Dharmapala emphasized integrating basic Buddhist beliefs such as the Eightfold Path in one's daily life, similar to the way the Ten Commandments provide rules for everyday living for Christians. Some have described the result as a "Protestant Buddhism," which focuses on spiritual teachings in one's everyday life.

He is best known for three lasting achievements. First, he revitalized Buddhism in Sri Lanka, the home of the religion's oldest school, and in India, the religion's birthplace. Second, he introduced Buddhist teachings throughout Asia, North America, and Europe. Third, he awakened a Sinhalese nationalism which had been inactive due to so many centuries of foreign rule. Dharmapala left behind a large body of published work, including *Return to Righteousness: A Collection of Speeches, Essays, and Letters of the Anagarika Dharmapala,* and many writings on Buddhism.

For More Information

BOOKS

Dharmapala, Anagarika. *Return to Righteousness: A Collection of Speeches, Essays, and Letters of the Anagarika Dharmapala.* Edited by Ananda Guruge. Colombo, Ceylon: Government Press, 1965.

Sangharakshita, Bhikksu. *Anagarika Dharmapala: A Biographical Sketch.* Kandy, Sri Lanka: Buddhist Publication Society, 1983.

Sangharakshita, Maha Sthavira. *Flame in the Darkness: The Life and Sayings of Anagarika Dharmapala.* Yerawada, India: Tiratna Grantha Mala for Trailokya Bauddha Mahasangha Sahayaka Gana, 1980.

PERIODICALS

Leithart, Peter J. "When East Is West." *First Things: A Monthly Journal of Religion and Public Life* (May 2005): 11–12.

Roberts, Michael. "For Humanity. For the Sinhalese. Dharmapala as Crusading Bosat." *Journal of Asian Studies* (November 1997): 1006–32.

Scott, Andrew. "Anagarika Dharmapala." *Maha Bodhi* (April–June 1981): 129.

WEB SITES

Jayawardene, Lakshman. "Versatile Anagarika Dharmapala—Communicator Par Excellence." *Daily News Online* (Sri Lanka). http://origin.dailynews.lk/2002/09/17/fea04.html (accessed on May 29, 2006).

Sangharakshita, Urgyen. "Anagarika Dharmapala's Achievement." *Writings by Sangharakshita.* http://www.sangharakshita.org/e-achievement.html (accessed on May 29, 2006).

Sangharakshita, Urgyen. "The Anniversaries of Anagarika Dharmapala and Mrs. Mary E. Foster." *Writings by Sangharakshita.* http://www.sangharakshita.org/e-anniversaries.html (accessed on May 29, 2006).

Sangharakshita, Urgyen. "Two Great Lives." *Writings by Sangharakshita.* http://www.sangharakshita.org/e-two.html (accessed on May 29, 2006).

Dipa Ma

BORN: March 25, 1911 • East Bengal, India

DIED: September, 1989 • Calcutta, West Bengal, India

Indian religious leader

"The whole path of mindfulness is this: 'Whatever you are doing, be aware of it.'"

During a lifetime that spanned most of the twentieth century, Dipa Ma overcame tragedy by meditating (engaging in continuous and profound thinking) and living quietly, surrounded by her family, friends, and students. She became an important figure in the history of modern Buddhism as a teacher and role model for ordinary people trying to achieve enlightenment while carrying out family responsibilities. Her life was a source of great inspiration to her students, many of whom went on to spread her version of the Buddhist message of *dharma* to others.

Dharma is a concept rooted in Hindu philosophy. Although the word means "protection," it can be used to refer to the basic principles of existence, which might be called divine law. Buddhists and others who follow dharma protect themselves from unhappiness and discontent by living in accord with these principles of existence. Buddhists, in particular, do so by following the teachings of the **Buddha,** Siddhartha Gautama (563–483 BCE; see entry), the founder of Buddhism. Some of these teachings address the importance of compassion, cherishing others, and transforming oneself in the face of difficulties. Followers of dharma believe that through meditation they can achieve happiness and enlightenment, even if they are suffering from poverty, tragedy, or simply the daily concerns of life. Dipa Ma made her life's work the teaching of dharma to those who sought her out.

Dipa Ma used meditation, like the Buddhist monk pictured here, to overcome the tragedy she faced during her life.
© CHRIS LISLE/CORBIS.

Birth and early life

Dipa Ma was born Nani Bala Barua on March 25, 1911. Her birthplace was a small village in the Indian province of East Bengal (modern-day Bangladesh), near the border with Burma (later called Myanmar). She was born to a clan that could trace its lineage back to the time of the Buddha. The people in her community practiced Buddhist rituals and customs, but they did not practice meditation, which was primarily left to monks and nuns.

From an early age Nani showed great interest in Buddhist rituals and practices. She helped monks at local temples and made statues of the Buddha. Instead of playing with other children, she read and studied, often discussing matters of Buddhist faith and practice with her father. Because she was a girl, she had little opportunity to obtain formal schooling in her village. Girls were expected to marry early. These marriages were typically arranged by the parents of the couple. When Nani was twelve years old, she was taken from her village and married to a twenty-five-year-old engineer named Rajani Ranjan Barua. She had been with her husband for just a week when he left to take a job in Rangoon (renamed Yangon in 1989), which was then the capital city of Burma. For two years she lived with her husband's parents until she was finally put on a boat to join him in Rangoon.

Soon after arriving in Rangoon, the teenage Nani, expressed interest in meditating. For a Buddhist, meditating is not simply a matter of sitting in a chair and thinking. The discipline of meditation has to be studied and practiced, often with the help of a Buddhist master. Without guidance and focus, Buddhists believe, meditation can turn into pointless daydreaming. Nani asked her husband for permission to study meditation. Her husband was not opposed to the idea, but he and his wife were "householders," the term used by Buddhists to refer to people who are not monks or nuns. Traditionally, householders did not engage in intense religious practice until after they had fulfilled their responsibilities as householders, especially the raising of children. Due to this Rajani told Nani to delay studying meditation until she was older.

Parenthood

Nani encountered great difficulty when she tried to have children. Because a woman in her circumstances was expected to be a mother, this was a source of shame to her. In time, she did become pregnant, but the child died in infancy. A second child also died while still very young. Finally, after she had been married for twenty-seven years, Nani gave birth to a daughter who survived. The daughter's name was Dipa, so Nani took the name Dipa Ma, which means "mother of Dipa." *Dipa* means "light" in the Bengali language, so Dipa Ma can also be translated as "mother of light." Dipa Ma and her husband also adopted Dipa Ma's younger brother Bijoy.

Soon after her daughter's birth, Dipa Ma's health began to decline. She suffered from severe hypertension, or high blood pressure, and for several years was unable to leave her bed. Her husband nursed her, but one day in 1957 he came home from work complaining that he was also feeling ill. He died a few hours later from a heart attack. Dipa Ma, overcome with grief and sickness, almost died herself. She concluded that the only way to survive would be through meditation. She said that during this period of sadness and confusion, she had a dream in which the Buddha chanted these verses from the Dhammapada, a sacred Buddhist text:

> Clinging to what is dear brings sorrow.
> Clinging to what is dear brings fear.
> To one who is entirely free from endearment
> There is no sorrow or fear.

Dipa Ma turned both her property and her daughter over to a neighbor and enrolled at the Kamayut Meditation Center in Rangoon. Her intention was to spend the remainder of her life there, but events took an unexpected turn. On her first day, she fell into a deep meditative state. She found that she was unable to move her leg, although she felt no pain. Finally, she realized that a dog had seized her leg and would not let go. Monks pried the dog off, and Dipa Ma was sent first to a hospital for treatment, then home to recover. Her daughter, glad to have her mother back, insisted that she not return to the center. Dipa Ma then decided that she would practice meditation at home.

Transformation

For several years Dipa Ma meditated at home. A friend then encouraged her to attend the Thathana Yeiktha meditation center in Burma, to study under the well-known teacher Mahasi Sayadaw. By this time Dipa Ma was

Buddhist nuns gather in a large room to pray. Dipa Ma challenged the notion that only men could become enlightened. Meditation is an important element on the path to enlightenment. © MICHAEL FREEMAN/CORBIS.

fifty-three years old and so frail that she could barely climb the stairs to the center. After a short period of study, Dipa Ma was able to enter stages of deep concentration and meditation that transformed her life. The condition of her heart improved. Her blood pressure went down. The weakness in her legs disappeared. Instead of feeling ill and grief stricken, Dipa Ma found herself a healthy, vigorous, happy woman.

Dipa Ma's friends and family were inspired by her changes. Several of them, including her daughter and Dipa Ma's sister, Hema, joined her at the center. For nearly a year, they followed the center's code of discipline, which involved maintaining silence, avoiding eye contact with others, sleeping for just four hours each night, and eating no food after noon. In 1967, however, the Burmese government ordered all foreigners to leave the country. The monks at the center believed that Dipa Ma could have stayed if she wanted to, but she decided to move to Calcutta (now Kolkata), India. She believed that in Calcutta her daughter would have more educational opportunities. She and Dipa moved and took up residence in a small room above a machine shop. The room had no running water, and the two had to share a toilet with another family. They cooked on a small charcoal grill on the floor. Dipa Ma slept on a thin straw pallet on the floor.

Teacher

Word quickly spread throughout the city that a gifted teacher of meditation had arrived from Burma. Soon people were appearing at Dipa Ma's door looking for instruction. Traditionally, teachers of meditation had been monks or spiritual masters, and were always men. In fact, traditional Buddhism taught that only men could become enlightened like the Buddha. A woman had to be reborn as a man in a future life in order to become enlightened. Dipa Ma, however, taught meditation to ordinary householders, many of them women, who were trying to balance domestic chores with a desire for spiritual enlightenment. Some of her followers referred to her as the "patron saint of householders."

The key lesson that Dipa Ma shared with the students who came to her was "mindfulness." This word refers to focusing intently on a task, whatever that task might be. For example, she would teach mothers of infants to become "mindful" as their infants were nursing. By becoming mindful, they would focus on their bodily sensations as the child nursed. Similarly, she taught busy shop owners to become mindful of their business or family, even if only for a few minutes each day. Her goal was to help people not go through their lives being unhappy because they had too much to do. Mindfulness made her students fully and deeply aware of their activities and made those activities important and a source of contentment.

Dipa Ma's students said that they learned not by what she did, but by who she was. They claimed her presence alone was enough to promote a

Vipassana

The type of meditation Dipa Ma taught is called *vipassana,* or "insight" meditation. This type of meditation was practiced by the Buddha. The purpose of vipassana is to focus awareness on the body and on the experiences of the senses. Some practitioners focus separately on the various parts of their bodies, doing what is sometimes called a "body sweep," concentrating in turn on their toes, their feet, their legs, and so forth. Others focus on their breathing. By intently concentrating on the rhythms of breathing, a person is said to be able to "breathe out" negative states of mind and "breathe in" such qualities as tolerance and patience. A person may also visualize his or her breath as a light that radiates from the body, spreading peace and happiness.

As a practitioner of vipassana becomes more relaxed and aware, unhappiness, confusion, and even tragedy can be overcome. Teachers of insight meditation stress that what a person concentrates on is not important. One can even concentrate on a pain or discomfort in the body. What is most important is the process of the concentrating. And as with any process, people improve their ability to concentrate over time. Through practice and discipline, they become more mindful both of the surrounding world and of their inner feelings.

sense of peace and mindfulness in them. She was a demanding teacher, insisting that her students not be lazy as they practiced meditation, but she was kind and loving as well. She would greet her students by blessing them and stroking their hair, and she shared her blessings with people, animals, and even inanimate objects on the street.

In the 1980s Dipa Ma traveled to the United States to teach her techniques at the Insight Meditation Society in Massachusetts. The society was created by three Westerners, Joseph Goldstein, Jack Kornfield, and Sharon Salzberg. These three had traveled to Calcutta frequently to meet with and learn from Dipa Ma. As quoted by Amy Schmidt in *Dipa Ma: The Life and Legacy of a Buddhist Master,* Goldstein said, "There may be a few times in our lives when we meet a person who is so unusual that she or he transforms the way we live just by being who they are. Dipa Ma was such a person. . . . 'Her' stillness and love were different from anything I had encountered before."

Dipa Ma died in September 1989. According to a neighbor who was at her side at the time of her death, in her last moments she folded her hands in prayer and bowed to a statue of the Buddha. She then stopped breathing, dying as calmly as she had lived during the last decades of her life. Her teachings have survived through the efforts of her students, many of whom went on to teach others.

For More Information

BOOKS

Glickman, Marshall. *Beyond the Breath: Extraordinary Mindfulness through Whole-Body Vipassana Meditation.* Boston, MA: Journey Editions, 2002.

Schmidt, Amy. *Dipa Ma: The Life and Legacy of a Buddhist Master.* New York, NY: BlueBridge, 2005. Excerpts available online at http://www.dharma.org/amys/bio.html (accessed on June 1, 2006).

WEB SITES

Salzberg, Sharon. "Awakening Confidence in Our Capacity: The Blessing of Dipa Ma." *Shambhala Sun Online.* March 2000. http://mambo.shambhalasun.com/index.php?option=com_content&task=view&id=1815&Itemid=243 (accessed on June 1, 2006).

Schmidt, Amy, and Sara Jenkins. "Mother of Light: The Inspiring Story of Dipa Ma." *Buddhadharma: The Practitioner's Quarterly.* Spring 2003. http://www.thebuddhadharma.com/issues/2003/spring/Schmidt_Jenkins_dipa_ma.html (accessed on June 1, 2006).

Enheduanna

BORN: c. 2300 BCE • Mesopotamia

DIED: c. 2260 BCE • Mesopotamia

Mesopotamian princess; priestess; poet

"The day was favorable for her, she was clothed sumptuously / she was garbed in womanly beauty. / Like the light of the rising moon, / how she was sumptuously attired."

Enheduanna is often referred to by historians as the first female poet and is even considered by some to be the first known author in all of literature. The daughter of the Sumerian king Sargon I of Akkad (ruled c. 2334–c. 2279 BCE), Enheduanna was a high priestess to the Sumerian moon god, Nanna. As a priestess, Enheduanna was regarded as having near-divine power herself. She chose Nanna's daughter, Inanna, a fertility goddess and the goddess of war, to be her personal goddess and protector. Enheduanna established the religious cult of Inanna and helped to spread belief in the goddess throughout the region. Enheduanna also composed several hymns to Inanna, including *The Exaltation of Inanna,* the oldest poem credited to a specific author.

Historical background

By the time of Enheduanna's birth in the twenty-fourth century BCE, the region of Mesopotamia, which consisted of parts of modern-day Iraq, Turkey, and Syria, had been settled for thousands of years. The local tribes were nomadic (had no permanent home) until the middle of the fourth millennium BCE. The first center of civilization formed in the south of modern-day Iraq, in what was called Sumer. Farming villages in this region grew into a series of a dozen powerful city-states

Enheduanna is depicted making offerings to Inanna. UNIVERSITY OF PENNSYLVANIA MUSEUM (IMAGE 166665).

which were sometimes at war with one another and sometimes fought together against common enemies. The earliest written records also date from about this time, in the form of clay tablets. These tablets detailed the operations of the large temple complexes in each city.

The stepped temple complexes, called ziggurats, averaged about 150 feet (46 meters) in height. Each ziggurat was built in honor of one of the many gods in the Mesopotamian pantheon, or collection of gods and goddesses. The most important of these were the sky god, An; the storm god and Earth god, Enlil; and the water god, Ea, who was sometimes also called the god of wisdom. These were followed in importance by a second threesome composed of the moon god, Nanna; the sun god, Utu; and the goddess of fertility and war, Inanna. The temple complex in the city of Ur honored Nanna. Uruk, one of the leading cultural centers of the early Sumerian period, had temples to Inanna and An. Priests managed the running of the temples. Ordinary citizens did not take part in the worship of the statues built to represent the various deities (gods and goddesses).

Sumer was conquered around 2330 BCE by the Akkadians, a Semitic group who had occupied the lands north of the city. Sumer and Akkad were combined under the rule Sargon I, the father of Enheduanna and the leader of the Akkadians. Sargon became the first Semitic king of Mesopotamia and the first ruler ever to conquer and hold an empire. His realm stretched from the Mediterranean Sea to the Persian Gulf. The empire lasted some 160 years, and Sargon himself ruled for fifty-five of those years.

Little is known of Sargon's early life. According to one Sumerian legend, he was born near the banks of the Euphrates River to a high priestess who found it necessary to hide her baby. She set him afloat in a reed basket that was later found by a gardener named Akki, who raised the baby as his own. The goddess Inanna took a liking to the boy and protected him. Before long he became a cupbearer to the king of Kish, a city in the north of Sumer, and then later king himself. He founded the city of Akkad, which archaeologists (people who study the remains of past human life) believe was located near the modern-day city of Baghdad, Iraq. Sargon fought many battles during his reign. Some accounts total his victories at thirty-four, including the victory over the Sumerian king that united Akkad and Sumer.

The Akkadians introduced many new gods when they conquered Sumer, but they did not forbid the Sumerians from continuing to worship their former gods. Sargon did take power away from the priest class by combining the offices of the *ensi,* the chief civil and religious leader, and the *lugal,* the temporary leader taken on in time of war. The new position was known as ensi. By incorporating these functions, Sargon fused the temporary civil leader with the permanent religious leader, and thereby reduced the political strength of the priests. In general, the Akkadians combined elements of Sumerian religion with their own rather than rejecting it.

Sargon appointed his firstborn daughter as the *en,* or priestess, to the Sumerian god Nanna in the city of Ur. This may have been done to encourage the Sumerian people to think of Sargon less as a foreign invader and more as a rightful ruler chosen by the gods. Nanna, the moon god, was the firstborn of Enlil and Ninlil, the goddess of Earth, heaven, and air. Sargon's daughter, whose birth name is unknown, took Enheduanna as her en name. Enheduanna means "chief priestess of the ornament of heaven." For the next five hundred years, royal princesses were traditionally installed as high priestesses at Ur, one of Mesopotamia's most

Inanna

Most gods and goddesses in the Mesopotamian pantheon represented some element of nature. Inanna, or Ishtar in Akkadian, was one of the pantheon's most complex deities. She was the goddess of such unalike forces as love, fertility, and war. A pantheon is a group of gods and goddesses. Inanna was described as cruel, vengeful, warlike, and destructive, but also as peaceful, tender, comforting, and mystical. She was seen as the protector of both Sargon and his daughter, Enheduanna. It was partly due to Enheduanna's focus on the goddess that Inanna became the most important deity in Mesopotamia for more than five hundred years.

Inanna was the daughter of Nanna, the moon god, and the twin sister of Utu, the sun god. She was represented in the heavens by the planet Venus. In fact, astronomers (scientists who study the planets and the stars) named a continent on that planet after her. In Sumerian the name Inanna means "Great Lady of An," with An being the god of heaven. When she first began to be worshipped by the Sumerians, Inanna symbolized the life force and was the goddess of both sexuality and fertility. When displeased, she could destroy crops and make women unable to bear children. Among the Assyrians and Akkadians to the north, she was worshipped as the goddess of war and the hunt and was often pictured in battle dress with bow and arrow.

Inanna is at the center of several powerful myths, including one that tells of her descent into the underworld to claim control of it. Her sister, Ereshkigal, who already ruled the underworld, was upset by this and sentenced Inanna to death. When Inanna died, however, the world dried up and crops would no longer grow. The water god, Ea, arranged to save Inanna, with the agreement that someone else would have to take her place in the underworld. Inanna chose her lover, Dumuzi. Dumuzi then ruled from the underworld for half of each year and rejoined Inanna for the other half.

important centers. This linked the royal daughters with Nanna, which in turn linked the kingship with the pantheon.

Princess, priestess, and poet

During digs conducted at Ur by English archaeologist Sir Leonard Wooley in 1925 and 1927, a thin, see-through limestone disk was found. The disk bears a likeness of Enheduanna on one side and an inscription identifying her as the "wife" of Nanna and the daughter of King Sargon on the other. Most likely a religious artifact from the temple, the disk shows the priestess performing a ritual.

The disk also serves as an introduction to the duties of a priestess, such as making daily offerings to the god or goddess honored by the temple. These offerings consisted of foods such as grain, honey, and dates that were carried in a basket called a *gimasab,* which is represented on the disk. Other duties included conducting a ceremony to purify water and caring for the *giparu,* the building attached to the temple that contained the priestess's private residence. Enheduanna's position took her to the other major cities of Mesopotamia, where she promoted not only her deity, Nanna, but also the goddess Inanna, whom Enheduanna took as her personal deity and protector.

The goddess Inanna, or Ishtar, was worshipped by the priestess Enheduanna. Innana was the Mesopotamian goddess of love, fertility, and war. HEAD OF A STATUE OF ISHTAR, WEARING A HEADDRESS FROM THE TEMPLE OF USHTAR AT MARI, SYRIAN, 2800–2300 BC (ALABASTER)/ASSYRIAN SCHOOL/NATIONAL MUSEUM, DAMASCUS, SYRIA, GIRAUDON/THE BRIDGEMAN ART LIBRARY INTERNATIONAL.

Priestesses were also responsible for composing hymns, songs, and poetry honoring the deities. Some of the historical knowledge of Enheduanna comes through the hymns she composed to Inanna. These hymns were later transcribed in cuneiform, wedge-shaped writing carved with a pointed stick on clay tablets. More than one hundred such tablets are believed to be the work of Enheduanna because they were written in Sumerian. Her father, Sargon, typically wrote in Akkadian. At least six different compositions have been attributed to Enheduanna from the tablets, the most well-known and completely translated of which is *The Exaltation of Inanna.* Historians and archaeologists have given these hymns Sumerian titles taken from their first lines. Therefore *The Exaltation of Inanna* is also sometimes called *Nin-me-sar-ra* (Queen of Countless Divine Powers).

The Exaltation of Inanna is 153 lines long and begins with a description of Inanna's characteristics. The second part details Inanna's powers as a goddess of battle. The third section tells of the trouble endured by Enheduanna when a local lugal (third-highest ranking military officer) rebelled against her father and she was banished from the temples in Ur and Uruk. She also mentions in the hymn the difficulty she has finding inspiration to write.

The *Electronic Text Corpus of Sumerian Literature* relays the *Exaltation* in translation for modern readers. This excerpt is from the section in which Enheduanna praises Innana's powers in battle:

> At your battle-cry, my lady, the foreign lands bow low. When humanity comes before you in awed silence at the terrifying radiance and tempest [storm or upheaval], you grasp the most terrible of all the divine powers. Because of you, the threshold

> [door] of tears is opened, and people walk along the path of the house of great lamentations [cries of grief]. In the van of battle, all is struck down before you. With your strength, my lady, teeth can crush flint. You charge forward like a charging storm. You roar with the roaring storm, you continually thunder with Ickur [god of storms]. You spread exhaustion with the stormwinds, while your own feet remain tireless. With the lamenting *balaj* drum a lament is struck up.

Another verse written by Enheduanna is *In-nin sa-gur-ra* (Stouthearted Lady), the longest of her surviving works at 274 lines. This hymn's main theme is the power that Inanna has over all aspects of human life. Another group of hymns that has been translated into English is *E-u-nir* (Temple Hymns). This is a collection of forty-two verses written or gathered by Enheduanna. Each verse is addressed to a different temple in Sumer or Akkad. More hymns to Inanna are included in *In-nin me-hus-a* (Inanna and Ebih). Fragments of verses and hymns are also found in two smaller collections, *E-u-gim e-a* (Hymn of Praise to Ekishnugal and Nanna on Assumption of En-ship) and *Hymn of Praise to Enheduanna.* In all of these collections, Enheduanna identifies herself somewhere in the text as the priestess of Nanna and the creator of the verses. Thus, it was possible that the copyists simply attributed these verses to the same person incorrectly. Later study of the texts, however, showed enough similarities to prove that they were all by the same person, Enheduanna.

In her dual roles as princess and priestess, Enheduanna helped merge the royal line with the line of Sumerian deities. She also raised Inanna to the position of one of the most worshipped goddesses in the Mesopotamian pantheon. As Inanna was also her father's patron deity, this worship was also extended to him, strengthening his kingship. Due to the skill displayed in her verses and the fact they have survived for thousands of years, some scholars refer to Enheduanna as the "Shakespeare of Sumerian literature."

For More Information

BOOKS

Barnstone, Aliki, and Willis Barnstone, eds. *A Book of Women Poets from Antiquity to Now.* New York, NY: Schocken Books, 1992.

Enheduanna. *The Exaltation of Inanna.* Translated by W. W. Hallo and J. J. A. van Dijk. New Haven, CT: Yale University Press, 1968.

Goodrich, Norma Lorre. *Priestesses.* New York, NY: Franklin Watts, 1989.

Hallo, W. W., and W. Simpson. *The Ancient Near East: A History.* New York, NY: Harcourt Brace Jovanovich, 1971.

Meador, Betty De Shong. *Inanna, Lady of Largest Heart: Poems of the Sumerian High Priestess Enheduanna.* Austin, TX: University of Texas Press, 2000.

Wolkstein, Diane, and Samuel Noah Kramer. *Inanna, Queen of Heaven and Earth: Her Stories and Hymns from Sumer.* New York, NY: Harper and Row, 1983.

WEB SITES

Binkley, Roberta. "Context: Who Was Enheduanna?" http://www.public.asu.edu/~rbinkle/enheduanna.htm (accessed on June 2, 2006).

Binkley, Roberta. "Enheduanna." *Feminist Theory Website.* http://www.cddc.vt.edu/feminism/Enheduanna.html (accessed on June 2, 2006).

"Enheduanna." *Gateways to Babylon.* http://www.gatewaystobabylon.com/gods/ladies/ladyenheduanna.html (accessed on June 2, 2006).

"Enheduanna." *Other Women's Voices.* http://home.infionline.net/~ddisse/enheduan.html (accessed on June 2, 2006).

"The Exaltation of Inana (Inana B): Translation." *The Electronic Text Corpus of Sumerian Literature.* http://www-etcsl.orient.ox.ac.uk/section4/tr4072.htm (accessed June 2, 2006).

Mahatma Gandhi

BORN: October 2, 1869 • Porbandar, India

DIED: January 30, 1948 • Delhi, India

Indian religious leader; reformer; lawyer

Mahatma Gandhi.
AP IMAGES.

"An eye for an eye makes the whole world blind."

Mahatma Gandhi was an Indian religious leader who led his country to independence from England in 1948 without striking a single blow. His policy of *satyagraha,* or nonviolent struggle, won his people their freedom and has influenced peaceful resistance movements around the world. This fragile-looking man, wearing only sandals, a loincloth (a piece of cloth worn around the hips), and round glasses, has become an international symbol of love and brotherhood. Gandhi was a devout Hindu, or follower of India's primary religion, Hinduism. He used the principles of his faith in his own life and in his work to seek peace and justice in India.

Out of India

Gandhi was born on October 2, 1869, in Porbandar, an Indian town on the coast near Bombay. He came from a wealthy family that was part of the merchant and business caste (a social division in Indian society) called Vaisya. His father had been a prime minister for several small states in India. His mother was a very religious woman who went to Hindu services every day. From her Gandhi learned some of the principles of her branch of Hinduism, such as not doing harm to any living thing, vegetarianism (not eating meat), fasting (going without food to purify the mind and body), and a respect for other branches of Hinduism and other beliefs. Gandhi was a quiet boy and an average student who did not take part in sports. He was shy but occasionally showed a violent temper.

As was the Indian tradition at the time, Gandhi's parents arranged a marriage for him when he was thirteen to a girl of the same age. Her name was Kasturbai Makharji. At first Gandhi treated her as his inferior, but later their relationship improved. Together they had four children, the first born in 1888 when Gandhi was nineteen. As a young man, Gandhi wanted to become a doctor, but such a profession was considered beneath his caste. Instead, after graduating from high school in India and spending a short time at college, he traveled to London, England, where he trained as a lawyer.

Before leaving for England, Gandhi promised his mother that he would continue to be true to his religion and not eat meat or drink alcohol. While in London, he paid close attention to his legal studies and also began to develop his own sense of spirituality and moral behavior. Because he was Indian, many of his fellow students treated him unfairly. He had occasionally experienced racism before in India from the British upper classes and military, but in London it was a daily experience. He became involved with a vegetarian society, and some of its members were part of a group called the Theosophical Society, a spiritual movement that follows a mixture of Hindu and Buddhist beliefs.

The founder of the movement, Helena Blavatsky (1831–1891), persuaded Gandhi to begin reading the Bhagavad Gita, one of the holy books of Hinduism. While in London, Gandhi not only became more interested in his own religion, but also in Christianity and Buddhism. Some of the other vegetarians he became friends with were Christians who were inspired by the religious principles of the Russian novelist Leo Tolstoy. Tolstoy preached nonviolence and living a simple life with few possessions.

Gandhi also became familiar with the writings of the American social critic and nature writer, Henry David Thoreau (1817–1862). Thoreau's essay "Civil Disobedience" taught the value of nonviolent resistance to government policies with which one does not agree. Gandhi was also influenced by the works of the English social and art critic John Ruskin (1819–1900). In his book *Unto This Last,* Ruskin complained about the harmful changes in society that came about with industrialization. He called for a return to the simpler life of farming and producing handmade goods that he claimed would heal society.

Gandhi returned to India in 1891 after receiving his law degree. His shyness was a major difficulty for him in his career, however. He became frightened and nervous when appearing in court and would stutter and forget what he was going to say. After two unsuccessful years of practicing law, he accepted a contract as an office clerk with an Indian business in South Africa.

Years in South Africa

When he arrived in South Africa in 1893, Gandhi was still a young man driven by personal ambition but with no great awareness of or concern for the welfare of others. His personal experiences in South Africa changed that. Gandhi visited the province of Natal where Indians (mostly Muslims, or followers of Islam) outnumbered the white residents. This had caused the ruling whites to pass laws stopping further immigration from India and encouraging Indians to leave South Africa. Gandhi experienced the prejudice that the other Indians in the country were facing immediately upon arriving in the country, when a white man demanded that he give up his first class train seat and sleeping berth because he was Indian. The man demanded that Gandhi go to the third-class coach where other Indians and black South Africans were supposed to sit. Gandhi refused and was forced off the train. He spent the night in a train station thinking about prejudice and how it could be cured. As he noted in his *Autobiography,* this incident convinced him never to give in to force but also never to use force to win a cause: "I object to violence because when it appears to do good, the good is only temporary, the evil it does is permanent."

Other incidents of this nature occurred to Gandhi during his time in South Africa. A judge once demanded that he take off his turban (headdress) in court, but Gandhi refused and left. Another time he was beaten by the driver of a stagecoach for refusing to ride on the outside to make room for a white passenger. His race barred him from hotels and restaurants. Experiences like these led to a major turning point in Gandhi's life. He began to see and understand the hardships of the people in South Africa under white rule. Finally he decided to do something about it,

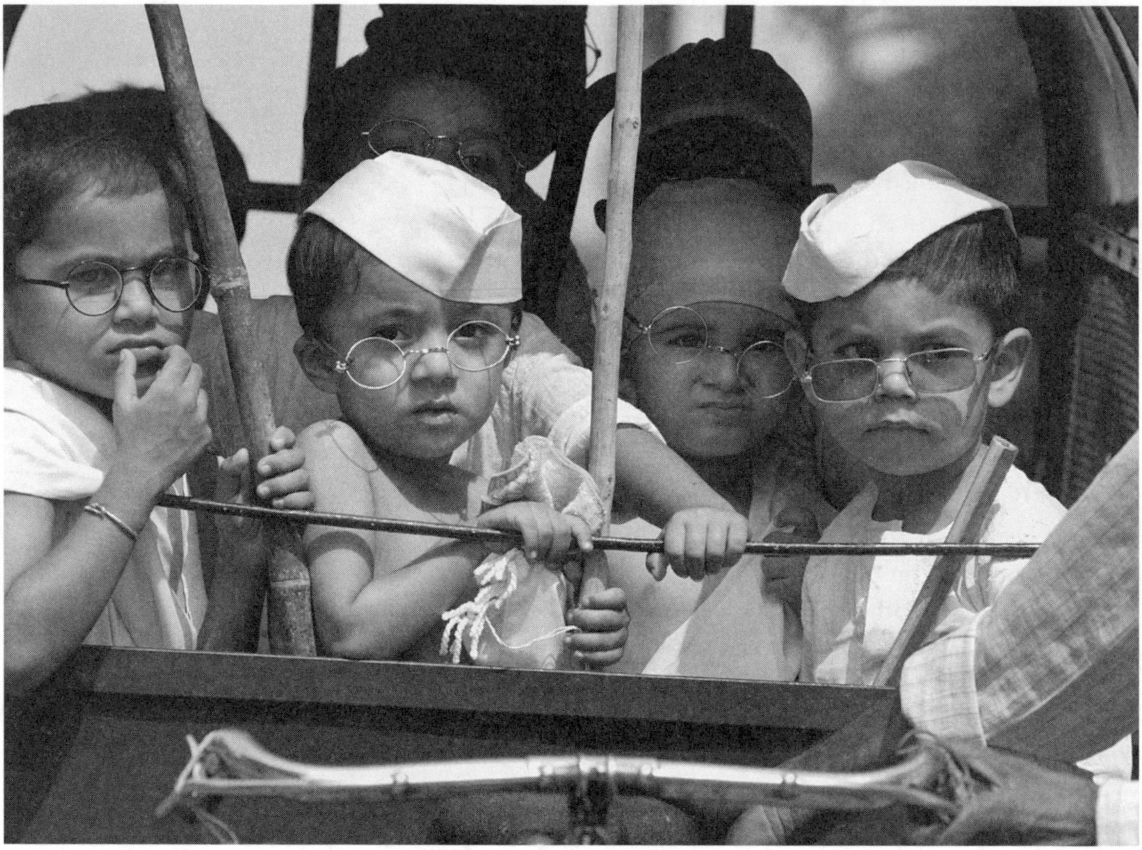

Indian children dressed as Mahatma Gandhi travel on a rickshaw to take part in Gandhi's birthday anniversary celebrations in the northern city of Lucknow, India. Gandhi's influences on peaceful movements are honored around the world. © PAWAN KUMAR/ RUETERS/CORBIS.

applying his idea of nonviolence, or *ahimsa* in the Hindi language, to the problem. He began a campaign to improve the legal status of Indians in South Africa, writing newspaper articles and founding the Natal Indian Congress in 1894 to educate the people. Gandhi had planned to stay in South Africa for only a year, but these and other political activities kept him in South Africa for more than twenty years.

In 1896 he returned briefly to India to bring his family to South Africa. When he arrived back in South Africa, a white mob tried to hang him. During the Boer War (1899–1902), in which the Dutch-descended population (called Boers) of southern Africa fought Great Britain for independence, Gandhi supported the British by organizing a volunteer ambulance corps. He was given a medal by the victorious

British government after the war. In spite of the help Great Britain had received from Indians during the fighting, however, they did not win the right of citizenship afterwards. In fact, the situation for South Africans of other than European origin slowly became worse.

In 1906 a law was passed requiring that Indians be fingerprinted and registered with the government. Gandhi called a mass meeting in protest and put into practice his new theory of nonviolent protest, or *satyagraha* ("devotion to truth," or the use of ahimsa for political protest), for the first time. He was arrested and imprisoned for two months, but the Indian population continued his protest. For the next seven years they ceased to work, refused to register, and burned their registration cards. Thousands were jailed, beaten, and even killed. Public and international reaction to such harsh treatment finally forced the government to compromise with Gandhi.

Prior to the protest, Gandhi had been working to create a new life for himself and his family. He had bought a farm in Natal and lived a simple life, abandoning his Western dress for the simple cotton loincloth and shawl of Indian peasants or poor farmers. By 1906 Gandhi had become celibate, which means that he did not have sexual intercourse, and lived in voluntary poverty. In 1910, as his nonviolent protests spread throughout Indian South Africa, he decided to build another colony near Johannesburg, South Africa. Known as Tolstoy Farm, it became a gathering place for those who resisted the government's policies.

Gandhi's nonviolent struggle in South Africa accomplished several things. In addition to achieving an eventual compromise over Indian registration, Gandhi also managed to make Hindu marriages legal and valid. Previously, only Christian marriages were recognized by the government. He was also successful in ending the practice of indentured labor. In this system, Indians would be brought to South Africa and forced to work for a specific period of time before they earned their freedom.

The fight for Indian independence

After more than twenty years in South Africa, Gandhi decided to return to his native India, where he spent the rest of his life. By this time, he had already been given the honorary title "Mahatma" ("Great Soul") by the poet Indian Rabindranath Tagore (1861–1941). For the first three years after his return, he did not draw attention to himself or get involved in politics. He supported the British during World War I (1914–18; a war in which Great Britain, France, the United States and their allies defeated Germany, Austria-Hungary, and their allies) by organizing an Indian ambulance training corps. He was forced out of the service, however, for protesting the racism of his English commanding officer.

In 1919 Gandhi was spurred into action by the passage of the Rowlatt Acts, which allowed the British-run government of India to put people accused of political crimes on trial without a jury. Gandhi organized a general strike and workers throughout the country refused to go to their jobs. He called this off when four hundred peaceful Indian protestors were killed by British-led soldiers. He was not ready to give up the fight for independence, however, and soon Indians throughout the country were expressing support for his movement. Gandhi became the leader of the Indian National Congress political party, and in 1920 he began a campaign to boycott (not buy) British goods. Instead, he advised the Indians to spin their own cotton and make their own clothes as he did. Gandhi hoped to create economic independence for each Indian village in this manner. This campaign led to Gandhi being imprisoned for two years. He was released in 1924 for medical reasons.

Gandhi developed several nonviolent methods of protest, including mass marches and fasting. In an attempt to try to bring Indian Muslims and Hindus together, he fasted for twenty-one days. When the British placed a salt tax on Indians in 1930, he organized a 24-day, 200-mile march to the sea with thousands of protestors. Once they reached the sea, they boiled seawater to make their own salt. In 1932 Gandhi also fasted to draw attention to the lives of the lowest caste in Indian society, the untouchables, whom Gandhi called the *harijans,* or "children of god."

Throughout the 1930s Gandhi concentrated on building a sense of national pride in Indians, promoting Hindi as the national language, and trying to establish basic education for the poor. He also continued to encourage fabric making as a way to self-sufficiency. Though he retired as the head of the National Congress, he remained its actual leader, working closely with others such as Jawaharlal Nehru (1889–1964). Nehru would later become the first prime minister of the independent republic of India.

The birth of India

Gandhi became convinced that there would be no real freedom for India as long as it remained part of the British Empire. When World War II (1939–45; a war in which Great Britain, France, the United States, and their allies defeated Germany, Italy, and Japan) began, Gandhi demanded that India be given its independence as "payment" for helping the British. England, however, managed to bring India into the war without making any such promises. The seventy-three-year-old Gandhi was sent to jail from 1942 until 1944, along with other Congress Party members such as Nehru. This set off violent protests throughout India.

In prison Gandhi fasted for three weeks. He became ill with malaria, a potentially deadly disease spread by mosquitoes. He also learned that his wife of sixty years, Kasturbai, had died. Finally Gandhi and the others were released. As the war reached its end, the British began to give clear indications that they were ready to transfer power to the Indians and leave the country. Gandhi's movement against British rule was largely responsible for this. Additionally, the costs of World War II had been high, and Britain could no longer afford the military price of maintaining its empire.

Gandhi's Ashes

After he was killed, the body of Gandhi was cremated, or burned. About twenty urns (vases) were filled with his ashes. All but one of these urns were sent around the country so that the ashes could be spread in the rivers of India, as Gandhi had wished. The final urn was sent to Cuttack, the capital of the Indian state of Orissa. There it was placed in a bank vault for safekeeping until a proper ceremony could be arranged. After India gained its independence, the capital of Orissa moved from Cuttack to a new location in Bubanshewar. Somehow the urn containing Gandhi's ashes was forgotten in the confusion.

In 1997, almost fifty years after Gandhi's death, the urn was rediscovered by a bank employee. Later that year Gandhi's final set of ashes was spread in India's Ganges River by his great-grandson, and Gandhi was finally put to rest in his native land.

However, independence was not as simple as the Indian people had hoped. Islam and Hinduism continued to divide the country. The leader of the Muslims, Muhammad Ali Jinnah (1876–1948), called for the creation of a separate Muslim state, to be called Pakistan. In August 1946 he declared a "Direct Action Day" that set Muslims against Hindus. The day turned violent and thousands were killed. Gandhi, now seventy-seven, fasted in protest of this violence, but the rioting continued in various parts of the country. By the time the British withdrew from India in 1948, the Congress Party had agreed to the division of the country the Muslims sought. Gandhi began his final fast on January 13, 1948, praying for unity in India. While attending prayers on January 30, he was shot and killed by a radical Hindu who did not approve of Gandhi's attempts to bring peace between the two religions.

Since his death Gandhi has come to represent peaceful protest and the power of nonviolence. Not only was he largely responsible for liberating his country from British rule, he also presented a model for other freedom activists. His satyagraha influenced protest movements and leaders around the world, including Martin Luther King Jr. (1929–1968) and his efforts to gain equality for African Americans in the United States; and Nelson Mandela (1918–), who spent twenty-five years in prison before becoming the first president of an independent South Africa.

Despite his many achievements, Gandhi remained humble. He was fond of saying, "I have nothing new to teach the world. Truth and nonviolence are as old as the hills." Known as the "Father of the Nation" by the people of India, his birthday, October 2, is celebrated as a national holiday. In 2000 *Time* magazine placed Gandhi second on its "Person of the Century" list.

For More Information

BOOKS

Barraclough, John. *Mohandas Gandhi.* Des Plaines, IL: Heinemann Interactive Library, 1997.

Chadha, Yogesh. *Gandhi: A Life.* New York, NY: Wiley, 1999.

Fischer, Louis. *Gandhi.* New York, NY: Signet, 1982.

Gandhi, Mahatma. *Autobiography: The Story of My Experiments with Truth.* Translated by Mahadev Desai. Ahmedabad, India: Navajivan Publishing House, 1927.

Gandhi, Mohandas K. *The Penguin Gandhi Reader.* New York, NY: Penguin Books, 1995.

Martin, Christopher. *Mohandas Gandhi.* Minneapolis, MN: Lerner, 2001.

"Mohandas Karamchand Gandhi." *Encyclopedia of World Biography.* 2nd ed. Detroit, MI: Gale Research, 1998.

Payne, Robert. *The Life and Death of Mahatma Gandhi.* New York, NY: E. P. Dutton, 1969.

PERIODICALS

McGeary, Johanna. "Person of the Century Runner-Up: Mohandas Gandhi." *Time* (January 3, 2000). This article can also be found online at http://www.time.com/time/time100/poc/magazine/mohandas_gandhi12a.html.

Rushdie, Salman. "Mohandas Gandhi." *Time* (April 13, 1998). This article can also be found online at http://www.time.com/time/time100/leaders/profile/gandhi.html.

WEB SITES

"About Gandhi," *M. K. Gandhi Institute for Nonviolence.* http://www.gandhiinstitute.org/AboutGandhi/index.cfm (accessed on June 1, 2006).

"Mohandas Karamchand Gandhi, 'The Mahatma'." *Kids Freesouls.* http://www.kidsfreesouls.com/gandhiji.htm (accessed on June 1, 2006).

Welcome to Mahatma Gandhi One Spot Complete Information Web site. http://www.mkgandhi.org/ (accessed on June 1, 2006).

Gerald Brousseau Gardner

BORN: June 13, 1884 • Blundellsands, England

DIED: February 12, 1964

British religious leader; witch; writer

"I think we must say good-bye to the witch. The cult is doomed, I am afraid, partly because of modern conditions, housing shortage, the smallness of families, and chiefly by education. The modern child is not interested. He knows witches are all bunk."

Gerald Gardner.

Gerald B. Gardner, the pioneer of the modern witchcraft revival movement, was a writer and occultist. An occultist is someone interested in supernatural powers and mystical knowledge. Gardner called himself a witch and founded the contemporary religion of witchcraft in England during the 1950s. This later led to the establishment of Wicca. Wicca is a form of white (benevolent and kind) witchcraft that comes from pre-Christian religious traditions that involve magic and a focus on the rhythms of nature. Gardner gathered beliefs and celebrations from a wide variety of sources to create what became known as the Gardnerian Tradition in witchcraft. He also initiated many people on both sides of the Atlantic Ocean into his coven, or assembly of witches.

A very British beginning

Gardner was born Gerald Brousseau Gardner on June 13, 1884, in the small northern English town of Blundellsands near Liverpool. He came from a moderately wealthy family, with a father who was an important local merchant and justice of the peace. Gardner later claimed that his grandfather had married a witch and that other members of the family had supernatural or psychic powers. There are also claims of a family connection to a woman named Grissell Gairdner, who was burned as a witch in 1610.

Gardner had asthma as a child and did not play with his two brothers. Instead he was cared for by a full-time Irish nursemaid who took him on trips across Europe and largely let the youth engage his curiosity as he pleased. Gardner formed early passions for both history and archaeology, which is the study of past human life and culture. When his nursemaid married and went to Ceylon (now Sri Lanka) to live with her husband, Gardner followed. The tropical climate was better for his asthma. Just sixteen, he took a job on a tea plantation. He worked on the plantation for nineteen years before moving to Borneo, a large island in the Malay Archipelago islands, where he became a rubber tree planter. In 1923 he moved to Malaysia, where he was employed for the next thirteen years as a rubber tree plantation inspector, a customs official, and an inspector of opium (an addictive drug made from opium poppies) establishments.

A student of local culture and magic

During his years in the East, Gardner turned his attention to local customs, religions, and supernatural and magical beliefs. He studied ritual weapons and the Malay *kris,* a type of dagger with a wave-shaped blade. His first published work, *Kris and Other Malay Weapons,* resulted from this interest. He conducted original research into the early civilizations of Malaya (now Malaysia), writing for the *Royal Asiatic Society* journal and becoming an expert on the native people of Malaya. He mounted archaeological expeditions in search of lost cities of the East. Gardner was able to finance his work with the income he made from the rubber trade.

Gardner retired at age fifty-two and returned to England with his wife, whom he had married in 1927. They settled in the south of England, in the area known as New Forest. He spent most of his time leading archaeological expeditions throughout Europe and Asia Minor. While on a visit to the island of Cyprus, he discovered what he described as places that he had dreamed about earlier. He became convinced that he had lived on Cyprus in another lifetime. He used this as the background and setting for his second book, the 1939 novel *A Goddess Arrives.* The book centered around the worship of the goddess Aphrodite 2,500 years earlier.

Gardner became fascinated with the idea of a goddess religion that supposedly ruled the peoples of Europe during the Stone Age, the earliest known period of human culture. According to this religion, the Mother Goddess was the creator and the center of religious power. This feminine-based religion, many say, was the primary form of religious belief for many centuries until it was finally replaced several thousand years ago by what is called the Sky God, or male-dominated religious systems that are known now. The existence of this religion was deemed uncertain by the early twenty-first century, but during the 1930s many people in England and the United States believed in it. According to legend, pre-Christian Europe was matriarchal, or controlled by women, and the supreme spiritual being was a mother goddess.

As a student of local folklore, Gardner soon became interested in the history of the region where he had settled, and he discovered that it had deep roots in witchcraft. He became involved with an occult group, the Fellowship of Crotona, which was led by the daughter of an early member of the Theosophical Society. The Theosophical Society is a mystical religious and philosophical movement founded in New York City in 1875. The society combines Buddhist and Hindu beliefs and seeks to investigate the universe and humanity's place in it. The Fellowship of Crotona practiced both Theosophy and Rosicrucian rituals. The Rosicrucians are an organization devoted to the study of ancient mystical, philosophical, and religious principles. The Crotona group claimed to be a line of hereditary witches, with secret knowledge passed down to them for hundreds of years. (Modern-day research indicates the group was only two decades old at the time of Gardner's involvement with them.) They had built a theater, and Gardner assisted them in the production of plays with occult themes. One member of the fellowship claimed to have known Gardner in his previous life on Cyprus.

Gardner claimed he was initiated into a coven, or group of witches, in 1939, by its leader, a woman he referred to as "Old Dorothy." Historians believe he was referring to a very prim and seemingly conservative lady named Dorothy Clutterbuck (1880–1951), who ran a small coven. (Gardner later claimed that he learned his witchcraft tradition from a coven that had a deep historical tradition, and that his writings were thus handed down from generation to generation. Clutterbuck's small coven, however, was one with

A woman reads from the Wiccan Book of Shadows during a séance. Gerald Gardner led a revival of Wicca in modern times. © THE COVER STORY/CORBIS.

recent roots only.) Once he was a member of the coven, Gardner began to study witchcraft ritual with the intent to publish a book. England still possessed laws against witchcraft at the time, however, so he wrote the 1949 novel *High Magic's Aid* using the false name of Scire. Though fiction, this book revealed much about witchcraft. Some of the material came from Gardner's association with Aleister Crowley (1875–1947), one of the more famous practitioners of the occult in England at the time.

When Gardner met Crowley, shortly before Crowley's death, Gardner persuaded him to write down the practices of a coven to which he had once belonged. Crowley also initiated Gardner into the Ordo Templi Orientis, a group that practiced the East Asian form of magic called Tantrism. Tantrism is a spiritual movement which involves mantras (verbal formulas), symbolic body postures and hand motions, and sexual rituals. Crowley's version of Tantrism was a corrupted form of tantra yoga, a Hindu discipline intended to awaken the energy in the body by using rituals to address relationships and sexuality. Gardner soon opened his own lodge of the Ordo Templi Orientis at his new home on the grounds of a nudist club to which he belonged. His lodge was made up mostly of men. In fact, the female membership of the group was often so low that he had to hire prostitutes from London to carry out the Great Rite, a ritual during which a high priestess was required to have sexual intercourse with male members.

England's chief witch

By 1951 the laws against witchcraft in England had been eliminated, and Gardner could speak publicly about the practice. He was also free to establish his own coven. Gardner moved to the Isle of Man where an acquaintance had opened the Museum of Magic and Witchcraft. Gardner soon bought the museum and operated it himself. In 1953 he met Doreen Valiente (1922–1999), whom he initiated into his coven of witches. Together they edited and expanded what Gardner called his Book of Shadows, a book of rules and rituals for the operation of a coven. Historians believe Valiente may have toned down some of Crowley's information regarding sexual practices and also helped to insert an emphasis on goddess worship.

In 1954 Gardner published *Witchcraft Today,* perhaps his most influential work. In it he acknowledged and drew from the theories of Egyptologist Margaret Murray (1863–1963) and her 1921 *Witchcraft: The Witch Cult in Western Europe.* Murray's book posed the theory that witchcraft was the remaining aspects of pagan religions that had survived the arrival of Christianity and the centuries of witch hunts that followed. Murray held that the practice of witchcraft went back to ancient times and was widespread throughout Europe. These ideas gained some popularity, although many of her professional colleagues mocked them. Gardner was intrigued by her theories and asked Murray to write the forward to his book.

In *Witchcraft Today* Gardner complained that witchcraft was in danger of dying out. He wrote: "I think we must say good-bye to the witch. The cult is doomed, I am afraid, partly because of modern conditions, housing shortage, the smallness of families, and chiefly by education. The modern child is not interested. He knows witches are all bunk." The book's publication, however, brought about a resurgence of interest in England and led to the formation of many new covens. Gardner was dubbed by the English media as "Britain's Chief Witch." He angered some witches in the country who felt that he was sharing too many secrets of the practice with outsiders. Others disapproved because Gardner incorporated his beliefs on naturism (nudism) with witchcraft.

By all accounts, Gardner was a difficult man with whom to work. Some considered him controlling and arrogant. Many of his followers, including Valiente, who had become the high priestess of his coven, split with him over personality clashes. The increasing media coverage of Gardner also did not please some of the other witches. Gardner continued to work, publishing *The Meaning of Witchcraft* in 1959. The following year he was invited to Buckingham Palace, not, however, because of his work in witchcraft, but for his government service in the Far East. Gardner's wife died that same year.

After a brief trip to Lebanon for health reasons, Gardner was returning by ship to England when he died of a heart attack on February 12, 1964. The captain of the ship was the only mourner at his funeral, and he was buried in Tunis, the capital of Tunisia, in Africa. Gardner had left his museum to the current high priestess of his coven, who, with her husband, continued to run it for a time. Soon, however, they sold the contents of the museum to the Ripley's Believe It or Not company, and the collected artifacts were distributed around the world to the Ripley's museums.

After Gardner's death his papers were made public, and it quickly became apparent that his claims to being initiated into a witchcraft tradition with a long and established ritual were untrue. The papers revealed that Gardner had created much of the ritual himself, blending elements he learned from Crowley with medieval texts, writings of other mystical orders, and bits of Asian ritual and folklore practices. The ritual knife he used, the *athame,* was developed from the Malaysian kris, which Gardner was very familiar with. He took eight different ancient pagan festivals and holy days and adapted them to become the witchcraft holy days, or Sabbats. He also instituted meetings, called Esbats, every other week.

Gardner has been credited with bringing the concept of witchcraft or Wicca to the United States, though he personally never traveled there. In 1963 he initiated a visiting Englishman named Raymond Buckley into the practice. Buckley then went back to the United States, where he was living. He began to spread Gardner's teachings in America, and they ultimately developed into the Wicca movement, which had more than fifty thousand practitioners by the early twenty-first century.

The Gardnerian Tradition

Gardner wrote about the sources he used for his witchcraft ritual in his Book of Shadows. Although it is a central sacred text to the religion of Wicca, this book was never published or made available to the general public. Instead, each coven possesses its own hand-written copy, and some of these are in code. They all supposedly contain the basic principles of Gardner's teachings and rituals, but differ somewhat from coven to coven, based on local preferences.

The Gardnerian Tradition contains mysteries and secrets that are supposedly passed on through three different levels, or degrees. When a person reaches the Third Degree, he has complete knowledge of the tradition and may break away, or hive, to form his own coven. The ideal number for a coven is considered to be thirteen. Wicca is a religion of initiation. That is, membership is not purely voluntary, but involves an initiation rite. A coven must find students serious about learning the rites in order for them to be accepted. Some witches, however, prefer to practice Wicca on their own and are called solitaries. Not all Wiccans practice witchcraft. Some merely believe in the nature elements of the religion.

Wiccans worship the Goddess and may also worship the God, according to Gardner's teachings, and celebrate Sabbats and Esbats. These Sabbats include the solstices (the two longest days of the year), the equinoxes (the two times a year when day and night are equal in length), Litha in the summer, Yule in the winter, Ostara in the spring, and Mabon in the autumn. Other Sabbats include Imbolic on February 1, Beltane on May 1, Lughnasadh on August 1, and Samhain on November 1. This celebration calendar, also called the Wheel of the Year, is used by most Neo-Pagan groups in the early twenty-first century.

Gardner developed rituals to accompany each of these holy days and for each degree of initiation into Wicca. One major ritual of the Gardnerian Tradition is called "Drawing Down the Moon." The high priestess of the coven enters a trance and becomes the Goddess, who is symbolized by the moon. The high priest of the coven calls on, or draws down, the Goddess into the high priestess. Wiccans generally celebrate inside a magic circle, holding hands and saying prayers to the Goddess and God. In the Gardnerian Tradition, such ceremonies are conducted in the nude.

A pentagram, or five-pointed star, is the general symbol of Wicca, and there are several interpretations of what these five points mean. Followers of the Gardnerian Tradition, however, deny that they have any meaning at all. A primary tenet, or principle, of the religion states "If no harm is done, do what you will." Gardner also applied the concept of karma to this tenet. Karma is a Hindu and Buddhist belief that one's actions will return to affect one positively or negatively in three ways: physically, mentally, and spiritually.

For More Information

BOOKS

Bracelin, Jack L. *Gerald Gardner: Witch.* London, England: Octagon Press, 1960.

Gardner, Gerald B. *Witchcraft Today.* New York, NY: Citadel Press, 2004.

"G(erald) B(rosseau) Gardner." In *Encyclopedia of Occultism and Parapsychology.* 5th ed. Detroit, MI: Gale Group, 2001.

Heselton, Philip. *Gerald Gardner and the Cauldron of Inspiration: An Investigation in the Sources of Gardnerian Witchcraft.* Milverton, England: Capall Bann, 2003.

Heselton, Philip. *Wiccan Roots: Gerald Gardner and the Modern Witchcraft Revival.* Milverton, England: Capall Bann, 2000.

Valiente, Doreen. *The Rebirth of Witchcraft.* London, England: Robert Hale Ltd., 1989.

PERIODICALS

Lawrence. M. J. "Modern Witchcraft Has Roots in '50s Britain." *Boston Herald* (October 22, 1998): 3.

WEB SITES

Gerald Gardner. http://www.geraldgardner.com/ (accessed on June 2, 2006).

"Gardner, Gerald B." *Mystica.* http://www.themystica.com/mystica/articles/g/gardner_gerald_b.html (accessed on June 2, 2006).

Abu Hāmid Muhammad al-Ghazālī

BORN: 1058 • Tus, Persia

DIED: 1111 • Tus, Persia

Persian religious scholar; writer

"What remained for me was not to be attained by oral instruction and study, but only by immediate experience and by walking in the mystic way."

Although Abu Hāmid Muhammad al-Ghazālī was a legal scholar and teacher, he is best known for his writings on religion and philosophy. In the middle of his life, al-Ghazālī gave up his academic career and spent years of deep thought on religion. He joined the Sufi sect of Islam, the mystical branch that emphasizes a direct connection with God through prayer and self-denial. Al-Ghazālī wrote more than four hundred works, including *Ihya' 'Ulum ad-Din* (The Revival of the Religious Sciences), which brought the mysticism of Sufism into the mainstream of Islam. Known as Algazel in the West, al-Ghazālī and his writings have influenced not only Islamic thinkers but Christian ones as well.

Period of learning

Al-Ghazālī was born in 1058 CE in the small village of Tus, near the town of Masshad in Persia (modern-day Iran). He may have been named after his father's business, as *ghazzali* means "wool merchant." His father was a

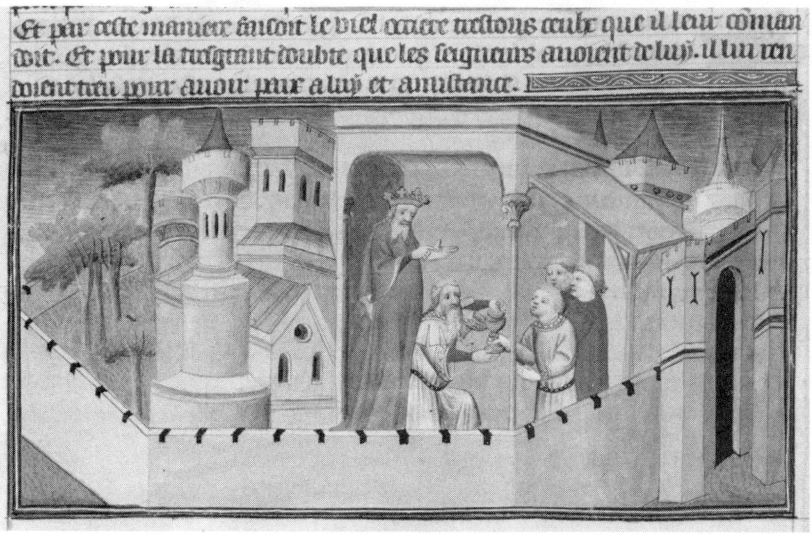

The Assassins share in some drugged wine before going to carry out their work of murder. The Assassins were responsible for the death of al-Ghazālī's sponsor, Nizam al-Mulk. MS FR 2810 F.17 HASSAN I SABBAH LEADING THE INITIATIONS AT ALAMUT GIVING HIS FOLLOWERS DRUGGED WINE (VELLUM), BOUCICAUT MASTER, (FL. 1390-1430) (AND WORKSHOP)/ BIBLIOTHEQUE NATIONALE, PARIS, FRANCE,/THE BRIDGEMAN ART LIBRARY INTERNATIONAL.

Sufi. He had several sisters and a brother, Ahmad, who became a Sufi poet. Al-Ghazālī's father died when he was very young, and he and his brother were left in the care of a Sufi friend, Ahmad al-Radkhani, who had promised to educate the boys. Economic conditions were not good, but by the age of fifteen, arrangements had been made for al-Ghazālī to continue his studies with a leading scholar, Abu Nasr al-Isma'ili, in the region of Jurgan, on the Caspian Sea.

Al-Ghazālī would later note in his autobiography, *al-Munkidh min al-Dalal* (Deliverance from Error), that he was more ambitious than religious as a young man. He pursued a scholarly religious path at first because that was what was available to a young man with little money or family standing. So, while studying with various teachers, he took notes, but did not bother to consider or memorize the lessons. One story tells how he was returning to his native Tus from Jurgan when his group was attacked by bandits. When al-Ghazālī begged that they not steal his school notebooks, the leader of the robbers laughed at him. The robber said that obviously al-Ghazālī was not much of a scholar if all his learning was kept in notebooks and not in his mind. From this point on, al-Ghazālī memorized his lessons instead of simply copying them down.

When al-Ghazālī was nineteen he earned a place at a religious college, or *madrasa,* in Nishapur, about 50 miles west of Tus. In Nishapur he studied with one of the major religious scholars of the generation,

Abu al-Malik al-Juwayni (died 1085), also known as Imam al-Haramayn. Al-Juwayni was the imam, or religious leader, of the two most sacred cities in Islam, Mecca and Medina. Al-Ghazālī studied both Islamic law and religion and was introduced to the work of two earlier Islamic thinkers, Abu al-Nasr al-Farabi (870–950) and Ibn Sina (980–1037). These men attempted to combine the use of reason and rational thought developed by ancient Greek philosophers with the Islamic belief in one supreme being, Allah.

Al-Ghazālī was a bright student and became a favorite of al-Juwayni. After finishing his studies, he remained for a time at the school and helped with teaching. The young Muslim scholar soon came to the attention of the powerful *vizier* (state official), Nizam al-Mulk (1018–1092). The minister had built the college in Nishapur, as well as several others in Persia and what is modern-day Iraq. After the death of al-Juwayni, Nizam al-Mulk invited al-Ghazālī to come to Baghdad, in modern-day Iraq, the administrative center of the Islamic empire.

A brilliant career

In Baghdad al-Ghazālī served Nizam al-Mulk as a legal advisor, taught, wrote, and enjoyed the company of other scholars. In 1091, at only thirty-three years old, he was named the chief professor at Baghdad's Nizamiyya college. This was one of the most prominent positions in the Muslim world. He lectured to large crowds of students on law and logic. He was noted for giving clear and easily understood presentations on complicated religious matters. He also wrote one of his best known works, *The Incoherence of the Philosophers,* in which he attempted to reveal the mistakes in the theories of al-Farabi and Ibn Sina. He believed these earlier thinkers had relied too much on rational thought, which he felt was not adequate for understanding concepts such as Allah and infinity, or something without boundaries.

Al-Ghazālī's philosophy was adopted by a group known as the Kalam thinkers, who attempted to prove that the universe had a beginning and therefore was created by Allah. The basic Kalam argument takes the following form: The universe had a beginning. Everything that has a beginning has a cause. Therefore, the universe has a cause, which is Allah. In their rejection of **Aristotle**'s (384–322 BCE; see entry) theory that the world of matter and motion is eternal, the Kalam thinkers and al-Ghazālī had much in common.

During his time in Baghdad, Al-Ghazālī also wrote *Fadaʿih al-Batiniyya* (The Obscenities of the Esoterics), a critical account of, among other things, the Assassins, a radical sect of Muslims organized in the late eleventh century. The Assassins often killed their enemies by using knives or poison. The name came from their practice of preparing themselves for their work by using *hashishin,* or the drug hashish. The word "assassination" later became used to describe a planned murder. The Assassins killed a number of prominent Muslims during al-Ghazālī's years in Baghdad, including his sponsor, Nizam al-Mulk.

Al-Ghazālī's rise in popularity came to a sudden halt. He suffered a crisis of belief, and maybe even a nervous collapse. In 1095 he developed a stutter that prevented him from lecturing and that ultimately made him mute, or unable to talk. Though he later recovered his voice and lost the stutter, al-Ghazālī gave up his teaching position and left Baghdad. It is possible he left the city in part because he feared being killed, due to his published criticism of the Assassins. In his autobiography, al-Ghazālī claims he could no longer stand the dishonesty he found in many of his fellow scholars. He believed they were more interested in money and fame than in real learning. He also decided that true religion could only come through a direct experience with Allah, not through scholarship. As he wrote in his autobiography: "I apprehended clearly that the mystics are men who had real experiences, not men of words, and that I had already progressed as far as possible by way of intellectual apprehension. What remained for me was not to be attained by oral instruction and study, but only by immediate experience and by walking in the mystic way."

Retires from the world

Al-Ghazālī moved his family back to Tus. He gave up his wealth and began to live the severe ascetic life of a Sufi. Such a life is marked by contemplation, prayer, self-denial, and poverty. The ultimate goal is to understand and become one with Allah. For Sufis, learning and education are the least important ways a person can experience Allah. More important is the physical experience of the divine, such as enjoying beautiful art or poetry, dancing, fasting (not eating), and even self-mortification, or beating and whipping oneself. For the next decade, al-Ghazālī traveled throughout the Middle East. He lived for a time in Damascus (in modern-day Syria), made a pilgrimage to Mecca (in modern-day Saudi Arabia), and visited Egypt. In 1099 he returned to

Sufis pray during an evening ceremony outside a mosque in Baghdad, Iraq. Later in life, Abu Hāmid al-Ghazālī turned towards the severe life of a Sufi, spending much time in prayer and contemplation. © BENJAMIN LOWY/CORBIS.

Tus, where he established a Sufi retreat and school. He lived a quiet life of prayer and writing, and became known as a mystic, one who seeks enlightenment or understanding through religious mysteries.

In 1106 Nizam al-Mulk's son persuaded al-Ghazālī to return to teaching. After much debate al-Ghazālī finally decided to teach at the Nizamiyya in Nishapur, where he had once studied. It was during these years that he completed his greatest work, *Ihyaʾ ʿUlum ad-Din.* In this book al-Ghazālī explains the rules and practices of Islam. It is basically an encyclopedia of the religion. Al-Ghazālī also attempts to show how devotion and practice of Islamic traditions ultimately lead to a higher mystical level of life for the believer. This principle brought Sufism into the orthodox, or traditional, practice of Islam. In another work, *Bidayat al-Hidayah* (The Beginning of Guidance), al-Ghazālī presents a simplified version of this same subject. A third major piece, *Michkat al-Anwar*

(Corner for Lights), compares the mystical experience to other ways of thinking and understanding.

After teaching in Nishapur for four years, al-Ghazālī returned to Tus in poor health. He died in 1111, but his influence has survived for centuries. He is known as a "Defender of the Faith," for his teachings and writings on Islamic practice. His arguments about the weakness of reason in understanding spiritual issues were later adopted by Christian scholars such as St. Thomas Aquinas (c. 1225–1274) to establish the power of Catholic Christianity in Europe. Indeed, al-Ghazālī was so successful in his arguments in favor of religion that some scholars have accused him of damaging the growth of philosophy.

About a century after al-Ghazālī's death, the great Spanish Muslim philosopher Ibn Rushd (1126–1198) attempted to disprove *The Incoherence of the Philosophers* with his own book, *Tahafut al-Tahafut* (The Incoherence of the Incoherence). Despite the fine reasoning in that work, al-Ghazālī's comments about the weakness of philosophy still influence Islam. Al-Ghazālī's own experiences provided examples of how a rich inner life and a mystical pursuit of Allah could be combined with the full observance of the rules of Islam. His work ended the suspicions of Islamic religious scholars regarding Sufism and made them look more favorably on the practice. This in turn ultimately made it easier for ordinary Muslims to participate in Sufi practices.

For More Information

BOOKS

"al-Ghazali." In *Encyclopedia of World Biography.* 2nd ed. Detroit, MI: Gale Research, 1998.

Campanini, Massimo. "al-Ghazali." In *History of Islamic Philosophy.* Edited by S. H. Nasr and O. Leaman. London: Routledge, 1996, 258–74. This chapter is also available online at http://www.ghazālī.org/articles/gz2.htm.

Ghazali, Abu Hamid Muhammad al-. *Freedom and Fulfillment: An Annotated Translation of al-Munqidh min al-Dalal and Other Relevant Works of al-Ghazali.* Translated by Richard J. H. McCarthy. Boston, MA: Twayne Publishers, 1980.

Ghazali, Abu Hamid Muhammad al-. *The Incoherence of the Philosophers.* Translated by Michael E. Marmura. Provo, UT: Brigham Young University, 2002.

Smith, Margaret. *Al-Ghazali, the Mystic.* London, England: Luzac and Co., 1944.

Watt, W. Montgomery. *Muslim Intellectual: A Study of al-Ghazālī.* Edinburgh, Scotland: Edinburgh University Press, 1963. Also available online at http://www.ghazali.org/articles/watt.htm.

PERIODICALS

Dallal, Ahmad. "Ghazali and the Perils of Interpretation." *Journal of the American Oriental Society* (October–December, 2002): 773–87.

WEB SITES

Abu Hamid al-Ghazali. http://www.ghazali.org/ (accessed on June 2, 2006).

"Abu Hamid Al-Ghazali." *Window: Philosophy on the Internet.* http://www.trincoll.edu/depts/phil/philo/phils/muslim/ghazali.html (accessed on June 2, 2006).

Halsall, Peter. "Medieval Sourcebook: Abu Hamid al-Ghazali (1058–1111 CE): Munkidh min al-Dalal (*Confessions,* or *Deliverance from Error*), c. 1100." *Fordham.edu.* http://www.fordham.edu/halsall/basis/1100ghazali-truth.html (accessed on June 2, 2006).

Nakamura, Kojiro. "al-Ghazali, Abu Hamid (1058–1111)." *Routledge Encyclopedia of Philosophy.* http://www.ghazali.org/articles/gz1.htm (accessed on June 2, 2006).

Watt, W. Montgomery. "Ghazali, Abu Hamid al-." *Encyclopedia of Religion.* http://www.ghazali.org/articles/gz-er.htm (accessed on June 2, 2006).

Gobind Singh

BORN: December 22, 1666 • Patna, Bihar, India

DIED: October 7, 1708 • Nanded, Maharashtra, India

Indian religious leader

"The Divine Guru hath sent me for religion's sake / On this account, I have come into the world; / Extend the faith everywhere/ Seize and destroy the evil and sinful."

Gobind Singh was the tenth and last living guru, or teacher and leader, of Sikhism. Sikhism is practiced by some twenty-three million people worldwide, with most living in the state of Punjab in India. Sikhism aims to create a close, loving relationship with God, particularly through prayer and meditation, or quiet reflection or thought on a single point. Gobind Singh was born Gobind Rai Sodhi on December 22, 1666, in the Indian city of Patna, and served as guru from 1676 until his death in 1708. His father was Sikhism's ninth guru, Teg Bahadur (1621–1675).

Gobind Singh is best remembered for two major accomplishments. The first was the establishment of the Khalsa, a militant brotherhood that helped define Sikhism and empowered Sikhs to resist persecution. (Persecution is when a person or group is mistreated because of their beliefs or other characteristics.) The other was proclaiming himself the last of the living gurus of Sikhism. He declared that after his death, the sacred Sikh scripture, the Shri Guru Granth Sahib, would represent the leader and final guru of the Sikh faith.

Political climate of the seventeenth century

Sikhism was founded 1499, after the faith's first guru, Nanak Dev (1469–1539), had a revelation, or vision of divine truth. He set off on

Gobind Singh offers amrit, *the elixir of life, to the Five Blessed Ones. It was through this ceremony, where five men of different social standings all shared from the same bowl, that Gobind Singh illustrated the Sikh belief in the unity of all men.* © DESAI NOSHIR/CORBIS SYGMA.

a pilgrimage to seek enlightenment, eventually returning to northern India in 1520. Enlightenment is a state of awareness in and understanding of spiritual matters than bring one closer to God. He began to share his teachings with followers he referred to as Sikhs. Following Nanek's death, leadership of the Sikh faith passed to a succession of gurus through the sixteenth and seventeenth centuries.

Prior to the creation of the Sikh religion, the Punjab region in India was dominated by Muslims, followers of the Islamic religion, who had drifted eastward from Pakistan and Afghanistan. During the time of Sikhism's first four gurus, Muslim emperors remained tolerant of Sikhism and other religious beliefs practiced in India. That changed, however, in the early seventeenth century, under emperor Jahangir (1569–1627). Jahangir was a fierce opponent of Sikhism and was determined to convert its followers to Islam. One of these followers was the fifth guru, Arjan Dev (1563–1606), who refused to convert and was put to death by the emperor. His successor, Guru Har Gobind (1595–1644), took steps to increase the military readiness of the Sikhs, who armed themselves and trained in various methods to defend their faith. Violent battles between Sikh and Muslim armies then frequently erupted. In the city of Kashmir at least half of the population, including both Sikhs and Hindus, were forced to convert to Islam.

In this climate of ongoing conflict, a delegation of Kashmiris (those from the Kashmir region in India) approached Gobind Rai's father, Guru Teg Bahadur, and asked for protection. In response, the guru traveled to Delhi, India, to meet with the Muslim emperor, Aurangzeb (1618–1707), in hopes of persuading him to abandon his persecution of Sikhs and Hindus. His effort, however, met with no success. The emperor offered the guru the same choice that he had offered the people of Kashmir and other cities: He could either convert to Islam or die. Even after being forced to witness the brutal execution of three of his close supporters, Guru Teg Bahadur chose to die rather than renounce his religion. His body was left exposed in the public square as a warning to others. This caused many Sikhs to become frightened and deny their faith. The religion began to lose its sense of identity and purpose.

Early life of Gobind Rai

As a child Gobind Rai showed an early interest in military activity, organizing mock battles with his friends. In 1672 Gobind Rai was taken to the town of Anandpur to begin his education. In school he learned not only the Punjabi language but also Hindi, Sanskrit, and Persian. After his father died on November 11, 1675, he was formally installed as guru on March 29, 1676. At just nine years of age, Gobind was already resolved to fight the persecution of the Sikhs. He maintained this resolve throughout his life, later saying famously that he would "train the sparrow to fight the hawk" and "teach one man to fight a legion."

Some Sikh leaders wanted to avenge the death of Guru Teg Bahadur, but Gobind seemed content to wait until the religion could attract more followers and be prepared to defend itself. Meanwhile, he continued his education. At age sixteen, he left Anandpur and founded the city of Paonta on the banks of the Yamuna River, where he remained for four years. During these years he devoted much of his time to physical pursuits such as swimming, archery, wrestling, horseback riding, and martial arts. He also wrote and translated a considerable amount of poetry that centered on religious issues, social justice, the equality of people, and the need to lead an ethical and moral life, or a life lived according to standards of proper and good behavior. Much of his poetry also dealt with military and warlike themes. Although some of his work seems to glorify warfare, the guru saw fighting as a way to achieve both self-respect and divine justice, not simply as a form of aggression.

Sikhism unsheathes the sword

As Gobind became more popular, he began to alarm the *rajas,* or local chiefs, in the surrounding areas. These rajas tended to support the emperor and used their own power to demand tributes, in the form of money, from surrounding communities. Furthermore, they objected to the teachings of Sikhism, especially the Sikhs' opposition to idol worship (the worship of a physical object as a god); their insistence on the equality of all people; and their rejection of the Indian caste system, which divides people into hereditary social classes. These beliefs were seen as threats to previously established traditions.

One of the chiefs who was angered by Gobind was Bhim Chand, the raja of the region surrounding Anandpur. Bhim Chand made repeated attempts to force Gobind out of power, in part by demanding that the Sikh community pay "rent" for the land they occupied. In response the guru hastened the buildup of his military force while keeping a close eye on Bhim Chand and his followers. Tensions between the two groups finally erupted into armed conflict when Bhim Chand's son was about to be married and the raja learned that Gobind was a close friend of the bride's father, Fateh Shah. Bhim Chand threatened to break off the wedding unless Fateh Shah joined him in battle in order to eliminate the Sikh threat. The two men then gathered an army of thirty thousand men and confronted the Sikhs, who numbered just four thousand men, in the October 1686 Battle of Bhangani. Despite having significantly fewer warriors, the Sikh forces emerged victorious.

Formation of the Khalsa

Gobind continued to earn the confidence of the people with his strength and leadership. Parties of Sikh pilgrims arrived in Anandpur almost daily to seek his advice and assistance. The leader of one such party reported being stopped on their way by a band of the emperor's

Sikhs perform Gatka, a Sikh traditional martial art, in a procession during a celebration in honor of the birth of the religion's founder, Nanak Dev. Gobind Singh established the Khalsa, a special order, in which Gatka is practiced.
© MUNISH SHARMA/ REUTERS/CORBIS.

soldiers, who robbed them. The soldiers even cut off the hair of some members of the party. When they resisted, others were killed. In response Gobind instructed Sikhs to assemble in Anandpur. The atmosphere at the gathering was almost festive, with singing and music. Then the guru appeared before his people bearing a sword, and to their astonishment he asked for a volunteer willing to give up his head for the faith. A man named Daya Ram came forward. The guru led Daya Ram into a tent, and when the guru reemerged alone, his sword was covered in blood. When he asked for a second volunteer, a peasant named Dharam Das came forward and followed the guru into the tent. Again, the guru emerged with a bloody sword. The people were beginning to think that he had gone mad. He asked for a third volunteer, and Mohkam Chand came forward. Two more volunteers, Sahib

Chand and Himmat Rai, then agreed to die for their faith and followed Gobind into the tent.

The volunteers, however, were not being killed; the blood on the guru's sword was that of a goat. The volunteers emerged from the tent wearing orange robes, and Gobind turned to the five and said to them that there was no difference among them. He called them his "five beloved ones" and went on to say to the assembled Sikhs that through his actions, he was creating an army called the Khalsa, which would travel about and spread Nanak's message of peace. He said that the Khalsa would bring about an age of peace, raising up the virtuous and destroying those who did evil.

A ritual was then held to initiate the five "beloved ones." The five, who were members of different castes, and the guru all drank from the same bowl during the ceremony, signifying the unity of all Sikhs regardless of their social status and background. The ceremony later became known as the *amrit* ceremony, after the drink the five members shared. Gobind announced that from then on, male Sikhs would take the name Singh, meaning "lion," and women would take the name Kaur, meaning "princess." Sikhs continue to practice this tradition in the twenty-first century.

The five Ks

On that day, as many as fifty thousand Sikhs joined the Khalsa. As a way to further inspire Sikhs and strengthen their identity with the faith, Gobind instructed his people to follow a number of principles. They were to practice their military skills and never retreat from an enemy; protect the weak and the poor; look on all people as equals and reject caste; believe in one supreme God; refrain from using drugs or tobacco and from consuming meat that is slaughtered according to the Islamic ritual (where the animal is bled to death instead of being killed by one quick stroke).

Most importantly, Sikhs were to carry the "five Ks," so called because each item begins with the letter *K*. The five Ks have remained emblems, or symbols, of the faith, allowing Sikhs to identify themselves as Sikhs to the world at large. The five Ks include the following:

- *Kesh,* uncut hair, which is seen as a gift from God and a sign of God's will. A male Sikh can often be recognized by the turban that is wound tightly around the head to contain his hair.

- *Kanga,* a wooden comb, which keeps the hair neat and generally symbolizes cleanliness
- *Kaccha,* an undergarment similar to shorts, which is worn to suggest chastity and cleanliness and serves as a reminder of the need to overcome earthly passions.
- *Kara,* a steel bracelet worn on the right wrist, which, being a perfect circle, with no beginning or end, symbolizes a connection with God.
- *Kirpan,* a saber, which is carried in readiness to defend the weak or uphold the right. The word literally means "mercy" or "grace." In modern times the kirpan is not an actual weapon but a small symbolic reminder.

The Shri Dasam Granth Sahib

Gobind Singh was the author of an important Sikh text, the Shri Dasam Granth Sahib, a 1,400-page compilation of prayers, mythical narratives, devotional works, and autobiographical details. Portions of the Shri Dasam Granth Sahib remain part of the daily devotions of Sikhs in the twenty-first century. One passage, the Jaap Sahib, is a prayer in praise of God:

> Thou has no form or feature,
> No caste no lineage;
> None can describe Thy appearance,
> Colour, mark or Garb.
> Thou art the source of all light,
> And the object of all praise;
> Thou art the supreme Lord of all,
> And the moon of the universe.
> Perfect is Thy discernment.
> All turn to Thee for refuge.
> Thou art the Great Companion;
> Thou art the sure Providence.

"Glimpses of Guru Gobind Singh Ji: The Dasam Granth Sahib." ***Info-Sikh.com.*** **http://www.info-sikh.com/PageG91.html (accessed June 1, 2006).**

Ongoing struggles

The years following the formation of the Khalsa were ones of continuing struggle for Gobind and his followers. From 1703 through 1705 a series of battles took place, collectively referred to as the Battle of Anandpur. A local raja, Ajmer Chand, conspired with other chiefs to kill the guru, but the hired assassins were themselves killed before they could carry out their mission. The emperor Aurangzeb agreed to march against the Sikhs if the local rajas agreed to join him, which they did. The Sikhs, however, drove off the emperor's army, which numbered ten thousand men, and killed his commander.

Numerous chiefs then met and agreed to lay siege to Anandpur. The siege lasted for months, the city was starving, and a number of Sikhs left the city, believing that the Sikh cause was hopeless. Gobind urged his remaining followers to fight on, and in time the Muslim commander grew equally weary of the fight and offered peace terms. Urged to do so by his followers, Gobind agreed to meet the commander, but the Muslim commander did not keep his word and attempted to capture the guru. Gobind and around forty of his followers were forced to take flight, finding refuge in the small village of Chamkaur in early December 1705. In the battle that followed, the Battle of Chamkaur, Gobind's two teenage sons volunteered to fight and were killed.

Gobind's generals, fearing for the guru's life, banded together and insisted that he and his family flee the village. Reluctantly, he agreed and departed, traveling across country sometimes on foot, sometimes on horseback, and sometimes disguised as a local saint and carried in a litter, or enclosed couch. At one point during the journey members of the guru's party became separated, and in the resulting confusion his two remaining sons were identified, captured, and imprisoned in a town called Sirhind. When they refused to convert to Islam, they were executed in December 1705 by the local ruler, Wazir Khan.

Gobind continued his flight. At one point he learned that the authorities knew his whereabouts, so he searched for a site where he could mount a defense. His small group was reinforced when the Sikhs who had abandoned him at Chamkaur rejoined his followers and expressed their willingness to fight. When the Muslim army approached the Sikh camp, they were driven off, and Gobind again resumed his journey. Eventually he arrived at the town of Talwandi Sabor. Then, finally, the guru was allowed to enjoy some peace, as the Islamic authorities issued orders commanding their followers to leave Gobind alone.

Wazir Khan, however, was alarmed by the peace that appeared to have been established between the guru and the Muslim emperor. He was afraid that if the two became allies, he would lose power and influence. He sent assassins to kill Gobind. One of the assassins pretended to be a Sikh worshipper and managed to enter Gobind's private apartment in the town of Nader and stabbed him. The guru lingered for a while but eventually died on October 7, 1708.

The Shri Guru Granth Sahib

In one of his last acts as guru, Gobind Singh made an unusual announcement. As he neared death, he declared that his successor would not be a living person. Rather, the final guru of Sikhism would be the sacred Sikh scripture, the Shri Guru Granth Sahib. The fifth guru, Arjan Dev, had compiled the Granth Sahib, sometimes called the Adi Granth, in 1603. It brought together the hymns and writings of Sikhism's first five gurus, particularly those of Nanak, as well as the writings of various

Hindu and Muslim saints. In the years that followed, the Granth Sahib was updated to include the writings of later gurus, and Gobind Singh had compiled all of these works into a final, complete version of the text. The Shri Guru Granth Sahib remains as the material representation of the final guru and all previous gurus, and as such is both the sacred scripture and spiritual guide of Sikhism. While the text is not regarded as the direct word of God, it is considered to be divinely inspired and is the focus of worship in Sikh temples, called *gurdwaras.*

For More Information

BOOKS

Grewal, J. S. *The Sikhs of the Punjab.* Cambridge, UK: Cambridge University Press, 1998.

Hoffman, Nancy. *Sikhism.* Detroit, MI: Lucent Books, 2005.

Kalsi, Sewa Singh. *Simple Guide to Sikhism.* Folkestone, UK: Global Press, 1999.

Mann, Gurinder Singh. *Sikhism.* Upper Saddle River, NJ: Prentice Hall, 2003.

Singh, Patwant. *The Sikhs.* New York, NY: Doubleday, 2001.

WEB SITES

"Glimpses of Guru Gobind Singh Ji: The Dasam Granth Sahib." *Info-Sikh.com.* http://www.info-sikh.com/PageG91.html (accessed June 1, 2006).

"Guru Gobind Singh." *Singh Sabha.* http://www.singhsabha.com/guru_gobind_singh.htm (accessed on May 26, 2006).

Sidhu, G. S., G. S. Sivia, and Kirpal Singh. "The Saint-Soldier (Guru Gobind Singh)." *Sikh Missionary Society U.K.* http://www.gurmat.info/sms/smspublications/thesaintsoldier (accessed on May 26, 2006).

"Sri Guru Gobind Singh Sahib Ji." *Gateway to Sikhism.* http://allaboutsikhs.com/gurus/gurugobind.htm (accessed on May 26, 2006).

Ibn Khaldūn

BORN: May 27, 1332 • Tunis, Tunisia

DIED: March 17, 1406 • Cairo, Egypt

Arab historian; legal scholar

"Whoever takes someone's property, or uses him for forced labor, or presses an unjustified claim upon him, it should be known that this is what the Lawgiver had in mind when he forbade injustice."

Abdahl-Rahman ibn Muhammad ibn Khaldūn, better known simply as Ibn Khaldūn, is generally considered to be one of the greatest Arab historians. Although he was a devout Muslim, or follower of the Islamic faith, Ibn Khaldun did not focus on religion in his work. He applied reason and logic to his study of history. He has been called the father of modern sociology (the study of the origin and development of human society) because he was the first to examine how social and historical factors combine. Instead of examining history through the major battles fought by armies, or through the reigns of kings, he studied how common people have shaped the world. He also developed a theory for the rise and fall of nations and empires that is still used in the twenty-first century.

Ibn Khaldūn believed civilizations rise and fall in constant cycles. He claimed that hard work and cooperation create a civilization and bring wealth and luxury to it. But then people become lazy, selfish, and dishonest, and the civilization declines. This theory was presented in his most famous work, the *Muqaddima* (Introduction), the first volume in his seven-volume history of the Arab world, *Kitab alʿibar* (Universal History).

Ibn Khaldūn closely read the works of Muslim scholars who had come before him, such as those by Ibn Sina, who is seated here surrounded by his students. © BETTMANN/CORBIS.

Childhood and early career

Ibn Khaldūn was born in Tunis, the capital of modern-day Tunisia in North Africa, in 1332. His family was well educated and had been part of the intellectual class for several generations. His clan, or family, originally came from Yemen, and was part of a tribe called the Hadhramaut. These people moved to Spain in the eighth century, at the start of the Muslim settlement in that region. The Khaldūn family settled in the city of Seville, where they stayed until the thirteenth century when the Islamic empire in Spain started to decline. The family then moved to the region of northwest Africa known in the Arab world as Ifriqiyah (modern-day Tunisia and eastern Algeria).

Ibn Khaldūn received a good education as a youth, studying Arabic and the holy book of Islam, the Qur'an. He was also schooled in *fiqh,* or Islamic law; *hadith,* or the sayings and deeds of the Prophet **Muhammad** (c. 570–632; the founder of Islam; see entry); mathematics; logic; and philosophy. He read the works of famous Muslim scholars who had come before him, such as Ibn Sina and Ibn Rushd.

When he was seventeen, Ibn Khaldūn's parents died during an outbreak of the plague, a deadly infectious disease that struck Tunis. After his parents' deaths, he took a post in a government office in Tunis. His job was to write the introductory notes to official documents. Despite this opportunity to see for the first time the inner workings of government, Ibn Khaldūn longed to leave his hometown for other parts of the Muslim world. He was given the opportunity to do so when a rival ruler, the emir, or governor, of Constantine (a city in Algeria) invaded Tunis. Ibn Khaldūn left the city and headed for Fez, Morocco, in the section of North Africa known as the Maghrib, or modern-day Tunisia, Morocco, and Algeria. Fez had been the capital city of several dynasties, or ruling families, and reached its high point under the Merinid *sultans,* or rulers, in the mid-fourteenth century.

Ibn Khaldūn soon earned a position as a writer of royal proclamations (announcements) for the Merinid sultan, Abu Inan, but he felt that the job was not worthy of him. He spent more time attending lectures at the Islamic *madrassa,* or college, in the city, where great scholars from all over the Muslim world came to speak. At the same time, he was suspected of plotting against the sultan and was imprisoned for two years, until the death of Abu Inan. Ibn Khaldūn was released from prison in 1358 and made the secretary to the new sultan. He also became a judge in the Islamic court in Fez. Again, however, jealous new enemies arose, and Ibn Khaldūn decided to move to Spain, where his family had once lived.

Spain and Africa

During his time in Fez, Ibn Khaldūn had befriended the sultan of Granada, Spain, Nasrid Muhammad V, who had been exiled (forced to leave) from his homeland. Ibn Khaldūn had helped Nasrid to regain his position, so he knew he would be welcome in Granada. He found a post at court with the ruling family and by 1364 had become important enough to be sent as a representative of Granada to sign a peace treaty with the Christians they had been fighting. He traveled to Seville, the original home of his family, where he went to speak with the King of Castile (a region of central and northern Spain).

The king was known as Pedro the Cruel (1334–1369) because of his harsh treatment of the enemies he fought. Ibn Khaldūn was successful in securing a peace treaty between Pedro's people and Granada, and Pedro was so impressed with the Muslim scholar and official that he offered to return his family estates if Ibn Khaldūn would join his court. Ibn Khaldūn politely refused and returned to Granada. After his return, the sultan's main advisor became mistrustful and jealous of him, so Ibn Khaldūn left Spain.

He moved back to North Africa and settled in Bougie (modern-day Bejaia, Algeria), an important port and cultural center at the time. In Bougie Ibn Khaldūn encountered an old friend, Abu Abdallah, who had been in prison with him in Fez. Abu Abdallah was now the sultan, and he made Ibn Khaldūn his prime minister, or chief political administrator. In his new position Ibn Khaldūn gained the trust of many of the Berber tribes, the native people of northern Africa. These Berbers had become Muslims when Islam spread into North Africa, but they resisted Arab rule, maintaining their independence. Ibn Khaldūn managed to collect

Berbers

The subject of several volumes of Ibn Khaldūn's *Kitab al-ʿibar,* the Berbers are non-Arabic tribes native to North Africa, where they number about twenty million. Berbers are also found outside the African continent. There is a large concentration of Berbers in Morocco and Algeria, and an estimated one million in France.

The Berbers speak their own language, called Tamazight, in addition to the languages of the regions they inhabit. No one is sure where the Berbers originally lived, but they have been in North Africa as long as any records show. They are Caucasoid, or white, as opposed to the black Africans who live south of the Sahara Desert.

When Islamic armies came into North Africa in the seventh century CE, the Berbers, many of whom were Christian at the time, quickly converted to Islam. Berbers then joined the armies and helped spread Islam, particularly in Spain where they created two strong Muslim dynasties. The Almoravids ruled Morocco and Muslim Spain in the eleventh and twelfth centuries, and the Almohads ruled the same areas in the twelfth and thirteenth centuries.

After the fall of these dynasties, the Berbers who lived on the plains gradually became part of the mainstream Arab culture. Other Berber tribes refused to conform and migrated to mountainous areas such as the Atlas Mountains. They have maintained their traditions for centuries. In the early twenty-first century Berber and Arab relations continue to be tense at times in Morocco and Algeria.

taxes from them, which was a major accomplishment. Again, however, a change of leadership in Bougie forced Ibn Khaldūn to alter his political loyalties. He was growing increasingly tired of all these disruptions in his political career. He longed for peace and the ability to pursue scholarly intellectual goals.

The years at Qalat ibn Salama

Ibn Khaldūn found an opportunity for such scholarly pursuits while he was working for yet another prince in the region. He was sent on a mission to a tribe of nomadic Arabs, people who had no permanent homes but who instead traveled with their herds of animals in search of food and water. On this mission he was welcomed by a branch of the tribe and decided to accept the hospitality they offered. He and his family were invited to live at an isolated castle called Qalat ibn Salama. For the next four years Ibn Khaldūn lived in the castle and began a large study on the history of the world and the Arab people. This was a turning point in his life, and his focus shifted from the chaos of political involvement to the creation of the *Muqaddima.*

In this work Ibn Khaldūn developed his theory for the rise and fall of civilizations. He based his conclusions on the concept of *asabiyya,* or group feeling and group solidarity (togetherness). Asabiyya can be examined in nomads such as the Bedouin tribes. These Bedouin ("desert dwellers" in Arabic) are of the same racial and ethnic background as other Arabs and are strong believers in Islam. Their lifestyle, however, isolates them from most of the population. Group loyalty is all-important for them, as they rely on each other to survive in the desert. According to Ibn Khaldūn, civilization was an eternal conflict between the

"Bedouin" type and the city dweller, or the desert versus the town. For Ibn Khaldūn, the Bedouin type represented the principle of disorder and restlessness, while the city dweller represented the idea of orderly behavior. Civilization is always a battle between these two elemental forces, he believed.

Later in life, Ibn Khaldūn moved from Bougie to his native city of Tunis, in modern-day Tunisia. It was here that he concentrated on his writing and completed most of his work. © G. ROSSENBACH/ZEFA/ CORBIS.

Ibn Khaldūn believed group solidarity was what made the establishment of dynasties possible. The group, family, or tribe with the strongest sense of such solidarity takes control. This solidarity can be increased by a commonly held religion, as with Islam, or with common social or cultural characteristics. Then cooperation makes division of labor in the society possible, and different people take on different jobs. The labor creates goods and services beyond the daily need of each person. This in turn leads to more free time and the growth of intellectual pursuits such as the sciences, arts, and music.

Ibn Khaldūn, however, went on to say in the *Muqaddima* that the production of such luxuries also creates a situation that causes the destruction of group solidarity. Individuals break away from the group, some people become nonproductive or lazy, and the civilization begins to fall apart. Eventually the empire is taken over by another group, usually a less civilized one with more group solidarity and energy. Then the process begins again.

This theory made Ibn Khaldūn the focus of much attention, because it traces the importance of people, rather than events, in the creation of history. Furthermore, he looked at the organization of society with relation to politics; city life; and economics, or the production, distribution, and use of goods and services in a society. This analysis of the importance of economics in history was one of the first such examinations.

Final years

Ibn Khaldūn finally left the castle and returned to his native city of Tunis in 1378, where he could find more resources to complete the next six volumes of his *Kitab al-ʿibar.* While the *Muqaddima* served as an introduction to the entire work, the next volumes concentrated on world history and on the history of the Berbers. For this Ibn Khaldūn needed libraries where he could do research. In Tunis he stayed out of politics and concentrated on his writing. By 1382 he had completed most of the work, but his influence with the ruler and his popularity with students caused jealousies at court, which put him in danger.

He accepted the invitation of the Egyptian sultan Barquq to come and live in Cairo. For the first time in his life, Ibn Khaldūn experienced a stable Islamic state, ruled by the Mamluke dynasty (1250–1517), who were former slaves and soldiers. In Cairo Ibn Khaldūn found peace, a high level of culture, and economic wealth. He became a professor at one of the major Islamic colleges and was appointed the *qadi,* or judge of Islamic law, several different times during his fourteen years in the city. Yet his later years were also filled with sadness. His wife and daughters died in a shipwreck off Alexandria, Egypt, on their way to join him.

After the death of Barquq in 1401, the sultan's son, Faraj, came to power. Soon thereafter, there was an invasion of the Middle East by the Mongols, warriors from Central Asia, led by the great conqueror Timur (c. 1336–1405). Timur and his Mongol soldiers were marching to Damascus, Syria, and the Egyptians feared that the troops would also attack their country. Faraj took his army to help defend Damascus, and the sixty-nine-year-old Ibn Khaldūn accompanied him as a diplomat. Once in Damascus, however, Faraj received word of a planned revolt against him in Cairo and hurried home, leaving Ibn Khaldūn and a small group behind. When Timur and the Mongols arrived, Ibn Khaldūn acted as a negotiator between the people of Damascus and the Mongol warrior, gaining a favorable peace for the city. He stayed in Timur's camp for five weeks, conducting talks and taking notes on life among the Mongols. Once back in Cairo, he wrote a description of this experience.

The next five years of Ibn Khaldūn's life were relatively peaceful, as he served as a judge and worked on various scholarly projects. He died in Cairo on March 17, 1406. His works have remained relevant throughout the centuries, and his theories on history and society bear many similarities to those discussed by modern-day historians and sociologists.

For More Information

BOOKS

"Abd al-Rahman ibn Muhammad ibn Khaldun." In *Encyclopedia of World Biography*. Detroit, MI: Gale Research, 1998.

Enan, Mohammad A. *Ibn Khaldun: His Life and Works.* New Delhi, India: Kitab Bhavan, 1979.

Ibn Khaldun. *The Muqaddimah.* Translated by Franz Rosenthal. Edited and abridged by N. J. Dawood. Princeton, NJ: Princeton University Press, 1967.

Lacoste, Yves. *Ibn Khaldun: The Birth of History and the Past of the Third World.* Translated by David Macy. London, England: Verso, 1984.

Lewis, Bernard. *The Arabs in History.* New York, NY: Oxford University Press, 2002.

WEB SITES

Hozien, Muhammad. "Ibn Khaldun: His Life and Work." *MuslimPhilosophy.com.* http://www.muslimphilosophy.com/ik/klf.htm (accessed on June 2, 2006).

"Ibn Khaldun (1332–1406)." *Religion & Liberty.* Acton Institute. http://www.acton.org/publicat/randl/liberal.php?id=197 (June 2, 2006).

Talbi, M. "Ibn Khaldun." *Encyclopedia of Islam Online.* http://www.muslimphilosophy.com/ei/KHALDUN.htm (accessed on June 2, 2006).

Israel ben Eliezer

BORN: August 27, c. 1700 • Okop, Poland

DIED: May 22, 1760 • Medzhibozh, Poland

Polish religious leader

"There is no act, word or thought in which the essence of divinity is not constricted and hiding. And so when you look and see with your mind's eye...You will see nothing but the divine power inside all things that is giving them life, being and existence at every moment."

Israel ben Eliezer gave new energy to Judaism in eastern Europe in the eighteenth century by reconnecting the common people to the religion. He was the founder of Hasidism, a Jewish mystical movement that emphasizes a direct connection to God through prayer and joyous experiences such as participation in the arts. For ben Eliezer, also known as Baal Shem Tov ("Master of the Good Name"), a pure heart was more pleasing to God than a great intellect. He taught that all Jews could grow closer to God by a constant focus on Him during a person's everyday life, rather than through studying the Torah, which is the body of Jewish literature and law.

For ben Eliezer, simple and sincere religious devotion was the true path to God. This meant that the unschooled as well as the intellectual could experience God and redemption, or the forgiveness of sins. This earned him a large following in central and eastern Europe, and ben Eliezer became one of the most influential spiritual leaders of the period.

He also became the subject of many tales and legends, which makes it difficult to separate the facts of his life from the fiction.

Early years

Tradition has it that Israel ben Eliezer was born in the village of Okop (also called Okopy) in the region of Podolia, long a part of Ukraine. At the time of ben Eliezer's birth, in 1700, this area was in the process of being returned to Poland after a lengthy Turkish occupation. Due to this, opinions differ as to the nationality of ben Eliezer. Most sources call him Polish, though some list him as being of Ukrainian heritage.

Confusion also exists about his family. Most sources agree that his parents, Eliezer and Sarah, were quite old when they had Israel. Some historians, however, say that his father was a rabbi (a person trained in Jewish law, ritual, and tradition), while others claim that the family, while very religious, was a poor one. Ben Eliezer was still a young child when his father died, but he was old enough to understand Eliezer's dying words, which were either "Israel my son, you have a very holy soul, don't fear anything but God," or "Fear nothing because God will take care of all." Soon after, his mother also passed away, and young ben Eliezer was put into the care of the community. This was a typical practice in the Jewish communities of Poland at the time.

Podolia, and the entire region of the Polish Ukraine, was an area that had been dominated by Judaism since the Middle Ages (c. 500–c. 1500). In the two centuries before ben Eliezer's birth, the Jewish population grew from only fifty thousand in 1500 to about five hundred thousand in 1650. The Jewish communities in the region enjoyed a degree of self-government and freedom from the rest of Christian Poland and Ukraine. Beginning in 1648, however, pogroms, or massacres of Jews, were carried out by the Christians of Poland and Russia. These pogroms were organized by the government of Russia in an attempt to channel the political discontent felt by the workers in the region away from the *tsars* (rulers) and onto the Jews, whose unfamiliar religious practices made many uneasy. More than one hundred thousand Jews were killed during the next half century, and more than seven hundred communities were destroyed. Those who survived were taxed highly by the Christian authorities and were threatened by attacks from wandering bandits unless they could pay to win their freedom.

As a result, Judaism in Podolia was on the decline at the time of ben Eliezer's birth. The intellectual community of scholars and Talmudic teachers (teachers of the Talmud, a collection of holy writings about the Jewish faith) had fled to Lithuania, leaving the lower classes and poorer Jews with no access to the scholarly pursuits of Judaism. Also, while Jews in other regions lived in thickly settled urban areas close to centers of Jewish learning and teaching, the Jews of Poland and Ukraine tended to live in scattered villages away from intellectual centers. A class division emerged in Poland, with the wealthier Jews and Talmudic scholars leading the communities but not contributing their fair share of the community taxes. This put a financial burden on the poorer Jews. Because this practice was not criticized by the rabbis, the common people began to distrust the established leaders of Judaism in the region.

This conflict led to many unusual religious practices in Poland and Ukraine. Some Jewish commoners and peasants turned to the Kabbalah, a mystical movement in Judaism developed during the Middle Ages. This tradition claimed to have come from the prophet **Abraham** (c. 2050–c. 1950 BCE; see entry) and provided a secret interpretation of the scriptures or holy books. Others were misled by mystics claiming to be prophets (people through whom the will of God is expressed), saviors, and miracle workers.

This was the cultural and historical backdrop of the region into which ben Eliezer was born and came of age. After being adopted by the community, he was educated in the village Jewish school. He learned to read Hebrew by age four, translated the Bible by age five, and began a serious study of the Talmud by age eight. As a student, ben Eliezer seems to have drawn attention to himself only because of his frequent absences from school. He was much more comfortable in the woods and fields surrounding Okop than he was in the classroom. At an early age, he began to see God in nature, not just in the teachings of the Torah (the first five books of the Hebrew scriptures) and the Talmud.

When he entered his teenage years, ben Eliezer was no longer considered a dependent of the community, and it was time for him to decide on a course for his life. His teachers felt it was obvious from his lack of interest in his studies that he would never become a rabbi, so he was hired as an assistant at the school. His duties included taking the children to and from school, and teaching them songs and prayers. He loved to tell the children parables, or stories that had a moral lesson to them. Later he became a caretaker at a local synagogue, or Jewish building of worship, where his chores included cleaning and keeping the books in order. This position gave him plenty of time for independent study, which he used to examine the writings of the Kabbalah and to educate himself in Jewish law. This study was done in secrecy, however, and the people of his village continued to think of him as a simple young man.

Ben Eliezer married at age eighteen, but his wife died not long after the ceremony. He then left Okop, traveling and working throughout the region of Galicia before settling in a village near the city of Brody. In Brody he worked as an assistant in the school and also as a mediator, or negotiator, between people with legal disputes. As a result of his efforts as a mediator, he came to the attention of Rabbi Ephraim of Brody, who was so impressed by ben Eliezer's intelligence and honesty that he promised him his daughter, Hannah, as his bride. Unfortunately, Ephriam died before the marriage could took place, and his son, Hannah's brother, was against the marriage, viewing ben Eliezer as a rough and uncultured peasant. Hannah, however, was in love with ben Eliezer, and the two eventually did marry and moved to a village in the Carpathian Mountains, far from Brody. Here ben Eliezer began working as a manual laborer, digging clay and lime.

Becomes Baal Shem Tov

Ben Eliezer's time in the Carpathians was spent in further mystical speculation and in an exploration of the woods and forests of the area. He became an expert on the plant life of the region and learned the use of herbal medicines for illnesses. Eventually ben Eliezer left his job as a laborer and become a butcher. He and Hannah, with whom he had two children by this time, also ran an inn or tavern. Soon ben Eliezer became a *baal shem,* or a healer that used medicinal herbs, and served Jews and Christians alike. He also began performing ceremonies to drive out ghosts and demons. He was said to have an angel, Achiyah HaShaloni, who taught him the mysteries of the Torah and helped him cure the bodies and souls of his patients. His fame began to spread, and ben Eliezer became known as Baal Shem Tov, with *tov,* meaning "good," added to the title to separate him from all other healers. He was also sometimes known as Besht, a name made up of the first letters of his honorary name.

At about age thirty-six ben Eliezer underwent a profound spiritual experience and began to formulate the basic principles of the movement that became known as Hasidism or Chasidism ("the pious"). These principles were a direct communion with God, a belief that even the simplest

Men dance at a Hasidic wedding. Israel ben Eliezer taught that singing and dancing to God's prayers was positive and healthy. © TED SPIEGEL/CORBIS.

human action could serve God, and a constant search for hints of godliness in the material world. He preached that salvation and redemption could be achieved through other means than an intense study of the Jewish religious texts. Ben Eliezer believed that God was present in everything, and therefore each human had God within him and was good. Sins and misdeeds were the result of error, not evil.

Another of ben Eliezer's lessons claimed that the common practice of asceticism, or the attainment of higher spiritual development through self-denial and self-punishment, was not favored by God. Instead ben Eliezer taught that God preferred joy to sadness or weeping. He added dancing and singing to his prayers and emphasized the importance of maintaining a healthy body. He said God's presence was in all surroundings and a person should serve God with their every deed and word. Ben Eliezer began to share these ideas with others, conveying his message in short tales and parables, just as he had with the schoolchildren he once taught. His message was welcomed by the common folk among the Jews of Poland. To aid these people in their religious lives, he added a new functionary, or official, in Judaism, the *Tzaddick*. This translates to "the righteous." This person had a highly developed spiritual awareness and could serve as a leader in the Hasidic movement.

Ben Eliezer was fond of saying that everything he accomplished was through prayer rather than study. He did not use prayer to ask for special requests, but simply to communicate with God and to feel as if he were one with Him. Ben Eliezer believed that this oneness, when a person gave up his separate existence and joined to God, created real joy and was the foundation of any true worship.

These beliefs won ben Eliezer followers but also earned him criticism and fierce attacks from many sides. The rabbis and Talmudic scholars found his encouragement of dancing and drinking to be unholy and against tradition, and they thought his lack of emphasis on scholarship posed a threat to the intellectual aspect of Judaism. However, although ben Eliezer taught that study of the Torah was not the only way to

Hasidism in the United States

Though Hasidism has spread throughout the world, some 200,000 of its estimated 250,000 followers live in the United States. Half of these reside in the state of New York, and most live in the Brooklyn neighborhoods of Crown Heights, Williamsburg, and Boro Park. Several branches of Hasidism are represented, one of which is the Lubavitch Hasidism. Crown Heights is the central location of this group, which has about fifteen thousand members. Another branch, Satmar, holds strongly to traditional beliefs, and there is a degree of friction between the two, especially over issues concerning the causes of World War II and differing views on the state of Israel.

While the Holocaust in Poland was the main reason that Hasidic Jews left that area, there were already congregations in the United States long before that time. In 1875 Rabbi Joshua Segal, also called the "Sherpser Rov," came to New York City. He soon became the leader of about twenty Hasidic congregations, known as the Congregations of Israel, Men of Poland and Austria. By the 1960s the number of Hasidic Jews in the state had grown to between forty and fifty thousand. Forty years later this amount had doubled. Such growth was due partly to immigration and partly to the high birthrate among the Jews in New York, who averaged five or six children per family.

become close to God, he never preached that such study was unimportant or unnecessary.

The final years

In 1740 ben Eliezer moved to the town of Medzhibozh, in Podolia. He lived in Medzhibozh for the rest of his life, spreading the word of Hasidism and continuing to work as a healer. He attracted new followers, including Rabbi Joseph, Rabbi Dov Baer of Merzeritz, and Rabbi Pinchas, all of whom helped to spread Hasidism after the death of ben Eliezer. Some of his followers, such as Baer of Merzeritz, were Talmudists, proving that ben Eliezer's teachings also reached intellectuals and scholars, not just common folk. He personally instructed visiting lay people (non-clergy members) and rabbis in the teachings of Hasidism.

Ben Eliezer died in 1760, shortly after falling ill on his way to a religious debate. The Hasidic movement continued to grow after his death, and his followers published many of his sayings and teachings in their works. One well-known example of this is *Shivhei ha-Besht* (In Praise of the Baal Shem Tov) a collection published in 1815 that contains more than two hundred legends and stories about ben Eliezer.

Israel ben Eliezer gave new life to Judaism in Poland with his popular teachings. For two hundred years after his death, the Hasidic community in Poland continued to grow and prosper. As a result of the Holocaust, the mass slaughter of millions of Jews by the German government during World War II (1939–45; a war in which Great Britain, France, the United States, and their allies defeated Germany, Italy, and Japan), Hasidic communities were transplanted around the world, with many relocating to Brooklyn, New York. A large and vital Hasidic community still functioned there in the early twenty-first century.

For More Information

BOOKS

Ben-Amos, Dan, and J. R. Mintz, eds. *In Praise of the Baal Shem Tov (Shivhei Ha-Besht): The Earliest Collection of Legends about the Founder of Hasidism.* Northvale, NJ: Jason Aronson Publishers, 1996.

Buber, Martin. *The Legend of the Baal-Shem.* Translated by Maurice Friedman. Princeton, NJ: Princeton University Press, 1995.

Herschel, Abraham Joshua. *A Passion for Truth.* Woodstock, VT: Jewish Lights Publishing, 1995.

Klein, Eliahu. *Meetings with Remarkable Souls: Legends of the Baal Shem Tov.* Northvale, NJ: Jason Aronson Publishers, 1995.

Rosman, Murray Jay. *Founder of Hasidism: A Quest for the Historical Baal Shem Tov.* Berkeley, CA: University of California Press, 1996.

PERIODICALS

Aberbach, David. "Mystical Union and Grief: The Ba'al Shem Tov and Krishnamurti." *Harvard Theological Review* (July 1993): 309.

WEB SITES

"The Ba'al Shem Tov." *OU.org.* http://ou.org/about/judaism/rabbis/baalshem.htm (accessed on May 25, 2006).

"Hasidism." *Religious Movements Homepage.* http://religiousmovements.lib.virginia.edu/nrms/hasid.html/ (accessed on May 25, 2006).

"Rabbi Yisrael Baal Shem Tov 1698–1760." *Jewish Virtual Library.* http://www.jewishvirtuallibrary.org/jsource/biography/baal.html (accessed on May 25, 2006).

Shulman, Yaacov Dovid, translator. "The Ten Principles of Baal Shem Tov." *Baal Shem Tov Foundation.* http://www.baalshemtov.com/ten-principals.htm (accessed on May 25, 2006).

Jalāl ad-Dīn ar-Rūmī

BORN: September 30, 1207 • Balkh, Persia

DIED: December 17, 1273 • Konya, Turkey

Persian poet; jurist; theologian

"The Prophet cried with a loud voice, 'Trust in God, yet tie the camel's leg.' . . . / If ye really have trust in God, exert yourselves,/ And strive, in constant reliance on the Almighty."

Jalāl ad-Dīn ar-Rūmī was a thirteenth-century mystic poet and a member of the Sufi sect, or division, of Islam. His name is sometimes given as Jalāl ad-Dīn ar-Rūmī. He is often referred to as *Mawlvi* in Arabic, *Mawlana* in Persian, or *Mevlana* in Turkish. All of these titles mean "our lord" or "our guide." Jalāl is widely regarded as the greatest poet to have written in the Persian language, the language of ancient Persia and modern-day Iran. In the late twentieth and early twenty-first centuries his poetry became widely popular in the West (the countries in Europe and the Americas). His name is also associated with the Whirling Dervishes. This name describes mystical Sufi Muslims called *Mawlawiyah,* who are noted for their joyful dances as they chant the many names of Allah, as God is called by Muslims.

Jalāl ad-Dīn ar-Rūmī
INSTITUTE OF ISLAMIC CULTURE. REPRODUCED BY PERMISSION.

Birth and early life

Jalāl was born on or about September 30, 1207, in the town of Balkh, a section of the Ghurid empire which later became part of Afghanistan.

His father, Baha ad-Din Walad, was a highly respected teacher, author, and theologian, or religious expert, whose work had strong mystical themes. ("Mysticism" has many meanings and is often associated with magic. In a religious sense, it generally refers to the notion of direct, mysterious communication with God.) Early in the thirteenth century, forces from Mongolia were invading Central Asia. Baha ad-Din recognized the threat they posed, so in about 1218 he left Balkh with his family and moved to Persia. Legend says that in the town of Nishapur, Persia, the family met a Persian mystical author named Farid od-Din Attar (c. 1142–c. 1220), who gave the eighteen-year-old Jalāl his blessing. This meeting with Attar made a deep impression on Jalāl, and when he began writing poetry himself, he thought of Attar as one of the people who inspired him.

The family continued its travels, careful to avoid both the Mongols to the east and the Christian Crusaders in Palestine to the west. (The Crusaders were soldiers who were attempting to bring the Holy Land of Palestine under Christian control.) They journeyed throughout the Middle East and made a pilgrimage to Mecca, the holiest city of Islam and the birthplace of the religion's founder, the prophet **Muhammad** (c. 570–632; see entry). Mecca is located in modern-day Saudi Arabia. The family then arrived in Anatolia, a part of modern-day Turkey also known as Asia Minor. In 1228 they moved to the capital, Konya, where Baha ad-Din secured a job teaching at a religious school. Jalāl was sent to the Syrian cities of Damascus and Aleppo for his religious education. After Baha ad-Din died in 1231, Jalāl took over his father's teaching position. He was twenty-four years old at the time, and he had already gained a favorable reputation for his scholarly, or intellectual, understanding of Islam.

Jalāl had engaged in years of study, but he had become displeased with the customary teachings about Allah and religion. He found the standard texts inadequate. He had come to believe that traditional Islam was placing too much emphasis on fine points of doctrine, or principle. In his view this method of worship was dry and without deep meaning. He was eager for something that would help him have a more intense relationship with Allah, and he did not believe that he would find that relationship in the accepted texts with their emphasis on law and tradition. In an attempt to achieve his goal Jalāl made contact with a number of well-known mystical teachers. In 1232 one of Baha ad-Din's earlier followers, Burhan ad-Din Muhaqqiq, came to Konya. He shared with Rumi the mystical theories he had developed in Persia. Burhan ad-Din left Konya in 1240, prompting Jalāl to journey to Syria. There he met other Sufi mystics, including Ibn al-Arabi and his stepson, Sadr ad-Din al-Qunawi, who became Jalāl's lifelong friend.

On November 30, 1244, Jalāl met a ragged, wandering dervish, or holy man, named Shams (sometimes spelled Shems) ad-Din. In Shams, Jalāl realized he had found what he had been looking for: a person with mystical knowledge of the beauty and greatness of Allah. The two immediately established a very close relationship. Jalāl lived with Shams and neglected his followers and his family. Jalāl's followers became so jealous of Shams that they forced the dervish to leave the city in early 1246.

Jalāl became so broken-hearted at the loss of his friend that his son, Walad, traveled to Syria to bring Shams back. The jealousy of both the family and the community, however, continued to grow, and one night Shams disappeared. For many years the source of this disappearance was a mystery. Some believed that Shams had simply left again, probably for Syria. Others believed that some of Jalāl's followers murdered Shams. Some even claimed that Jalāl's own sons murdered him. Only recently has it been proven that Shams was indeed murdered and buried near a well that still exists in Konya. Who was responsible for his death remains uncertain.

Sufi Islam

Sufism is often referred to as a sect, or subgroup, of Islam. This is only partially true. Sufism is less a sect than a way of approaching Islam. Members of the two main branches of Islam, the Sunnis and the Shi'ites, can also be Sufis. Sufism is the esoteric division of Islam, meaning that its members believe in mystical knowledge held by a small, restricted circle of people. Sufis can be recognized by their characteristic long robes and the wound turbans on their heads.

Sufism emerged during Islam's early years in the seventh and eighth centuries, when the religion was expanding and wealth was flowing into the Islamic empire throughout the Middle East. The Sufis believed that Islam placed too much emphasis on worldly concerns, rituals, and laws. They wanted a form of religion that led to inner ecstasy, or intense emotion and communion with Allah. Sufis believe that a devoted Muslim can experience Allah only through consistent chanting, meditation (focused and concentrated thought), love for other people, self-discipline, and self-denial. They also believe that the way to achieve spiritual wealth is through owning few material goods. Excessive worldly possessions, they believe, can corrupt the soul. Sufis are well known for their charitable work. They practice patience, a total reliance on Allah's knowledge of the future, and thankfulness to Allah.

Mystical poet

Jalāl was grief-stricken. His sense of loss and mourning served as the spark that turned him into a poet. He identified himself so strongly with Shams that he even signed Shams's name at the end of most of his early poems. Many scholars believe that Jalāl composed most of these and later poems while in a state of mystical ecstasy, or intense joy or delight. They suggest that Jalāl wrote while listening to the sound of drums or flutes, or to the sound of a watermill, or even while just enjoying nature with his friends and followers. He often chanted his verses while taking part in the "whirling" dances of the Sufi mystics who came to be known as the Whirling Dervishes.

In the years that followed, Jalāl had relationships with other men similar to that which he had with Shams. One of these men was a goldsmith named Salah ad-Din Zarkub, whose daughter eventually married Jalāl's eldest son. His relationship with Salah ad-Din encouraged him to continue writing poetry. Legend holds that Jalāl would hear the sound of Salah ad-Din's hammer and begin his whirling dance on the street outside, chanting his verses as he did so. After Salah ad-Din died, Jalāl found another spiritual companion in Husan ad-Din Chelebi. Husan ad-Din inspired Jalāl to write his most famous work, the *Masnavi-ye Ma'anavi,* often called simply the *Masnavi* or *Mathnawa.*

The *Masnavi* was written over a long period of time. It is said that Jalāl wrote the verses in it on any and all occasions, such as when he was taking a bath or just walking down a road. He was always accompanied by Husan ad-Din, who wrote the verses down. Jalāl probably completed the work sometime around 1270. In the meantime he had become a respected member of Konya society. Many students, teachers, and even Christian priests visited him, both to pay their respects and to learn what they could about Sufi mysticism.

Jalāl died on December 17, 1273. He was so well known and respected that representatives of all the religions in the city attended his funeral. Rumi is buried in a mausoleum (a building that contains burial sites) called the Green Dome in Konya. The mausoleum is also a museum and is visited by thousands of people each year. Jalāl's son, Walad, organized Jalāl's followers into the *Mawlawiyah,* part of the Whirling Dervishes. Thus, although Jalāl did not create the Whirling Dervishes (who could be found in Baghdad, Iraq, at least one century before he lived), his name and teachings are associated with the group, which became a specific sect shortly after his death.

Jalāl's works

Jalāl's earliest work was titled *Diwan-e Shams-e Tabriz-i* (The Works of Shams of Tabriz). This was a collection of about forty thousand verses named in honor of Jalāl's companion and spiritual inspiration, Shams. The poems in this collection were written primarily in the voice of Shams. Many of the poems are odes, which are a form of poetry marked by intense feeling and emotion. Some read almost like love poems to

Allah, but many readers believe that they were written as much in honor of Shams as they were to Allah.

Jalāl's major work is the *Masnavi* (Spiritual Couplets). (A couplet is a two-line poetic verse.) Written in three volumes, the book contains more than twenty-five thousand lines of poetry. It includes folktales, fables, philosophy, lyrical poetry, and parables, which are simple stories that illustrate moral or religious lessons. The book's subjects include the saints of Islam, commentaries on the Qur'an (the sacred text of Islam), and mystical interpretations of a large number of subjects, both religious and nonreligious. The *Masnavi* is the most widely read poem among Muslims. In fact, among Muslim texts, it is regarded by some as second in importance only to the Qur'an. It is sometimes even called the *Qur'an-e Farsi* (The Qur'an in Persian).

The *Fihi Ma Fih* is a collection of Jalāl's speeches. They were written down and collected by his son, Wahad. The *Majalis-i Sab-a* is a collection of seven of Jalāl's sermons.

A man prays in the Rumi Mevlana Mausoleum in Konya, Turkey. The mausoleum houses Jalāl's body. Also on the grounds are a mosque, dance hall, living quarters and school. It is a popular site for Muslim pilgrims and others.

The chief theme that runs throughout Jalāl's work, especially his poetry, is *tawhid,* meaning "unity." The unity he sought was a mystical unity with Allah and with all of Allah's creations. The poetry is dominated by a sense of longing for a complete love for and from Allah. Jalāl believed this love was at the center of everything, from the smallest details of life to the most complex philosophical theories. Much of the poetry has a double meaning. Jalāl's words could apply to his intense feelings for Shams and his other companions, but they also relate to his love of Allah.

One of the reasons Jalāl's poetry became and has remained so popular is that it does not deal with doctrine, or formal teachings. Jalāl, like most Muslims, believed in the truth of the Qur'an, but he had little interest in disputes about its meaning or which of its laws Muslims should follow. Many readers enjoy his poetry because it makes use of numerous simple, easy-to-understand symbols. He often used images of wine and taverns, for example, to suggest that life is like a big feast at which people celebrate out of sheer joy. He spoke of drunkenness to suggest how people might feel when they experience closeness with Allah. Other simple symbols Jalāl used include the nightingale, which represents the soul; the sun, which represents teaching and enlightenment; and winter, which suggests a soul that is somehow cut off from Allah and the joy of Allah's creations.

A representative sample of Jalāl poetry can come from virtually any page of his works. In the *Diwan-e Shams-e Tabriz-i,* he wrote an untitled ode about death. The theme of the poem, reproduced on *Poetseers.org,* is that death is not something to be feared or regretted, for it represents a unity with Allah, a "coming together." While death may look like a prison, it is really a release that allows one to experience the beauty of Allah.

> On the day I die, when I'm being
> carried toward the grave, don't weep.
>
> Don't say, "He's gone! He's gone!"
> Death has nothing to do with going away.
>
> The sun sets and the moon sets,
> but they're not gone. Death
> is a coming together.
>
> The tomb looks like a prison,
> but it's really release into Union.
>
> The human seed goes down in the ground
> like a bucket into the well where Joseph is.
>
> It grows and comes up full
> of some unimagined beauty.
>
> Your mouth closes here
> and immediately opens
> with a shout of joy there.

The Jalāl's "industry"

Jalāl and his poetry became somewhat of a commercial enterprise in the West in the late twentieth and early twenty-first centuries. Many western readers found meaning in Jalāl's poetry because of its simplicity and its efforts to find a direct connection with God. In 1995 a major publisher in the United States released a collection of his verse under the title *The*

Essential Rumi, and the book sold about 250,000 copies. Publishers regard this as an amazingly large number for a book of poetry, which tend to be published by smaller companies and academic presses. A later collection, titled *The Soul of Rumi,* also became very popular with English-speaking readers.

The Sufi mystic also became popular outside of the publishing world. Singer Madonna (1958–) set Jalāl's poetry to music on a 1998 compact disc. Fashion designer Donna Karan (1948–) included recitations of Jalāl's poetry in some of her fashion shows, and film director Oliver Stone (1946–) talked about making a film of Jalāl's life. People can buy all manner of Jalāl products, including prayer books, collections of his verse around various themes, and calendars. Illustrated editions of his poems are also available, and oral readings can be found on compact discs.

For More Information

BOOKS

Barks, Coleman, trans. *The Essential Rumi.* San Francisco, CA: HarperCollins-SanFrancisco, 1995.

Barks, Coleman, trans. *The Soul of Rumi.* San Francisco, CA: HarperSanFrancisco, 2002.

Salam, Muhammad Nur Abdus. *Rumi: Stories for Young Adults.* Chicago, IL: Kazi Publications, 2000.

WEB SITES

"About Mawlana Jalaluddin Rumi." *Dar Al Masnavi.* http://www.dar-al-masnavi.org/about-rumi.html (accessed on June 2, 2006).

"Life of Rumi." http://www.khamush.com/life.html (accessed on June 2, 2006).

Rumi. "Ode 911." Translated by Coleman Banks. *Poet Seers.* http://www.poetseers.org/the_poetseers/rumi/odes_of_rumi/7/ (accessed on June 2, 2006).

Jesus Christ

BORN: c. 6 BCE • Bethlehem, Judea

DIED: c. 30 CE • Jerusalem, Judea

religious leader

Jesus Christ.

"Father, forgive them; for they know not what they do."

Jesus Christ, originally known as Jesus of Nazareth, is the founder of Christianity and the central figure in the early writings of the religion. A Jewish healer, spiritual guide, and teacher who lived during the first century CE, Jesus is both a historical figure and a member of the Christian divine triumvirate (group of three, or Trinity). He is considered the Son of God, sent to Earth to atone, or make amends for, the sins of humanity. God and the Holy Spirit complete the Trinity.

Born approximately 6 BCE, Jesus died around the age of thirty-three after preaching for only three years. In that time, he gathered twelve followers, who were known as his disciples, and attracted the attention of much of the population in his home region of Palestine. In addition to preaching about universal love and everlasting life, Christians believe Jesus performed many miracles during his lifetime. Ultimately, he was crucified, or killed by being nailed to a cross, by the Romans, who occupied Palestine and were afraid of the power Jesus was gaining over the population. Three days after his death, Jesus was said to have risen from the dead and later he returned to heaven. His disciples spread the word about his life and miraculous resurrection. These teachings formed the core of the Christian religion, which would become the largest in the world. The life of Jesus was recorded in the Gospels ("good news"), or books, of Matthew, Mark, Luke, and John in the New Testament. The New Testament is the second half of the Bible, the primary sacred text of Christianity. The first half of the Bible is referred to by Christians as the Old Testament. To Jews (followers of Judaism), it is known as the Tanakh and may be referred to by non-Jews as the Hebrew Bible.

Historical Jesus

Despite his importance in Western religious history, Jesus is largely a mystery. The majority of his life is unrecorded, and much of the reality of his ministry and work became clouded by the myths that arose after his death. The main points of his life are detailed in the first four Gospels of the New Testament, but as these accounts concentrate more on his teachings than his personal activities, they reveal little about the actual man he was. Although thousands of authors have written about Jesus, broad areas of disagreement persist. Some focus on the miracles he supposedly performed, while others deny he possessed any supernatural powers and emphasize his message of love. Some call him a pacifist, or a person who believes disputes should be settled peacefully. Others see the attitude of a warrior in his words, such as in Matthew chapter 10, verse 34 (10:34): "Think not that I am come to send peace on earth; I am come not to send peace, but a sword." Indeed, in the words recorded in the Gospels, Jesus often seems to contradict himself, making the job of a biographer even more difficult.

Jesus lived during an era of political unrest. Palestine, which was supposedly the Promised Land that God had given to the children of Israel, had been invaded by the Greeks and then by the Romans. In 63 BCE the Romans made certain areas of Palestine, such as Judea and Galilee, semi-independent kingdoms whose rulers answered to Rome. By the time Jesus was an adolescent, however, the entire region had become a province of Rome and had lost all its independence. The Jewish people of Palestine, however, often rebelled against Roman rule.

From the activities of shepherds recorded in the Gospels, Jesus would appear to have been born in the spring or summer. The birth date of December 25 is widely accepted to be a later invention by his followers, who wanted to blend his birthday with the much older festival of the winter solstice, the shortest day of the year, because that festival was already widely celebrated. The estimated year of his birth did, however, establish the

Western calendar system. Dating began with AD 1, where AD stands for *anno Domini,* which is Latin for "in the year of the Lord." Dates before Jesus's birth were labeled BC, or "before Christ." These designations have since been widely replaced by the more academic terms CE, meaning "Common Era," and BCE, meaning "Before the Common Era."

According to the Gospels, Jesus was born in Bethlehem, to Mary, a virgin (someone who had never had sexual relations). She was engaged to a much older man, Joseph, who was supposedly related to David, the second king of Israel. Joseph and Mary had gone to Bethlehem because it was Joseph's native town and he needed to be present for a Roman census (count of the population). Upon arriving in the town, Joseph and Mary discovered that there were no rooms to be rented, so they stayed in the stable behind the inn. There, Mary gave birth to Jesus. Signs announced his arrival. Over Bethlehem, the Star of David rose, while an angel appeared to shepherds nearby to tell them that the savior had been born. Magi, or wise men, from the East were also guided to the stable by a star.

The Old Testament refers in many places to a messiah, a savior who would come to help the Jews in difficult times. At the time of Jesus's birth, the ruler of Judea was Herod Agrippa I (c. 10 BCE–44 CE). Herod feared the coming of the messiah, thinking that this would cause unrest among the people he ruled. When word reached him that the savior had arrived, he ordered that all male children under the age of two in Bethlehem should be killed. When he heard of this order, Joseph left with Mary and the baby Jesus for Egypt, where they remained until Herod's death. Afterwards they returned to Palestine, to the town of Nazareth.

Joseph and Mary had a large family. In addition to Jesus, they had at least two daughters and four other sons. Some Christian scholars claim that these other children were cousins, or perhaps Joseph's children from another marriage, and that Mary remained a virgin all her life. As a youth Jesus studied the Jewish scriptures, or holy writings. Little else is known of his childhood, aside from one event. When he was twelve, he accompanied his parents to Jerusalem for Passover, an important weeklong Jewish festival held in the spring. This was perhaps the first time that Jesus had made such a long journey (excluding those made in his infancy) or that he had visited such a large city. After the celebration, Joseph and Mary left for home, only to discover that Jesus was not with them. Hurrying back to Jerusalem, they found their son in the temple, listening to and discussing religious matters with the Jewish scholars.

The Virgin Mary

Mary, the mother of Jesus of Nazareth, has become one of the major figures of the Christian Church. The Mary cult, a smaller group within Christianity that places special focus Mary, has been strong for two thousand years. Also known as Mariam or Miriam, Mary is "the most celebrated female religious figure in the Christian tradition," according to historian Elizabeth A. Johnson, writing in *U.S. Catholic.* Little is known about this famed woman, however. What stories have been preserved are found mostly in the Bible's Gospels, as are the events of the life of her son, Jesus.

Mary is believed to have been born around 22 BCE, and the year of her death is unknown. Tradition holds that she was the child of Saint Joachim and Saint Anne and that she was conceived without Original Sin. (Original Sin refers to the sin of Adam and Eve, who disobeyed God's order and ate from the Tree of the Knowledge of Good and Evil in the Garden of Eden; it is the notion that all humans are born sinners.) Mary's birth without this Original Sin is called the Immaculate Conception. Because of her own Immaculate Conception, Mary was able to give birth to a pure Son of God, without sin, while also remaining a virgin. She is often referred to as the Virgin Mary or the Blessed Virgin. As a young woman Mary was engaged to Joseph, a carpenter. During this time she was visited by the angel Gabriel, who told her not to be afraid, for a son would be conceived by her who would be the Son of God. When Joseph discovered that his future wife was already pregnant, he decided to dissolve the engagement. He was then visited in his sleep by an angel and told to wed Mary.

Mary plays a major role in a number of events in the New Testament, including Jesus's birth; the time when Jesus went missing for several days at age twelve; the marriage in the town of Cana when Jesus turned water into wine; her son's Crucifixion, when she remained by his side; her visit to Christ's tomb after his Resurrection; and Pentecost, the seventh Sunday after Easter, when the Holy Spirit descended upon the twelve apostles. A tradition arose in the fifth century CE that Mary was taken, or assumed, directly into Heaven after her death, still a virgin. This event came to be celebrated on August 15 as the Assumption.

Catholic tradition holds that Mary remained a virgin throughout her life. This had led to much speculation by scholars about not only the miraculous birth of Jesus but also those of his brothers and sisters. In 1854 the Roman Catholic Church made the Immaculate Conception an article of faith, while in 1950 Pope Pius XII announced that Mary's body had not decayed in her grave. Instead, he claimed, God had taken both her body and her soul directly to heaven.

Tradition holds that Joseph was a carpenter, and that Jesus adopted the same trade. Upon Joseph's death, Jesus assumed the role of supporting his family. Some accounts also hold that Jesus became a self-taught rabbi, or Jewish religious scholar and teacher, and devoted hours each day to study.

Becomes a healer and preacher

At about the age of thirty, Jesus encountered the prophet and preacher John the Baptist, who told people to repent for their sins and be baptized, or cleansed spiritually by immersion or dunking in water. Jesus was among the crowd who came to John at the Jordan River, and he was baptized. At this point, Jesus is said to have heard a voice from heaven telling him that he was the Son of God. He went into the desert, fasting (not eating) and meditating (thinking deeply) for forty days. During this period the devil is said to have tried to convince Jesus to worship him, but Jesus resisted.

Upon his return, he discovered that John the Baptist had been arrested, so he took up John's work, preaching repentance and the coming of the kingdom of God. Initially he preached near Nazareth, but he attracted few followers as people there had known him since he was a boy. He moved to different locations in Palestine and soon found followers among fishermen and common workers. In time he gathered twelve disciples, whom he personally educated. These disciples also claimed Jesus was the Messiah, and he was given the title of Christ, which came from the Greek word *christos. Christos,* like the word *messiah,* means "anointed one."

Jesus and his disciples established a headquarters in the town of Capernaum, on the Sea of Galilee, and from there went out to advocate love and forgiveness. Jesus taught by using parables, or stories with moral lessons. Accounts claim that he healed the sick, restored the ability to walk to the lame, and cured those with the dreaded skin disease of leprosy. Jesus had no intention of becoming the warrior messiah of Jewish tradition. He did not want to gather armies around him and defeat the Romans. Rather, he wanted to improve society by changing the ways individuals dealt with one another and establishing a community built on love and trust.

Before long, the radical preachings of Jesus began to anger the Romans who occupied Palestine. The Pharisees, a Jewish religious group that insisted on the strict observance of Jewish law, were also growing alarmed. They felt that Jesus was a threat to their position of power, especially as more and more of the populace looked to him as the Messiah. Around 30 CE Jesus entered Jerusalem for Passover week, with crowds laying palm fronds (leaves) before him and calling him the son of David and the Messiah. In the temple he overturned the tables of the merchants, who had largely overrun the holy place. During the

The Virgin Mary cradles Jesus in her arms. © RICHARD CUMMINS/CORBIS.

following days he engaged in heated debate with Pharisees and other religious scholars. These activities and disagreements further angered the priests, who then sought to eliminate Jesus.

On Thursday night of Passover week, Jesus and his disciples had a final meal together, the reenactment of which would become one of the main sacraments, or religious rituals, of Christianity: Holy Communion, also known as Mass or the Eucharist. Following the meal, Jesus went to the Garden of Gethsemane to pray. Jesus's disciple, Judas Iscariot, betrayed Jesus by leaking his whereabouts to his enemies. It was at Gethsemane that Jesus was arrested and taken to trial for blasphemy, or words and action that show irreverence to God. Jesus was sentenced to death and taken to the Roman authorities to have the sentence carried out. The Roman governor of Judea, Pontius Pilate, attempted to satisfy the demands of a screaming crowd by ordering Jesus's crucifixion. The punishment was carried out on Friday, later called Good Friday in Christian tradition, on the hill of Golgotha, also known as Calvary. Among Jesus's last words were, as quoted in Luke 23:24, "Father, forgive them; for they know not what they do."

The Resurrection

On the following Sunday, celebrated afterwards as Easter Sunday, when followers went to the tomb where Jesus was buried, they discovered the stone covering the entrance pushed aside and Jesus gone. His disciples supposedly shared a meal with him after he rose from the dead. Others, including his mother, Mary, were said to have seen him after this miraculous Resurrection. Forty days later, after telling his disciples to spread his teachings far and wide, Jesus was taken up to heaven.

Over time the life and death of Jesus took on a more deeply symbolic form. Though historians debate whether or not Jesus called himself the Son of God, his followers soon made this claim a fact of the budding religion of Christianity, named after Jesus Christ. In this context, he was seen as a sacrifice on the part of a loving God, the Father, who had offered up his only Son to redeem humanity's sins. The Crucifixion of Jesus and his subsequent Resurrection became major elements of Christian belief and reflect an idea that Jesus himself preached: that by believing in God, one could have life everlasting.

Jesus led a simple, humble life, which he preached others should do as well. He lived by his words, and his life became an example of what could be achieved by loving one's fellow humans and forgiving the wrongdoings of others. The Christian religion teaches that by having faith in Jesus Christ as both the Son of God and as a man who once walked among other men, one may reach personal salvation and have eternal life.

For More Information

BOOKS

Allison, Dale C., Jr. "Jesus." In *Encyclopedia of Religion.* Edited by Lindsay Jones. Vol. 3. 2nd ed. Detroit, MI: Macmillan Reference USA, 2005, 4843–52.

Johnson, Paul. *A History of Christianity.* New York, NY: Atheneum, 1976.

Pentecost, J. Dwight. *The Words and Works of Jesus Christ: A Study of the Life of Christ.* Grand Rapids, MI: Zondervan Publishing House, 1981.

Porter, J. R. *Jesus Christ: The Jesus of History, the Christ of Faith.* New York, NY: Oxford University Press, 1999.

Reumann, John. "Mary: An Overview." In *Encyclopedia of Religion.* Edited by Lindsay Jones. Vol. 3. 2nd ed. Detroit, MI: Macmillan Reference USA, 2005, 5751–5.

Wilson, A. N. *Jesus: A Life.* New York, NY: W. W. Norton & Co., 1992.

PERIODICALS

George, Timothy. "The Blessed Evangelical Mary." *Christianity Today* (December 2003): 34–9.

Johnson, Elizabeth A. "Mary, Mary, Quite Contrary." *U.S. Catholic* (December 2003): 12–7.

WEB SITES

"From Jesus to Christ: The First Christians." *PBS Frontline.* http://www.pbs.org/wgbh/pages/frontline/shows/religion/ (accessed on June 2, 2006).

"Historical Jesus: Books, Articles and Reviews." *New Testament Gateway.* http://www.ntgateway.com/Jesus/biblio.htm (accessed on June 2, 2006).

Lindemans, Micha F. "Jesus Christ." *Encyclopedia Mythica.* http://www.pantheon.org/articles/j/jesus_christ.html (accessed on June 2, 2006).

Maas, A. J. "Chronology of the Life of Jesus Christ." *New Advent.* http://www.newadvent.org/cathen/08377a.htm (accessed on June 2, 2006).

Khadijah

BORN: c. 555 • Mecca, Arabia

DIED: 619 • Mecca, Arabia

Arabian religious leader

"And whoever does good deeds whether male or female and he (or she) is a believer—these shall enter the garden, and they shall not be dealt with a jot unjustly."

— *The Holy Qur'an,* 4:124

Khadijah was the first wife of **Muhammad** (c. 570–632; see entry), the founder of the Islamic faith. She was his first convert to the new religion, and she helped him spread its teachings by using her wealth and influence. Khadijah was forty when she took Muhammad as her husband. At the time he was employed by the international trading system that she ran. She supported him when he declared he had received a vision from Allah and pronounced himself the prophet, or divine messenger, of a new religion. Khadijah has been seen as playing a significant role in Islamic history because of her loyalty to her husband. She is also a fascinating figure in her own right. Despite the fact that women were seen as second-class citizens during the period in which she lived, she became one of the world's first successful international businesswomen.

A woman on her own

Khadijah al-Kubra, or tul Kubra, was born around 555 CE in the city of Mecca in Arabia (modern-day Saudia Arabia). At the time Mecca was an important trading center at the crossroads of major trade routes such as India's Spice Road and Arabia's Incense Road. Spices from India, silk from China, and farm products from east Africa all arrived at the port of Yemen and were then taken by camel caravan to Mecca. From there the goods were transported to Syria and then on to the rest of the Mediterranean world.

Mecca was considered the region's trading capital, and its leading citizens were merchants. Foremost in the merchant class was a tribe of ancient and powerful Bedouins ("desert dwellers" in Arabic) called the Quraysh. In addition to their trading business, the Quraysh had gained custody of the Ka'aba in the fifth century. The Ka'aba was the central shrine for pre-Islamic Arabs. It held idols, or images used as objects of worship, and the Black Stone, a sacred stone which was said to come from heaven. The Ka'aba was a major holy site of the Arab people, and the Quraysh made money from the many pilgrims that came to worship.

Khadijah was from the Quraysh tribe. Her father was Khuwalid bin Asad bin Abdul Uzza bin Qusayy. Khuwalid was both a member of the Quraysh of Mecca and distantly related to members of the Bani Hashim clan. The Bani Hashim was the clan of Muhammad Mustafa, who would later become the Prophet Muhammad. Like the other Quraysh of Mecca, Khuwalid had made his fortune in the trading business. He sent out two caravans every year: one to Yemen in the winter to retrieve goods, and one to Syria in the summer to deliver goods.

At the age of fifteen Khadijah was married for the first time to Abu Halah Hind ibn Zarah, a member of the Makhzumi clan. The couple had three sons named al-Tahir, Halah, and Hind. Historians believe that Khadijah's first husband died and that she later was married a second time, to Ateeq ibn ʿAaith, also of the Makhzumi clan. The fate of her second husband is unclear, with some sources reporting that he also died and others that he and Khadijah divorced.

Khadijah's mother died in 575, when Khadijah was around twenty. Her father died a decade later, and the children then inherited the family's wealth. Only Khadijah seemed to inherit her father's commercial skills as well. Her brothers were apparently uninterested in the caravan business, so Khadijah took over its operation. She was advised by an uncle but made decisions on her own. This was very unusual for a woman in Arab society at the time, as women were generally considered much less important and intelligent than men. Typically only male children could inherit lands or

Mount Hira, near Mecca, is the site of the Prophet Muhammad's first revelation of the Qur'an by the angel Jabra'il. Khadija's husband would go to the mountain to meditate. © KAZUYOSHI NOMACHI/CORBIS.

businesses from their parents. Women had no rights and were thought to bring bad luck. Sometimes female infants were even buried alive by fathers who were disappointed not to have had a son.

Khadijah proved to be a worthy successor to her father, however, eventually mounting caravans as large as those of all her competitors in Mecca combined. She had a clever business sense and was able to buy and sell goods at the right time to make the most money. She was also a skilled judge of men, hiring caravan agents, or guides, who later demonstrated excellent navigation skills through the desert. The business prospered under her leadership.

Khadijah was known in Mecca as "the Pure One," "the Princess of Quraysh," and "the Princess of Mecca" because of her noble ancestry and the good deeds she performed. She helped provide for the poor in the city and supported all of her relatives financially. Historians believe that Khadijah, unlike her other family members and most Arabs of the time, did not worship idols. The pre-Islamic world had many deities (gods and goddesses) to whom the people prayed, and more than three hundred of these were housed in the Ka'aba. Among these deities, Allah was considered by most Arabs to be the supreme god.

Khadijah was most likely influenced religiously by a distant cousin named Waraqah ibn Nawfal. He was a religious scholar and a believer in the unity of the creator, or in the existence of a single supreme being. Waraqah claimed that the Arabs were wrong to worship many different idols and deities. Historians believe that Waraqah's teachings caused Khadijah to reject polytheism, or the belief in many deities, in favor of monotheism, the belief in a single deity.

Wife of Muhammad

Although many men sought to wed Khadijah after her second marriage had ended, she instead devoted herself to her children and her business. One of the most important responsibilities Khadijah had as a caravan owner was the selection of caravan agents. These agents were essential to her business, as it was their duty to cross the desert to Syria in the summer leading huge caravans of camels. In the summer of 595, Khadijah had difficulty finding an agent. A relative of hers, Abu Talib, learned of her problem through the guild of merchants. Abu Talib went to her to offer the services of his young nephew, Muhammad, for whom he had become responsible after the death of Muhammad's parents. Though the young man had never led a caravan alone, he had accompanied his uncle on trips and was considered trustworthy. Khadijah hired the young man for a trial run, and the caravan proved a huge success.

Muhammad was accompanied on the caravan by a servant of Khadijah's named Maysara. They traveled by night to avoid the heat of the day and reached Syria in a month. They sold their goods, which included raisins, dried dates, perfumes, animal hides, and woven items, for cash or traded them for other goods that they could bring back for sale in Mecca. The servant Maysara observed the negotiations carried out by Muhammad and was pleased. Muhammad managed to make twice the profit of the usual caravan. When Muhammad returned to Mecca several months later, Khadijah was impressed by the stories Maysara told about him. Maysara told Khadijah how Muhammad had handled himself well in his business dealings and how absolute strangers had come to respect him quickly. Khadijah assigned him a managerial

Women in Islam

Khadijah was just one of several strong wives taken by Muhammad over his lifetime. In total he married more than twenty women. One of his favorites, A'isha, was not only a judge but also a political activist and clever battlefield commander. Another of Muhammad's wives was an *imam,* or Muslim religious leader.

Yet if these women were living in parts of the modern-day Muslim world, as Lisa Beyer observed in *Time* magazine, "they might be paying a high price for their independence." The Qur'an regards women as individuals responsible for their moral actions, and many Muslim women have taken leadership positions in religion and government. Since the Islamic revolution in Iran in 1979, however, extremists in many Muslim countries have taken away women's rights, confining them to their homes and requiring them to wear veils.

To these extremists, women are wives and mothers and should always be obedient to men. So-called honor killings, or the slaying of women who have been raped or have committed adultery (had sexual intercourse with someone other than their spouse), are seldom investigated by the law. In most Muslim countries women must wear the Islamic veil at all times, are forbidden to drive, and may travel only when accompanied by a husband or male relative. Muhammad himself would likely disapprove of these restrictions to personal liberty that are occurring among followers of the religion he founded. He was a believer in strong women like his wife, Khadijah. He outlawed female infanticide and established the rights of women to obtain education and to hold property.

position until the winter, when she hired him to lead the winter caravan to Yemen and paid him three times the usual rate. The second trip was also successful.

Respect apparently turned to love, as Khadijah had either her servant or a close friend ask Muhammad if he would be interested in marrying her. She was forty at the time; Muhammad was twenty-five. He agreed to the proposal, and the two were married in 595. By all accounts the marriage was a happy one. The two lived in Khadijah's residence, which was off the main bazaar, or marketplace, in Mecca. Shortly after the marriage, the wealthy Khadijah retired from the caravan trade and focused on her husband and family. Muhammad, who had always been a thoughtful young man, also left the business world and began meditating on the nature of the world.

Together the couple had two sons, Qasim and Abdullah, both of whom died in infancy. Many sources claim that all four of Khadijah's daughters, including the youngest, Fatima (c. 605–633), were born to Khadijah and Muhammad. As Khadijah was forty at the time of her third marriage, however, it is possible some of these daughters were

Muslim women on the haj *pray at Mount Arafat in Saudi Arabia. During the haj Muslim pilgrims retrace the steps of the Prophet Muhammad in Mecca to fulfill a journey of faith.* © REUTERS/CORBIS.

actually from her second marriage. In 606 the couple become responsible for the upbringing of **ʿAlī ibn Abī Tālib** (c. 600–661; see entry), the six-year-old son of Abu Talib. Ali was a much younger cousin of Muhammad but was raised as his son. He later became one of Muhammad's most famous followers and married his daughter, Fatima.

As he grew older, Muhammad became increasingly thoughtful and reflective and went on trips to Mount Hira, near Mecca, to meditate. On one such trip in 610 he experienced a powerful vision in which the angel Jabraʾil, or Gabriel, appeared to him and had him recite the words that later became part of the Qurʾan, the Muslim holy book:

> Recite in the name of thy Lord who created
> Man from the blood coagulated.
> Recite! The Lord is wondrous kind

Who by the pen has taught mankind
Things they knew not.

Shaken by this experience, Muhammad returned to his wife, Khadijah, who assured him that he was not insane. She convinced him that he had indeed received a message from Allah. Her cousin, Waraqah ibn Nawfal, spoke with Muhammad and also became convinced that he was a messenger from Allah, and said that his coming had been foretold in Jewish and Christian scriptures. Muhammad continued to have visions, telling only those closest to him about them.

Midwife of Islam

Khadijah's support helped Muhammad believe in his visions and establish a new faith that he called Islam, which means "submission" in Arabic. Its followers were called *Muslims,* or "ones who submit." Muhammad began to travel and spread the word of Islam throughout Mecca. He preached belief in one god, Allah, who he claimed created the world and sat in judgment over humanity. Muhammad spoke of a life after death and of a god who was fair and would reward good deeds on Earth. Many poor Meccans and some merchants responded to Muhammad's call, but the new religion quickly earned Muhammad and Khadijah enemies. Many Meccans resented Muhammad saying that the traditional gods and goddesses were to be replaced by his Allah. They were satisfied with life the way it was. The powerful Quraysh fought against the new religion because they feared that Muhammad would destroy the Ka'aba rather than embrace it for Islam.

Khadijah and her husband became increasingly isolated in Mecca as many of the new Muslim converts left the city for Abyssinia (modern-day Ethiopia). Abu Talib, Muhammad's uncle, made clear to the town that Muhammad was under the protection of the Bani Hashim clan and that no harm should come to him. Eventually, however, Muhammad, Khadijah, their family, and their remaining followers had to hide from the powerful Quraysh in a wild mountain valley. They lived a grim and difficult life, and Khadijah was forced to use most of her money to buy water and supplies for the faithful. This isolation lasted for several years, until 619. In the end, however, the fight against Muhammad and the Bani Hashim clan was given up, and Muhammad and his family returned to Mecca. Worn out by the harsh conditions she had lived under, Khadijah died not long after returning home. Abu Talib also died soon thereafter. Muhammad remained in Mecca for three more years before leaving for Medina, where he was welcomed as the Prophet and Islam began to thrive.

Khadijah guided the religion of Islam through its early hardships by her love and devotion to her husband. Her belief in Muhammad's visions helped give him the faith to create his new religion. She also selflessly used her wealth to insure the survival of both their family and their new faith. Khadijah has long been revered in the Muslim world as a symbol of virtue and loyalty.

For More Information

BOOKS

Razwy, Syed A. A. *Khadijah tul Kubra: The Wife of the Prophet Muhammad: May Allah Be Pleased with Her: A Short History of Her Life.* Elmhurst, NY: Tahrike Tarsile Qur'an, 1944.

PERIODICALS

Beyer, Lisa. "Life Behind the Veil." *Time* (November 1, 1990): 37.

WEB SITES

al-Jibouri, Yasin T. "Khadijah Daughter of Khuwaylid: Wife of Prophet Muhammad (pbuh)." *Al-Islam.org.* http://al-islam.org/biographies/Khadijah.htm (accessed on June 2, 2006).

"Marriage of Khadijah." *Islamic Web.* http://www.islamicweb.com/history/Khadijah.htm (accessed on June 2, 2006).

Where to Learn More

The following list focuses on works written for readers of middle school and high school age. Books aimed at adult readers have been included when they are especially important in providing information or analysis that would otherwise be unavailable.

Books

Armstrong, Karen. *Islam: A Short History,* rev. ed. New York: Modern Library, 2002.

Bottero, Jean. *Religion in Ancient Mesopotamia.* Chicago, IL: University of Chicago Press, 2001.

Boyer, P. *Religion Explained: The Human Instincts That Fashion Gods, Spirits, and Ancestors.* London: William Heinemann, 2001.

Buswell, Robert E., Jr., ed. *Encyclopedia of Buddhism.* 2 vols. New York: Macmillan Reference, 2003.

De Lange, Nicholas. *An Introduction to Judaism.* Cambridge, U.K.: Cambridge University Press, 2000.

Dundas, Paul. *The Jains.* 2nd ed. London and New York, NY: Routledge, 2002.

Flood, Gavin D. *An Introduction to Hinduism.* Cambridge, U.K.: Cambridge University Press, 1996.

Glazier, Stephen D. *Encyclopedia of African and African-American Religions.* New York: Routledge, 2001.

Grimassi, Raven. *Encyclopedia of Wicca and Witchcraft.* St. Paul, MN: Llewellyn Publications, 2000.

Hartz, Paula. *Zoroastrianism,* 2nd ed. New York: Facts On File, 2004.

Higginbotham, Joyce. *Paganism: An Introduction to Earth-centered Religions.* St. Paul, MN: Llewellyn Publications, 2002.

Hirschfelder, Arlene, and Paulette Molin. *Encyclopedia of Native American Religions: An Introduction.* 2nd ed. New York: Facts On File, 2001.

Hoffman, Nancy. *Sikhism.* Detroit, MI: Lucent Books, 2006.

Jones, Lindsay. *Encyclopedia of Religion,* 2nd ed. Detroit, MI: Macmillan Reference USA, 2005.

Keown, Damien. *Dictionary of Buddhism.* New York: Oxford University Press, 2003.

Lace, William W. *Christianity.* San Diego, CA: Lucent Books, Inc., 2005.

Martin, Michael, ed. *The Cambridge Companion to Atheism.* Cambridge, U.K.: Cambridge University Press, 2005.

Momen, Moojan. *A Short Introduction to the Baha'i Faith.* Oxford, U.K.: Oneworld Publications, 1997.

Nasr, Seyyed Hossein. *Islam: Religion, History, Civilization.* San Francisco: Harper San Francisco, 2003.

Oldstone-Moore, Jennifer. *Confucianism: Origins, Beliefs, Practices, Holy Texts, Sacred Places.* New York: Oxford University Press, 2002.

Oldstone-Moore, Jennifer. *Taoism: Origins, Beliefs, Practices, Holy Texts, Sacred Places.* New York: Oxford University Press, 2003.

Robinson, George. *Essential Judaism: A Complete Guide to Beliefs, Customs and Rituals.* Rev. ed. New York: Pocket Books, 2000.

Roochnick, David. *Retrieving the Ancients: An Introduction to Greek Philosophy.* New York: Blackwell, 2004.

Tiele, C. P. *Comparative History of the Egyptian and Mesopotamian Religions.* New York: Routledge, 2001.

Tomkins, Steven. *A Short History of Christianity.* London: Lion Books, 2005.

Web Site

URI Kids: World Religions. United Religions Initiative. http://www.uri.org/kids/world.htm (accessed on July 24, 2006).

Religions, Faith Groups, and Ethical Systems. Ontario Consultants on Religious Tolerance. http://www.religioustolerance.org/var_rel.htm (accessed on July 24, 2006).

World Religions Index. http://wri.leaderu.com/ (accessed on July 24, 2006).

Index

Italic type indicates volume numbers; **boldface** type indicates main entries and their page numbers; Illustrations are marked by (ill.).

A

C

D

E

F

G

K

L

N

O

P

Y

Z